Exploring the "Little" Books of the Old Testament

Series One, Book Two

Hosea, Lamentations, Joel

Exploring the "Little" Books of the Old Testament

Series One, Book Two

Hosea, Lamentations, Joel

by

Sylvia Bambola

Heritage Publishing House

Copy right © 2026 by Sylvia Bambola. All rights reserved. No part of this book may be used or reproduced in any manner whatsoever without written permission of the publisher.

ISBN: 978-0-9657389-8-9

Unless otherwise indicated, all Scriptures taken from Holy Bible, King James version, Cambridge, 1769

Also by Sylvia Bambola

Non-Fiction

Exploring the "Little" Books of the Old Testament-Book 1

Discovering God's Attributes

Destination Hell

Biblical Gardens of God and Valleys of Man

Encountering Jesus Throughout the Bible

The Coming Deception

12 Questions New Christians Frequently Ask

Following the Blood Trail from Genesis to Revelation

Fiction:

Mercy at Midnight

The Babel Conspiracy

The Daughters of Jim Farrell

The Salt Covenants

Rebekah's Treasure

Return to Appleton

Waters of Marah

Tears in a Bottle

Refiner's Fire

To

My Children and Grandchildren

With Love

Table of Contents

Introduction

The first book in this series covered *Ruth, Esther,* and *Song of Solomon,* all human love stories that also portray God's love for us and the lengths to which He went to restore us to Himself.

Book Two covers *Hosea, Lamentations,* and *Joel*. In them we see a different side of God, that of His righteous anger and judgment. On the heels of Book One, the obvious question is, "Can such a loving God also be wrathful?" The answer is, "Yes."

Every book in the Bible reveals some unique insight into God's character, His love, mercy, longsuffering, patience, etcetera. But because He is holy, His justice is also evident. That's why we need to study the Scriptures, even these "little books." They help us understand Who God is, what He requires of us, and how we fit into His plans. They also contain embedded life lessons that are just as relevant today as they were then.

I must confess, I prefer reading about God's love more than His justice. Like most people, I want to be reminded that His love never fails even if I do. But Scripture indicates that God's judgments are really offshoots of His love because they are meant to bring the offending party back to Him. In addition, His incredible mercy can be found even in the midst of these judgments. Ever ready to forgive, God always prefers repentance to punishment.

And that's comforting!

Hosea

Chapter 1

Although Hosea is listed after Lamentations in the Bible, I have put it first because historically it preceded the events in Lamentations. Hosea, a prophet to the northern kingdom, was one of twelve to be considered a minor prophet due to the size of his work. His name means salvation. Facts about his early life are sketchy. Some claim his occupation was either a farmer or baker; his birthplace, Gilead. Neither are known for certain. It is believed his ministry began prior to 753 B.C. and ended around 723 B.C. After that, nothing further is known.

He was a contemporary of Amos, Isaiah, and Micah, though only Amos was a prophet to the northern kingdom. After king Solomon's death in 931 B.C., the kingdom split into two. Ten tribes formed the northern kingdom called Israel. The remaining two tribes formed the southern kingdom of Judah.

During Hosea's day, Israel experienced prosperity almost equal to that of the golden age of Solomon. Syria's decline as a military threat left Israel free to pursue commercial interests. Their mineral resources and newly acquired control of the prized Damascus trade routes revived their economy. As merchants became wealthier, the divide between rich and poor widened. Before long, the wealthy began abusing the poor, stealing their land, and forcing them into rigorous servitude.

In the midst of this, Israel became even more susceptible to pagan influence. The Canaanite religion had already infiltrated the nation during Joshua and Caleb's day. Now, Baal and Ashtoreth were openly worshipped in rituals that included drunkenness, violence, and prostitution. Eventually, these abominations also flourished in Judah. Within a hundred years after Israel's demise, prostitutes openly practiced their trade near Jerusalem's Temple.

Hosea functioned as a prophet during the reign of seven northern kings: Jeroboam II, Zechariah, Shallum, Menahem, Pekahiah, Pekah, Hoshea. Though he was a northern prophet, his revelations were well known throughout Judah. Grieved over his people's flagrant idolatry, greed, and immorality, Hosea knew if they didn't repent and return to Yahweh, judgment would fall.

Let's look at the seven kings mentioned.

Jeroboam II:

The thirteenth king of Israel and son of Jehu, Jeroboam II, extended Israel's territory, capturing Damascus and its important trade routes from the Assyrians. He also oversaw Israel's moral and spiritual decay. Just thirty years after he died, the northern kingdom of Israel ceased to exist.

Zechariah:

Son of Jeroboam II, Zechariah's name means "God remembers." Murdered by Shallum, who would become his successor, Zechariah ruled for only six months and was the last of the Jehu dynasty.

Shallum:

After murdering Zechariah, Shallum ruled one month before he himself was murdered by Menahem, who then replaced him on the throne.

Menahem:

Menahem employed brutal warfare against his enemies. Exact dates and times are disputed by scholars, but the consensus is that he ruled eight to ten years (752-742 B.C.). He, too, was murdered. His assassin, Pekah, eventually became king.

Pekahiah:

Son of Menahem, Pekahiah ruled from 741-740 B.C., a span of two years. Because he followed his father's policy of paying tribute to Assyria, he was assassinated by Pekah, the very one who also assassinated Pekahiah's father. Israel had become divided between those who wanted to continue the policy of compliance to Assyria and those who didn't. Pekah was in the opposing camp. Like his predecessors, Pekahiah allowed idolatry to continue in Israel, and was as evil as Jeroboam II. He was murdered in his Samarian palace.

Pekah:

He was king for eight years (740 B.C. to 732 B.C.) His resistance to Assyria eventually made king Tiglath-pileser III remove him. Many scholars believe it was through assassination at the hands of Hoshea, Pekah's replacement. Whether Tiglath ordered it or just sanctioned it, the result was the same.

Hoshea:

Israel's last king, Hoshea, ruled for nine years (732 B.C. to 724 B.C.). His conspiracy against Pekah paid off and allowed him to ascend the throne. He was considered evil, but not as evil as the kings who preceded him. At the time of his rule, Israel was Assyria's vassal. Though only the capital in Samaria and the Ephraim hill country remained in Israel's hands, Hoshea was still forced to pay a heavy tribute. His unwillingness to oppose Tiglath-pileser had secured Hoshea his crown. But when Tiglath-pileser died in 727 B.C., Hoshea saw a chance to get out from under the tribute and refused further payment. In response, Tiglath's successor, Shalmaneser, in 725/724 B.C., came against Israel. He imprisoned Hoshea and laid siege to Samaria. After almost three years of fighting, the city finally fell in 722 B.C., thus ending Israel's northern kingdom.

Scripture says these seven kings *"did evil in the sight of the Lord."* This was Hosea's world, a world of violence, intrigue, assassinations, immorality, and idolatry.

Just a side note: In Hosea, Lamentations, and Joel, collective Israel is referred to by God as either she, he, they, or Jacob. While I'm not dogmatic about it, I believe each word distinguishes how God viewed His people during those times. When Israel or Judah are mentioned as "he," I believe it implies that God is referring to them as His son, either beloved or prodigal. When Israel is "she," God is referring to her as His beloved or unfaithful wife. "They" refers to rulers, elites, or kings. And when God talks about Jacob, I believe He is showing His contempt over Israel reverting to the old nature of supplanter, heel catcher, deceiver, and conniver.

Now, turning to the text:

"The word of the LORD that came unto Hosea, the son of Beeri, in the days of Uzziah, Jotham, Ahaz, and Hezekiah, kings of Judah, and in the days of Jeroboam the son of Joash king of Israel. The beginning of the word of the LORD by Hosea. And the LORD said to Hosea, Go, take unto thee a wife of whoredoms and children of whoredoms: for the land hath committed great whoredom, departing from the LORD." Hosea 1:1-2

Though Hosea was a northern prophet, it is interesting to note that four southern kings were mentioned first, then followed by only one from the northern kingdom. These four kings of Judah ruled during Hosea's time and during the time of the seven northern kings mentioned above. In contrast to the northern kings, whom God declared were all evil, only one of the southern kings (Ahaz) was. Perhaps that's why they are mentioned before Jeroboam II. In addition, Hosea's desire that his warning be a deterrence, compelled him to alert both north and south.

On the other hand, some scholars believe this first mention of the south was due to Hosea considering that only David's line (southern kingdom) valid, while the line of the northern kings were illegitimate.

Because the land was riddled with idolatry, God asked Hosea to do something surprising: marry a whore and have a family. In the next sentence, God identified with this by saying His people had become whores by following after other gods.

Their idolatry was a blow to God on many levels. As the One Who had freed them from Egyptian slavery, brought them into the Promised Land, enabled them to conquer their enemies, then elevated them as a nation, He had every right to be incensed. But as a relational God, One who desired a deep love relationship with Israel as both Husband and Father, He was brokenhearted. I've detailed this relational aspect of God in several of my books and will include only a portion now.

What is the relationship between a bridegroom and bride? Between a husband and wife? It is intimate, caring, exclusive, and deep. And throughout the Bible we see references to this relationship, both natural and spiritual.

Leviticus contains God's statutes concerning the type of wife a priest should marry as well as the type he should not. *"They* (the priests*) shall not take a wife that is a **whore**, or profane; neither shall they take a woman put away from her husband* (divorced*): for he* (the priest) *is holy unto his God,"* (Leviticus 21:7).

We see that priests were only to marry respectable women; women who had kept themselves pure for their husbands. But what does it tell us on a deeper level? Just this—since God is also holy, in fact the very definition of holiness, then He, too, would never take a whore for a wife. And why is that important? Because the marriage relationship is the very relationship God desired with His people, and He was describing the necessary qualifications of *His* wife, Israel.

Early on, God made His intentions to His bride, clear. *"In the day that I* (God) *took them by the hand to bring them out of the land of Egypt; which my covenant they brake, although I was an **husband** unto them, saith the LORD,"* (Jeremiah 31:32b). So, Israel's adultery began early and continued in varying degrees throughout their history.

In Jeremiah 2:32, God laments, *"Can a maid forget her ornaments, or a bride her attire? yet my people have forgotten me days without number."* You can almost feel God's heartache. His accusations become more pronounced in Jeremiah 3:20. *"Surely as a wife treacherously departeth from her husband, so have ye dealt treacherously with me, O house of Israel, saith the LORD."* That's how God saw Israel's idolatry. It was treachery itself; a faithless wife dishonoring her husband.

In Ezekiel 16, God listed Israel's duplicity. He talked about how He made a special covenant with her; how He raised her above other nations; how He provided and protected her. But despite all this, she offered her children as human sacrifices to Molech, served other gods, and played the whore. Ezekiel 16:30-32 says, *"How weak is thine heart, saith the Lord GOD, seeing thou doest all these things, the work of an imperious* ***whorish*** *woman; In that thou buildest thine eminent place in the head of every way, and makest thine high place in every street; and hast not been as an harlot, in that thou scornest hire; But as a* ***wife*** *that committeth adultery, which taketh strangers instead of her* ***husband****!"* What a sad description of how Israel had degraded herself!

Even so, God made this promise in Isaiah 54:5-7, *"For thy Maker is thine* ***husband****; the LORD of hosts is his name; and thy Redeemer the Holy One of Israel; The God of the whole earth shall he be called. For the LORD hath called thee as a woman forsaken and grieved in spirit, and a* ***wife*** *of youth, when thou wast refused, saith thy God. For a small moment have I forsaken thee; but* ***with great mercies will I gather thee****."*

What a beautiful picture! God was telling Israel that though they had sinned, though they had prostituted themselves by following after other gods, He would, once again, have mercy on them. Not only that, He would still be their *husband,* One who would tenderly love, protect, and provide for them.

Though mercy and restoration were coming, Israel's whoredoms could not go unpunished. Inevitable judgment would fall. The story of Hosea and Gomer is a touching illustration of this, depicting God's heartbreak, anger, and mercy.

Now, let's look at prostitution during the time of the Old Testament:

The Bible uses different words for this practice. According to Zondervan's *Pictorial Encyclopedia of the Bible,* these different words can, though not always, have different meanings. The *Pictorial Encyclopedia* infers "harlot" (*zanah*) denotes a professional, someone paid for sex, while "whore" (*qedeshah*) most often refers to a devotee, a cult prostitute who engages in ritual sex during pagan worship. However, the *Theological Wordbook of the Old Testament* infers these words are often interchangeable and can be literal or figurative, referring to people as well as nations. Sometimes both.

Cult prostitutes:

Cult prostitutes were "set apart" or dedicated to a specific deity. Since many of the pagan gods represented fertility, their ceremonies heavily involved sexual practices meant to mirror the power of their gods to reproduce a bounteous harvest. During harvest time, it was common for cult prostitutes to travel from one threshing floor to another, then engage in orgies to ensure the fertility of both future crops and animals.

What an insult to Yahweh, the Creator of all things, the One Who controls the weather (Job 38:22-23, Psalm 107:29, Mark 4:39) and growing seasons (Genesis 8:21-22)! Israel had benefited from God's blessings, had seen His great power, yet still turned to lesser deities. Thus, cult prostitution became commonplace throughout both the northern and southern kingdoms.

Since threshing floors were sites of pagan rituals, it's interesting that God commanded David to purchase the threshing floor of Ornan the Jebusite and build an altar there. This altar reclaimed that threshing floor for God and stayed the wrath He had unleashed upon Israel for David's sin of counting the people in a census. It was also the future site of Israel's Temple where other sacrifices would be offered in order to stay God's anger.

The professionals:

In addition to the cult prostitutes, there were the professionals, those who sold themselves for monetary gain. Neither their money, nor the money of the cult prostitutes were acceptable tithes to the Temple. Though these professionals were tolerated, they were looked down upon and occupied a low social standing.

Then there was the selling of children by their parents for "wine." That thought is so reprehensible it staggers the imagination. Yet, it was not uncommon. Since wine is unnecessary to sustain life, it infers these parents sold their children for gain, to obtain things they might not otherwise afford. That makes it all the more depraved. It's a good illustration of how Israel had sold herself and her progeny for gain by making alliances with those she shouldn't have.

God called His people and nation an adulterous whore (cult prostitute for following other gods) and harlot (one who sold herself to other nations, like Egypt, for their protection). This is how He saw His "wife" Israel, in Hosea.

While priests and Levites were forbidden to marry a prostitute, it was not forbidden for a prophet to do so, though it would be unseemly. Yet, Hosea obeyed God's command to *"Go take unto thee a wife of whoredoms and children of whoredoms."*

Continuing with the text:

"So he went and took Gomer the daughter of Diblaim; which conceived, and bare him a son. And the LORD said unto him, Call his name Jezreel; for yet a little while and I will avenge the blood of Jezreel upon the house of Jehu, and will cause to cease the kingdom of the house of Israel. And it shall come to pass at that day, that I will break the bow of Israel in the valley of Jezreel." Hosea 1:3-5

Hosea married the prostitute, Gomer. Her name means "complete, finish, to end, failure." She symbolized the northern kingdom of Israel as a failed state; one God was going to end. Her father's name, Diblaim, means "two fig cakes." Fig cakes were a symbol of God's blessings and faithfulness. Gomer's lineage, like Israel's, came from a heritage (Father Abraham) set apart, protected, and nurtured by God only to disintegrate into an ungrateful, faithless prostitute. The "**two** fig cakes" symbolize both the northern and southern kingdoms. Though Israel would fall first (in 722 B.C. when they were conquered by Assyria), Judah would also be judged nearly 135 years later during Jeremiah's day.

A nod to fig cakes can be seen in Song of Solomon 2:5-7. *"Stay me with **flagons**, comfort me with apples: for I am sick of love. His* *left hand is under my head, and his right hand doth embrace me. I charge you, O ye daughters of Jerusalem, by the roes, and by the hinds of the field, that ye stir not up, nor awake my love, till he please."*

It's a picture of the believer acknowledging her constant need of Jesus by asking Him to support (*stay*) her with flagons. According to the *Theological Wordbook of the Old Testament*, "*stay*" implies the laying on of hands, especially the laying on of hands in a sacrificial sin offering, where sin is transferred from the one offering the sacrifice to that which is being sacrificed. It also implies a surrender to God in consecration and dedication. What an awesome picture of the "Great Exchange" where Jesus takes our sins upon Himself, and we get His righteousness! "*For he* (God the Father) *hath made him* (Jesus) *to be sin for us, who knew no sin; that we might be made the righteousness of God in him*" (2 Corinthians 5:21). The bride in Song of Solomon was reminding herself of who she is in Christ.

Then that word "flagons" (*ashiyshah*) means "something closely pressed together such as a raisin or fig cake, flagons of wine, a grape vine covered with berries." The bride in Solomon's Song was saying, "Keep me strong by remaining so close to me that we are as intertwined and inseparable as a fig cake or a vine and its fruit." She understood that the only way she could successfully live this new life is for them to remain close. In John 15:5, Jesus said, *"I am the vine, ye are the branches. He that abideth in me, and I in him, the same bringeth forth much fruit: for without me ye can do nothing."*

This was also to be the type of relationship God had with His wife, Israel. She was to love Yahweh, live inseparable and tightly pressed to Him, guided and protected. Instead, she chose the world and other gods.

Hosea and Gomer's union produced a son God named Jezreel. There's a lot here. Jezreel means "God will sow or scatter." This is a play on words. It's an obvious insult and taunt to the fertility gods Israel, and probably Gomer, were worshipping. While the Israelites committed unspeakable acts in hopes of inducing their pagan gods to give them a plentiful harvest, there was God, the One Who sows, the One Whose sowing never fails but always produces the harvest He intends, whether positive or negative.

The name "Jezreel" is also a prophetic warning that judgment was coming. In the not-so-distant future, God would scatter Israel. This happened after Assyria conquered Israel, then dispersed the Jews throughout their kingdom.

Next, Jezreel refers to Judah's hill country, the name of several cities, a valley, as well as king Ahab's palace. The downfall of Israel was greatly accelerated at Jezreel, specifically at Ahab's Samarian citadel. It was here that his wife, Jezebel, daughter of the pagan Phoenician king, initiated the Canaanite worship of Asherah and Baal, making Samaria the center of it all. She elevated its priests while executing the priests and prophets of Yahweh.

Though it was the beginning of the end for the northern kingdom, the "bow" or strength of the southern kingdom would also be broken about 265 years later when Judah's king Josiah was slain at Jezreel (609 B.C.).

Jezebel was eventually killed by Jehu who then took Israel's throne by force. As God's chosen, Jehu was anointed by the prophet Elijah, then instructed to eradicate the house of Ahab. He did this during the slaughter at Jezreel (2 Kings 10:10-11). Unfortunately, he exceeded his orders by also massacring

Judah's king Ahaziah (who had aligned himself with Ahab) and forty-two of Ahaziah's kinsmen. Because Jehu had shed their blood, God, as the ultimate "blood avenger" promised, in Hosea, that this blood would be avenged.

I have covered God as blood avenger in some of my books and will cover it more later. But we must understand that blood has a voice and cries out to God when spilled unjustly (Genesis 4:10). Thus, all the innocent blood shed throughout the ages (murders, abortions, etcetera) will one day be avenged.

To further understand this passage in Hosea about God breaking the "bow" of Israel, which refers first to Israel then Judah, we need to see what happened to king Josiah in the Jezreel Valley. The prophecy in Zechariah 12:10-11 states that in the last days Israel would acknowledge their Messiah. *"And I will pour upon the house of David, and upon the inhabitants of Jerusalem, the spirit of grace and of supplication: and they shall look upon me whom they have pierced, and they shall* ***mourn*** *for him, as one* ***mourneth*** *for his only son, and shall be in bitterness for him, as one that is in bitterness for his firstborn. In that day shall there be a great* ***mourning*** *in Jerusalem, as the* ***mourning*** *of* ***Hadadrimmon*** *in the valley of Megiddon."*

Hadadrimmon is the name of a vegetation god and the combined names of two storm gods, Hadad and Rimmon. It's also the name of a city in the Megiddon valley (Valley of Jezreel) where Israel's godly king, Josiah, was killed in battle against the Egyptians. Judah had been steadily declining spiritually prior to Josiah's reign. In many ways, he was his nation's last hope, thus, his death was catastrophic. And the mourning of his death symbolized the mourning of the death of Israel's southern kingdom. Just twelve short years later, Babylon would conquer Judah and take many of its inhabitants back as captives.

It's interesting to note that according to *Strong's Exhaustive Concordance*, Josiah means "foundation, self-existent or eternal, Jehovah." He is a type or shadow of Jesus. Just as the Jews mourned the death of king Josiah at Megiddon, so, at the end of the Tribulation, the remnant Jews, at Megiddon, will mourn the fact that they rejected Jesus when He came as their self-existent, eternal Lamb, their foundation and cornerstone. And just as Josiah's death signaled the southern kingdom's upcoming "death" by Babylon, so the Jews will finally realize their rejection of Jesus signaled their national "death" for nearly two millennia. But Megiddon will also be the site of their "resurrection" when Jesus restores them as the head of nations, indicating that the place of their downfall would be the very place of their restoration.

Continuing with the text:

"And she conceived again, and bare a daughter. And God said unto him (Hosea), *Call her name Loruhamah: for I will no more have mercy upon the house of Israel; but I will utterly take them away. But I will have mercy upon the house of Judah, and will save them by the LORD their God, and will not save them by bow, nor by sword, nor by battle, by horse, nor by horsemen."* Hosea 1:6-7

In the previous verses God commanded Hosea to name his first born "Jezreel," as a warning that judgment was coming. God then instructed Hosea to name his second child, Loruhamah, meaning "God will show no compassion or mercy." God had had it with Israel's immorality and idolatry. A terrible judgment awaited, a judgment without mercy or compassion.

But God also made it clear that Judah was not to be part of Israel's judgment. Though Judah was not sinless, God's mercy still extended to her. It's interesting to note that God declared Judah's salvation would be by His hand alone and not by any war weapons or skill in battle. Unfortunately, Judah forgot this because these are the very things she relied on prior to being destroyed by Babylon.

Continuing with the text:

"Now when she had weaned Loruhamah, she conceived, and bare a son. Then said God, Call his name Loammi: for ye are not my people, and I will not be your God. Yet the number of the ***children of Israel shall be as the sand of the sea****, which cannot be measured nor numbered; and it shall come to pass, that in the place where it was said unto them, Ye are not my people, there it shall be said unto them, Ye are the* ***sons*** *of the living God. Then shall the children of Judah and the children of Israel be gathered together, and* ***appoint themselves one head****, and they shall come up out of the land: for great shall be the day of Jezreel."* Hosea 1:8-11

Loammi, *"You are not my people."* What sad words! God was divorcing his wife. The people He loved as a husband loves a wife, the apple of His eye, the very people He wanted to gather to Himself and protect, had committed adultery with other gods and become repulsive to Him. Long after Israel's demise, when God saw Judah going down this same path, He reminded her of Israel's fate in Jeremiah 3:6-8. *"The LORD said also unto me* (Jeremiah) *in the days of Josiah the king, Hast thou seen that which backsliding Israel hath done? she is gone up upon every high mountain and under every green tree, and there hath played the harlot. And I said after she had done all these things, Turn thou unto me. But she returned not. And her treacherous sister* ***Judah*** *saw it. And I saw, when for all the causes whereby backsliding*

Israel committed adultery I had put her away, and given her a ***bill of divorce****; yet her treacherous sister* ***Judah*** *feared not, but went and played the harlot also."*

Even so, chapter one of Hosea ends on a high note. After declaring that Israel was no longer His people, God then promised they would again thrive. They would become as numerous as sand on a beach. He was reaffirming the covenant He made with Abraham in Genesis 22:17. *"That in blessing I* (God) *will bless thee, and in multiplying I will multiply thy seed as the stars of the heaven, and as* ***the sand which is upon the sea shore****; and thy seed shall possess the gate of his enemies."*

Oh, the great love of God! His heart was surely broken over His people becoming an unfaithful wife and prodigal son, yet He looked forward to the day when they would be restored!

Chapter 2

"Say ye unto your brethren, Ammi; and to your sisters, Ruhamah. Plead with your mother, plead: for ***she is not my wife,*** *neither am I her husband: let her therefore put away her whoredoms out of her sight, and her adulteries from between her breasts; Lest I strip her naked, and set her as in the day that she was born, and make her as a wilderness, and set her like a dry land and slay her with thirst."* Hosea 2:1-3

It's obvious that God didn't want to judge Israel but desired she return to Him before it was too late. He instructed Hosea to tell the people they are "His people" (*Ammi*) and that He loved them and would have mercy on them (*Ruhamah*). Hosea was also to plead with the nation (*your mother*) to turn from idolatry.

Notice, God commanded Israel to remove *"her adulteries from between her breasts."* In Song of Solomon 1:13, it is Jesus Who lies between the bride's breasts, symbolic of Him filling her heart. He is the One who purifies and strengthens her. He is her breastplate of righteousness (Ephesians 6:10-18). But here in Hosea, other gods were positioned there. If this didn't change, judgment would fall.

And this is what God threatened to do:

- *"strip her naked."* According to Tim Lahaye and Ed Hindson's *Exploring Bible Prophecy from Genesis to Revelation,* women caught in adultery during Biblical times were stripped naked as a public punishment. Perhaps that's what God was referring to symbolically, stating He would strip Israel of her glory, wealth, and position by removing His hand of protection and provision.
- *"set her as in the day she was born."* If you connect this with the above, it reinforces the picture of stripping her as naked as a newborn baby. But I also believe it could have a deeper meaning. Israel, as a nation, was born when she was liberated from Egyptian bondage, specifically when her people crossed the Red Sea. It was a type of baptism, a *mikveh* of cleansing as well as a symbol of dying to the old and beginning anew with the Lord. It was a type of born-again experience, with Israel having faith and trust enough to follow the God of Abraham, Isaac, and Jacob. But as newborns, they were defenseless, in great need of God's mighty hand for protection and guidance. If God returned Israel to that same state, she would be at the mercy of her enemies, as defenseless as a newborn baby.
- *"make her as a wilderness."* Israel knew all about the wilderness. She had wandered in one for forty years. Being made a wilderness meant she would be dry, barren.
- *"slay her with thirst."* Slay means to kill. God was threatening to kill Israel with thirst. If Israel was physically made a wilderness and a dry land, thirst would naturally occur. Again, it points to Israel's time in the wilderness. Psalm 107:4-5 says, *"They wandered in the wilderness in a solitary way; they found no city to dwell in. Hungry and* ***thirsty****, their soul fainted in them."*
    - But it also has spiritual connotations. A nation once spiritually alive can dry up and become

spiritually dead. Psalm 63:1 says, *"O God, thou art my God; early will I seek thee: my soul* ***thirsteth*** *for thee, my flesh longeth for thee in a dry and* ***thirsty*** *land, where no water is."*

- Matthew 5:6 says, *"Blessed are they which do hunger and* ***thirst*** *after righteousness: for they shall be filled."*
- Blaise Pascal, 17th century French philosopher, said there is a God-shaped vacuum in the heart of each man that only God can fill. I believe that's true. Trying to fill it with other things like money, power, success, drugs, sex, etcetera, will never satisfy. And that's just what God was saying. Thirsting after other gods, Israel turned her back on Yahweh making her spiritually dry. And she would never be satisfied until she returned to Him.
- Jesus said in John 4:13-14, *"Whosoever drinketh of this water* (the world's water) *shall thirst again: But whosoever drinketh of the water that I shall give him shall never thirst; but the water that I shall give him shall be in him a well of water springing up into everlasting life."*

Continuing with the text:

"And I will not have mercy upon her children; for they be the children of whoredoms. For their mother hath played the ***harlot****: she that conceived them hath done shamefully: for she said, I will go after my lovers, that give me my bread and my water, my wool and my flax, mine oil and my drink. Therefore, behold, I will hedge up thy way with thorns, and make a wall, that she shall not find her paths. And she shall follow after her lovers, but she shall not overtake them; and she shall seek them, but shall not find them: then shall she say, I will go and return to my first husband; for then was it better with me than*

now. For she did not know that I gave her corn, and wine, and oil, and multiplied her silver and gold, which they prepared for Baal." Hosea 2:4-8

Due to her whoredoms, God called Israel a "harlot" (*zanah*), one who sold herself for gain. Israel's control of the Damascus trade routes and the sale of her minerals had made her rich. This necessitated making pacts with other nations or "lovers" for trade and protection. Eventually, Israel even became vassals, forced to pay tribute. Greed and pride caused Israel to sell herself to these lovers; lovers who abandoned her when it mattered most.

Because Israel did this, Yahweh would *"hedge up"* her way *"with thorns."* A Hebraic idiom, it means that God was going to make her way difficult. He would not go before her as in days past. She had disqualified herself from receiving the benefits of Deuteronomy 31:8: *"And the LORD, he it is that doth go before thee; he will be with thee, he will not fail thee, neither forsake thee: fear not, neither be dismayed."*

Does this mean God was through with Israel? Absolutely not! His actions are not ones of total or permanent repudiation, but of love. He desired Israel to see the futility of trusting in other gods and nations. He wanted her to realize that He had been the One Who provided protection and brought her prosperity, the very prosperity she squandered in the worship of other gods. And His desire was that this realization would cause her to return to Him.

Continuing with the text:

"Therefore will I return, and take away my corn in the time thereof, and my wine in the season thereof, and will recover my wool and my

flax given to cover her nakedness. And now will I discover her lewdness in the sight of her lovers, and none shall deliver her out of mine hand. I will also cause all her mirth to cease, her feast days, her new moons, and her sabbaths, and all her solemn feasts. And I will destroy her vines and her fig trees, whereof she hath said, These are my rewards that my lovers have given me: and I will make them a forest, and the beasts of the field shall eat them. And I will visit upon her in the days of Baalim, wherein she burned incense to them, and she decked herself with her earrings and her jewels, and she went after her lovers, and forgat me, saith the LORD." Hosea 2:9-13

If repentance wasn't forthcoming, God would act. He again listed some of the things He would do, including stripping Israel of her wealth, possessions, crops. Notice, He called these things *"my."* That's because they *were* His. As the God Who owns the cattle on a thousand hills (Psalm 50:10) and because *"The earth is the Lord's and the fullness there of"* (Psalm 24:1), He could say that. And when He chooses to withhold His blessings, no one can prevent it.

God also mentioned He would destroy Israel's vines and fig trees. According to the *Theological Wordbook of the Old Testament,* vine/s can be emblematic for "a faithful wife." Because the fig tree, Israel, was faithless, God would destroy her. Her land would be given to the *"beasts of the field."* This could mean that the fruit of Israel's labors, her vineyards and crops, would be eaten by wild animals. But since heathens are often called beasts (Daniel 7:3, Titus 1:12, 2 Peter 2:12), it could also refer to these fruits being confiscated by Israel's captors. In addition, since animals such as the bull, lion, eagle, and serpent were associated with Baal worship, it suggests that in God's eyes, only beasts were the fitting recipient of Israel's endeavors.

In addition, God said He would cause all feasts to end. While these feasts were meant to be holy convocations, appointed times when Israel met with God, they had become times of Baal worship or *"the days of Baalim."* Now, God would stop them by dispersing the Jews throughout the Assyrian Empire.

Baal was known by various names: Baal-peor, Baal-zebub, Baal-berith, Baal-hermon. Each indicated the town where he was worshiped, thus the plural use of "Baalim." A Phoenician deity, his name means "master, owner, **husband**." And the insult was that instead of Yahweh as their husband, Israel had espoused herself to Baal.

The Israelites not only burned incense to these Baalim, they wore idolatrous jewels and earrings. Jewelry was not only worn as ornaments and displays of wealth, but as talismans. Certain gems were believed to have supernatural powers, some to ward off sickness or disease, others as a defense against evil spirits or to impart power. Still others were believed to bring "good luck." Diamonds were purported to give warriors strength. Amethysts prevented drunkenness. Rubies were worn for love. Sapphires for happiness and bliss. Both men and women wore them, especially when participating in pagan rituals. And sometimes these jewels were even offered to these idols.

This practice, as well as the use of charms and amulets, was offensive to God. It inferred ***He*** was not enough. Therefore, God wanted to show His people the utter uselessness of their jewels as well as the utter impotence of their Baalim. As a god of fertility, Baal was responsible for the abundance of food and livestock. He was even credited for making women fertile. Now, instead of abundance and prosperity, there would be destruction and want. And neither the Baalim nor all the people's amulets or jewels would be able to prevent it.

Continuing with the text:

"Therefore, behold, I will allure her, and bring her into the wilderness, and speak comfortably unto her. And I will give her her vineyards from thence, and the ***valley of Achor for a door of hope****: and she shall sing there, as in the days of her youth, and as in the day when she came up out of the land of Egypt. And it shall be as that day, saith the LORD, that thou shalt call me Ishi; and shalt call me no more Baali. For I will take away the names of Baalim out of her mouth, and they shall no more be remembered by their name. And in that day will I make a covenant for them with the beasts of the field, and with the fowls of heaven, and with the creeping things of the ground: and I will break the bow and the sword and the battle out of the earth, and will make them to lie down safely. And I will betroth thee unto me for ever; yea, I will betroth thee unto me in righteousness, and in judgment, and in lovingkindness, and in mercies. I will even betroth thee unto me in faithfulness: and thou shall know the LORD."* Hosea 2:14-20

God said He would bring Israel *"into the wilderness,"* symbolically to the place of their Mt. Sinai covenant, and start all over. He would once again love her, provide for her, prosper her, and make her sing as she did when rescued from Egyptian bondage. Micah 2:12-13 prophesied of this future event which will occur during the second half of the Tribulation. Then God will, once again, rescue Israel, this time from the hands of the antichrist (Revelation 12:6).

God promised Israel she would again have a reason to sing His praises just as she did after safely passing through the Red Sea

(Exodus 15:21). Their valley of Achor, meaning trouble, would become a door of hope.

In my book, *Biblical Gardens of God and Valleys of Man,* I detailed the Valley of Achor and have included it below to give a better under-standing of what happened there.

Valley of Achor:

This is not a valley you want to visit. Something terrible happened here. The Israelites had just experienced a stunning victory. God had collapsed the walls of Jericho so their army could breach the city and destroy it. In Joshua 6:17, God declared Jericho cursed and therefore its destruction was to be complete. *"And the city shall be* ***accursed****, even it, and all that are therein, to the LORD: only Rahab the harlot shall live, she and all that are with her in the house, because she hid the messengers that we sent."* When God declared something "accursed" nothing was to be left standing, not people, animals, or buildings. In addition, Jericho was a type of "first fruits" to be offered to God as they began their conquest of the Promised Land.

Unbeknown to Joshua, God's command was violated and not everything was destroyed in Jericho. So, when Joshua sent three thousand of his soldiers to besiege the small city of Ai, he thought victory was assured. But to his surprise, Ai's smaller contingency rousted Israel's larger army, sending them packing and even killing thirty-six. How could that be? Especially after their spectacular victory at Jericho? Something was wrong.

After Joshua tore his clothes in grief and shame, prostrated himself before the Ark of the Covenant, God gave him the answer. *"Israel hath sinned, and they have also transgressed my covenant which I commanded them:* ***for they have even taken of the accursed thing****, and have also stolen, and dissemble also, and they have put it even among their own stuff. Therefore the children of Israel could not stand before their enemies, but turned their backs before their enemies* (ran away), *because they were* ***accursed****: neither will I be with you any more, except ye destroy the* ***accursed*** *from among you,"* Joshua 7:11-12.

So, that was it. Someone had kept spoils from Jericho, polluting Israel's entire camp. And God would have none of it. He would not protect them or go before them in battle until this sin was expunged.

Joshua understood the ramifications of what had happened. Word would get out how Israel's larger army was cowered and made to run away by Ai's smaller one. Now, the pagan inhabitants of the Promised Land would have no fear of Israel. Unless God intervened, their campaign was lost before it barely got started.

Knowing this, Joshua was careful to follow God's ensuing instructions: *"Up, sanctify the people, and say, Sanctify yourselves against to morrow: for thus saith the LORD God of Israel, There is an* ***accursed*** *thing in the midst of thee, O Israel: thou canst not stand before thine enemies, until ye take away the* ***accursed*** *thing from among you,"* (Joshua 7:13). Though God's anger was kindled, He was merciful. He, Himself, would expose the offending party.

This is what they did next: the following morning all the tribes assembled, and God called out the tribe of Judah. From them, He called out the families, then the households, then the men of each household until only Achan was left. After being questioned by Joshua, Achan confessed. *"When I saw among the spoils a goodly Babylonish garment, and two hundred shekels of silver, and a wedge of gold of fifty shekels weight, then I coveted them, and took them; and behold, they are hid in the earth in the midst of my tent, and the silver under it,"* (Joshua 7:21). The sin was exposed. Achan's covetousness and greed had caused Israel to lose the battle at Ai. But more importantly, they had caused Israel to lose the favor of God.

One must understand that Jericho, like other cities in the Promised Land, was a place of gross idolatry. Evil spirits can inhabit idols as well as people, and it is not a stretch to say this was a place and people possessed by demons. Also, it was a Canaanite custom to sacrifice babies and place their bones in the foundation or walls of homes in dedication to their gods. Therefore, it is not unreasonable to believe that those in Jericho, a Canaanite city, practiced this as well. In addition, Jericho was a place of temple prostitutes and gross sexual sins, which included bestiality. In the occult, ritual sex is often used to transmit demons from person to person. Thus, all Jericho was to be dedicated to God for destruction.

Jericho was considered so evil, even Joshua cursed it. *"And Joshua adjured them at that time, saying, Cursed be the man before the Lord, that riseth up and buildeth this city Jericho: he shall lay the foundation thereof in his firstborn, and in his youngest son shall he set up the gates of it,"* (Joshua 6:26). This curse was fulfilled years later. Hiel's eldest son, the Bethelite, died when Hiel laid Jericho's foundation. Hiel's youngest son died when he hung the gates.

God has a reason for everything He does. Even when we don't comprehend it or we believe God's actions are severe, we need to understand that there are things in the spiritual realm that are beyond our knowing. Perhaps we'll understand when we get to heaven. For more about why cities like Jericho were so accursed, see my book, *The Coming Deception*.

Because of what happened at Ai, Joshua could not let Achan's sin stand. Israel's future rested on making it right. And the remedy? Enter the Valley of Achor. *"And Joshua, and all Israel with him, took Achan the son of Zerah, and the silver, and the garment, and the wedge of gold, and his sons, and his daughters, and his oxen, and his asses, and his sheep, and his tent, and all that he had: and they brought them unto the* ***valley of Achor****. And Joshua said, Why hast thou troubled us? the LORD shall trouble thee this day. And all Israel stoned him with stones, and burned them with fire, after they had stoned them with stones,"* Joshua 7:24-25.

What a valley! Achor means, "trouble." *The Theological Wordbook of the Old Testament* goes further and talks about how a person's action can bring trouble not only to himself but others and even his nation, necessitating man's or God's judgment. This is what Israel had done. Like Achan, Israel had brought trouble on themselves, forcing God to act. Their greed made them covet alliances with ungodly nations and pagan gods. As a result, they became "cursed." And like Achan, his family, and possessions, they would be turned into a pile of ash.

But there's an important application for us, too. Like the Israelites, as believers we are trying to possess our Promised Land. Then some "accursed" thing hinders our progress, and we can't go any further. God won't allow it. He loves us too much because having an accursed thing will make us accursed. In addition, holding on to accursed things can bring trouble not only to ourselves but to others, our family, friends, even our neighborhoods. So, God will act. 1 Peter 4:17 tells us that judgment begins in the house of the Lord.

Just what are these "accursed" things? Those who have come out of the occult will instantly recognize them. They are the paraphernalia of witchcraft, objects or books used in their former life. If any remain, they can be a source of demonic contact. What about ill-gotten gain? Things stolen from others or during a crime are also accursed. So are illicit drugs, for they are gateways to the demonic realm. So are busts of idols, which are popular in home décor today. Accursed things can also include certain movies or types of music. Rest assured, God will reveal whatever is offensive. And if we obey and relinquish them, there will be no need to travel to the Valley of Achor and feel God's burning displeasure.

This is a necessary step because believers are admonished to be separated. 2 Corinthians 6:16-17 says, *"And what agreement hath the temple of God with idols? for ye are the temple of the living God; as God hath said, I will dwell in them, and walk in them; and I will be their God, and they shall be my people. Wherefore come out from among them, and be ye separate, saith the Lord, and touch not the unclean thing; and I will receive you."*

But here's the good news. Even if we are taken to the Valley of Achor because we failed to rid ourselves of some accursed thing, then finally repent, destroy it, and return to God, He can turn the burning ash pile of Achor to a place of plush growth as in Isaiah 65:10; and a door of hope as in Hosea 2:15.

But while God promised in Hosea to turn Israel's Achor into a door of hope, He also wanted to rid her of the mention or memory of Baal. Thus, He instructed the Jews to no longer call Him Baali but Ishi only. The Israelites were calling both Yahweh and Baal, "Baali," meaning "my husband" and "master." Ishi, on the other hand, means "my husband, one's beloved." All traces of Baal were to be erased.

God then promised Israel a time of peace, not only between man and animals, but through the total eradication of war. *"The wolf also shall dwell with the lamb, and the leopard shall lie down with the kid; and the calf and the young lion and the fatling together; and a little child shall lead them,"* (Isaiah 11:6). *"And he* (God/Jesus) *shall judge among the nations, and shall rebuke many people: and they shall beat their swords into plowshares, and their spears into pruninghooks: nation shall not lift up sword against nation, neither shall they learn war any more,"* (Isaiah 2:4). This happens in the millennial reign of Christ.

Then God, in Hosea, said something wonderful. He promised to *"betroth"* Israel to Him "forever." As their forever Husband, He promised them five things, the very number of grace. Their marriage would be characterized by righteousness, judgment, lovingkindness, mercies, and faithfulness.

What an amazing God! Despite Israel's unfaithfulness, evil, idolatry, and immorality, He promised her eternal restoration and a beautiful, intimate relationship with Him, all illustrating the depth of His love and stunning character.

Continuing with the text:

*"And it shall come to pass in that day, I will hear, saith the LORD, I will hear the heavens, and they shall hear the earth; And the earth shall hear the corn, and the wine, and the oil; and they shall hear Jezreel. And I will sow her unto me in the earth; and I will have mercy upon her that had not obtained mercy; and I will say to them which were not my people, Thou art my people; and they shall say, **Thou art my God.**"* Hosea 2:21-23

God promises that heaven would respond to earth's need for rain, sunshine, etcetera to produce abundant crops. He would "sow" Israel. Recall that Jezreel means "God will judge, sow, scatter." Though God must judge Israel during Hosea's day by allowing them to be conquered and scattered, there will come a time when He will "sow" or plant them in their land, prosper them, and call them by His name.

Prior to 1948, when Israel became a nation, many had trouble believing this prophecy. The land produced little, was deserted, and was considered a barren wilderness. Mark Twain, in his 1867 book, *The Innocence Abroad,* describes what he saw during his visit: "A desolate country whose soil is rich enough, but is given over wholly to weeds . . . a silent mournful expanse. . . a desolation. . . we never saw a human being on the whole route. . . hardly a tree or shrub anywhere. Even the olive tree and the cactus, those fast friends of a worthless soil, had almost deserted the country."

But after Israel's return, the land began yielding again. Today, the Jezreel Valley is lush and green, full of farms, vineyards, and olive groves. Even so, most of Israel's population are secular, living in unbelief. This will only change during the Tribulation when the remnant Jews acknowledge Jesus as their Messiah, and say, *"Thou art my God."*

In Matthew 23:39, Jesus told the scribes and Pharisees they would not see Him again (come the second time) until *"Ye shall say, Blessed is he that cometh in the name of the Lord."* Zechariah 12:10 predicts this event. *"And I* (Jesus) *will pour upon the house of David, and upon the inhabitants of Jerusalem, the spirit of grace and of supplications: and they shall look upon me whom they have pierced, and they shall mourn for him, as one mourneth for his only son, and shall be in bitterness for him, as one that is in bitterness for his firstborn."* And Romans 11:26 says, *"And so all Israel shall be saved: as it is written, There shall come out of Sion the Deliverer, and shall turn away ungodliness from Jacob."*

For two thousand years, God has gathered Gentiles and Jews into His Church as referenced in both Romans and Peter. *"As he* (God) *saith also in O'see, I will call them* (the Gentiles) *my people, which were not my people; and her beloved, which was not beloved. And it shall come to pass, that in the place where it was said unto them, Ye are not my people; there shall they be called the children of the living God,"* (Romans 9:25-26). And *"But ye* (born-again believers, the Church) *are a chosen generation, a royal priesthood, an holy nation, a peculiar people; that ye should shew forth the praises of him who hath called you out of darkness into his marvellous light: Which in time past were not a people, but are now the people of God: which had not obtained mercy, but now have obtained mercy,"* (1 Peter 2:9-10).

There is no end to God's mercy. He loves everyone, both Jew and Gentile. It cannot be said too often that He wishes no one to perish. How He longs for everyone to come into His loving arms and say, *"Thou art my God!"*

Chapter 3

*"Then said the LORD unto me, Go yet, love a woman beloved of her friend, yet an adulteress, according to the love of the LORD toward the children of Israel, who look to other gods, and love **flagons of wine**. So I bought her to me for **fifteen pieces of silver**, and for **an homer of barley, and an half homer of barley**: And I said unto her, Thou shalt abide for me many days; thou shalt not play the harlot, and thou shalt not be for another man: so will I also be for thee. For the children of Israel shall abide many days without a king, and without a prince, and without a sacrifice, and without an image, and without an ephod, and without teraphim: Afterward shall the children of Israel return, and seek the LORD their God, and David their king; and shall fear the LORD and his goodness in the **latter days**."* Hosea 3:1-5

This is a small chapter but packed with spiritual nuggets. God again instructed Hosea to love a woman who is *"yet an adulteress."* That word "woman" is *ishshah*. And while it means "woman, female," it also means "mortal man, mankind." And that word "yet" (*owd*) means "continuance, again." Though this specifically refers to Gomer, who continually engaged in prostitution, it also points to the human race that also continually engages in spiritual prostitution by rejecting God.

Notice, Gomer is *"beloved of her friend."* Several commentaries suggest that this indicates she had a specific lover while engaged in prostitution. There is certainly no reason to refute that. However, I see a deeper meaning. This woman is *"beloved of her friend"* even though she continually prostitutes herself. I believe *"her friend"* is God Himself, and Gomer, of course, is Israel. Though Yahweh no longer called Israel His wife, she was still His friend. This is a reference to Abraham, the friend of God, and the Abrahamic Covenant. Because Abraham was God's friend and because God made an everlasting covenant with him and his descendants, the prostitute, Israel, was still "beloved" by God. And because of God's promise to Abraham, He would always be Israel's friend. Though friendship is not as intense or intimate as the relationship between husband and wife, it suggests that a covenant was still in effect.

But there's more. Although that word "barley" (*seowrah*) means "barley," it also conveys the general meaning for "plant, grain." It points to Jesus' death on the cross. In John 12:24, Jesus said, *"Verily, verily, I say unto you, Except a **corn** of **wheat** fall into the ground and die, it abideth alone: but if it die, it bringeth forth much fruit."* In Greek, that word "corn" is *kikos* and means "a kernel of seed, corn, grain." And wheat" is *sitos* meaning "grain, corn, wheat." Jesus, the "Seed" of woman, is the "grain" that falls to the ground and dies as our sacrificial Lamb in order to produce a harvest.

Then Hosea gave the reason for this shift in relationship from husband to friend. Israel had loved other gods as well as *"flagons of wine."* According to the *Theological Wordbook of the Old Testament*, "the King James Bible constantly translated raisin cakes as flagons of wine." Thus, this passage refers to raisin cakes.

Leaven symbolizes sin. Leviticus 2:4, 7:12 details how unleavened cakes were to be given as an offering to Yahweh. This cake was punctured, again pointing to Jesus. It prophetically symbolizes that Jesus, the Bread of Life, would be pierced for us as the sinless sacrifice.

Instead of offering unleavened bread to Yahweh, those in the northern kingdom offered raisin cakes to the queen of heaven. Eventually, those in the southern kingdom did as well, (Jeremiah 7:18, 44:19).

In the last chapter, we also saw how raisin or fig cakes can refer to the tightly pressed and entwined relationship Israel and all believers are to have with God. But prostituting Israel had become pressed together and entwined with demons.

God then instructed Hosea to buy back his wife, Gomer, who had left him and was now owned by and working for the local prostitution ring. Hosea obeyed and purchased her for fifteen pieces of silver and a homer and a half of barley (about 64 ounces, also valued at fifteen pieces of silver). Thus, her total slave price equaled thirty pieces of silver.

Homer (*chomer*) means not only a "measure for dry goods" but also "mire, clay, heap, human bodies, mere man." The *Theological Wordbook of the Old Testament* adds that *chomer* is "likened metaphorically to men in their creaturely relationship to their Maker, to the potter-clay relationship." On the other hand, silver symbolizes redemption. It points to redemption through the God-man, Jesus, Who became clay to pay for our sins.

Numbers in Scripture are also relevant. In the Old Testament, thirty pieces of silver was the going price for a slave. It's no coincidence that Jesus was betrayed (actually purchased) for thirty pieces of silver as the Lamb of God, our sin substitute. In turn, His sacrifice bought us back from the slave markets of the world.

This is not just a story of a prophet reclaiming his debauched wife. It's not even just the story of God's love for and reclamation of the nation of Israel. It goes far beyond that. It's the story of Jesus reclaiming and restoring mankind itself!

God then said Israel would be tested a long time (*many days*). This test was to see if she would refrain from idolatry. During that time, she would be scattered with no king or prince, no cohesive nation.

In addition, she would have neither Temple nor priest (ephod). The ephod was an outer garment worn by the high priest. An onyx stone was affixed to the fabric over each shoulder and inscribed with the names of the twelve tribes of Israel. Attached to the ephod was the breastplate containing twelve different gemstones, each representing one of the twelve tribes. In addition, the ephod contained the Urim and Thummim, used to determine God's will, as both Saul and David did. But instead of consulting their priests and seeking God's will, the Israelites had turned to teraphim (household gods), graven images, and divination. As a result, Israel would now lose the benefit of God's guidance.

Prophetically speaking, God, like Hosea, would keep Himself from His wife, Israel. And for almost 2000 years He has. Since Israel was destroyed by Rome in 70 A.D. until 1948, she has been scattered and without a king or high priest. Her Temple was destroyed. Sacrifices ceased. But now, God is in the process of fulfilling Hosea 3:5. *"Afterward shall the children of*

Israel return, and seek the LORD their God, and David their king: and shall fear the LORD and his goodness ***in the latter days.****"*

God repeated this promise in Jeremiah 31:31, *"Behold, the days come, saith the LORD, that I will make a new covenant with the house of Israel, and with the house of Judah."* Notice, both kingdoms are mentioned indicating divided Israel would be united. This was a hope they could count on. God was not finished with them.

As unbelievers, before we came to Christ, we, too, like Hosea's wife, were spiritual prostitutes. We worshipped other gods—the gods of materialism, pleasure, fame, position, money, etcetera. But just as Hosea purchased Gomer from slavery and the prostitution ring, so Jesus purchased us from the slave markets of the world, cleaned us up, and called us His own.

Oh, how faithful God is! Yes, Israel has experienced judgment for her many sins, but God has begun her restoration and will complete it during the Tribulation or Jacob's Trouble, and once again be her Husband. And Jesus will be the Husband to Gentile born-again believers. Isaiah 61:10-11, speaking about these believers (the church) says, *"I will greatly rejoice in the LORD, my soul shall be joyful in my God; for he hath clothed me with the garments of salvation, he hath covered me with the robe of righteousness, as a* ***bridegroom*** *decketh himself with ornaments, and as a bride adorneth herself with her jewels. For as the earth bringeth forth her bud, and as the garden causeth the things that are sown in it to spring forth; so the Lord GOD will cause righteousness and praise to spring forth before all the nations."*

Here, the church is likened to a lavishly adorned bride and Jesus as our bridegroom during His millennial kingdom when

He reigns in glory and causes *"righteousness and praise to spring forth before all the nations."*

Isaiah 62:5b goes on to say, *"As the* ***bridegroom*** *rejoiceth over the bride, so shall thy God rejoice over thee."* God *wants* to be our husband. He loves us and *wants* to protect, guide, and bless us. This is His heart of love.

Song of Solomon gives us an even deeper picture. It is more than a love story between king Solomon and the Shulamite woman, or between God and His wife, Israel. It's a foreshadowing of the love between Jesus, the King, and His bride, the Church. I've covered this in detail in my first book of *Exploring the "Little" Books of the Old Testament"* series and will not repeat it now.

It is interesting to note that when Jesus was in the synagogue and quoted Isaiah 61, which speaks of both Messiah ben Joseph, the Suffering Servant, and Messiah ben David, the King, and announced His ministry, He stopped at verse 2 and didn't proclaim *"the day of vengeance of our God."* Why? Because that part would not be fulfilled until the Tribulation.

And here's the amazing thing: after those terrible seven years of tribulation, we, His bride, will reign with Him in His millennial kingdom! Can God be any more forgiving, or loving, or generous? What a wonderful future He offers those who love Him!

Chapter 4

"Hear the word of the LORD, ye children of Israel: for the LORD hath a controversy with the inhabitants of the land, because there is no truth, nor mercy, nor knowledge of God in the land. By swearing, and lying, and killing, and stealing, and committing adultery, they break out, and ***blood toucheth blood****. Therefore shall* ***the land mourn****, and every one that dwelleth therein shall languish, with the beasts of the field, and with the fowls of heaven; yea, the fishes of the sea also shall be taken away."* Hosea 4:1-3

Due to Israel's sins and lack of repentance, God continued warning of His judgment. His people were devoid of truth. They no longer followed or served Him. Proverbs 1:7 says, *"The fear of the LORD is the beginning of knowledge: but fools despise wisdom and instruction."* Those in Israel had become fools, despising God's instruction and following their own inclinations.

And what had this folly produced? A nation of liars, killers, thieves, swearers, adulterers. A nation where *"blood toucheth blood,"* meaning it was full of violence and murder.

This sounds all too familiar! Look around. What has our nation become? A mirror image of Israel! Yes, politics has always been associated with deception, backstabbing, and backroom deals. But I remember a time when it was civil, at least superficially. I never thought I'd hear one politician advocating the murder of his opponent or hear such blatant lies that no one even believes them. And the rest of it, the swearing, killing, stealing, adultery, is blatant, too, and becoming all too acceptable.

Today's statistics on violence are all over the place. Some claim it has steadily declined. Others say these statistics don't include all violence; that property crimes and youth violence have actually gone up. Still others say gang violence has increased 30% over the past five years. Then a National Crime Victimization Survey claims violent crime has increased by 44%! And that doesn't include mob violence. Those "mostly peaceful" protests are hardly that. Stores are looted, cars and buildings damaged. And the disgrace is this: many of these protesters are paid by liberal socialist groups and can't even articulate what they are protesting.

In 2020, the George Floyd riots damaged 700 buildings and completely destroyed twelve others. The estimated cost of ensured damage was 1-2 **billion** dollars. That doesn't count the uninsured structures, property, or items.[1] In 2024, Portland State University spent 1.2 million repairing their library after it was damaged by pro-Palestinian protesters.[2] LA spent 2 million in 2025 on cleanup and repair after just one anti-ICE protest.[3] This does not count the cost of the mass looting in that city or elsewhere. The list goes on.

President Trump's hard line on crime has helped. But what happens when a new president is elected? One who believes in "defunding the police"? We must realize that things can change quickly from one administration to another. Currently, our streets, homes, businesses reflect a society lacking "knowledge of God." If that doesn't change, expect things to get worse. And when they do, at some point, expect God to act.

I'd like to digress here and drill down on why blood touching blood is so serious. To begin with, it implies that blood is being spilled. And spilling blood, especially innocent blood, has far reaching consequences. I've written about this in some of my other books but will include it now because it can taint a nation and make *"the land mourn."* It's also important because it addresses the issue of capital punishment which many sincere Christians oppose. What they don't understand is that it was instituted by God Himself.

Let's see why.

When Noah's ark rested safely after the flood, and he and his family disembarked, the first thing Noah did was offer one of every clean animal as a sacrifice to God. Because this pleased Yahweh, He removed the curse from the ground. That's why, later, various types of produce were acceptable sacrifices in the Jewish Temple. Then He told Noah he could now eat the flesh of animals (Genesis 9:3-4) but prohibited the eating or drinking of blood. *"But flesh with the life thereof, which is the blood thereof, shall ye not eat."*

Later, in Leviticus 17:10-12, this restriction was repeated and the reason given: *"For the life of the flesh is in the blood and* ***I have given it to you upon the altar to make an atonement for your souls: for it is the blood that maketh an atonement for the soul.****"*

Here, God spelled it out. Only blood can make an atonement. Only blood covers sin. Under Levitical Law, a whole system of animal sacrifices and blood handling was established. By it, the

Israelites clearly understood that blood was holy and reserved only for God.

After Noah's sacrifice, God, in Genesis 9:5-6, told him if a beast or man takes the life of a man, the blood of that man or beast will be required. Then God gave the reason: *"Whoso sheddeth man's blood, by man shall his blood be shed: for in the image of God made he man."* Only blood was payment for blood because man was made in God's image.

This law precedes the Law of Moses and was never cancelled in the Old or New Testament. God still forbids the willful killing of one man by another. This includes abortion, but not the killing in war, self-defense, or an accidental slaying.

In ancient Israel, six cities of refuge were established for those who killed in self-defense or accidently (Numbers 35:6-34). These cities were a place the killer could go in order to escape the blood avenger who was duty-bound to avenge the shedding of innocent blood. The blood avenger could not kill a person if he remained in one of these cities. Again, this did not apply to someone who willfully murdered another. That person continued to remain at the mercy of the blood avenger.

Thus, it's clear that God established capital punishment. This was also understood by the Israelites under Levitical Law. Numbers 35:33-34 tells us why it was necessary: *"**So ye shall not pollute the land** wherein ye are: for blood it **defileth the land**: and the land cannot be cleansed of the blood that is shed therein, but by the blood of him that shed it. Defile not therefore the land which ye shall inhabit."*

So, if we do not put murderers to death, *"We pollute and defile our land."* And Deuteronomy 19:13 adds, *"Thine eye shall not pity him* (the murderer), *but thou shall put away the guilt of innocent blood from Israel, that it may go well with thee."*

If the guilt of innocent blood is not put away, if the murderer is not made to pay with his blood, it will not go well with that nation.

Christians who oppose capital punishment are subordinating God's Word to their own viewpoint and feelings. Proverbs 3:5-6 warns, *"Lean not unto thine own understanding. In all thy ways acknowledge him* (God), *and he shall direct thy paths."* In the end, it doesn't matter what we ***think*** is right. It only matters what God ***says*** is right. We need to align our thinking with God's Word because God is never going to align His with ours.

So, we know that:

God Himself instituted the death penalty. He made it clear that only blood can pay for the shedding of innocent blood. And we are not to pity the murderer. If a murderer does not pay with his blood, the land becomes defiled and polluted, and it will not go well for that nation. Since murder is still forbidden in the New Testament (Matthew 19:18, Romans 13:9, 1Peter 4:15, 1 John 3:15) that still applies today.

What happens if the murderer accepts Jesus? He will naturally have to face the consequences set forth in his nation's legal system. But spiritually speaking, if that murderer confesses his sin and puts it under the blood of Jesus, the blood requirement is considered paid. Jesus' blood satisfies the requirements of the blood avenger.

Has the shedding of innocent blood been sufficiently paid for in our nation? The answer is, "No." Our nation is awash with blood through abortion and violent crimes. Though it may seem that there are no consequences for this, rest assured, God keeps detailed accounts. His Word doesn't change. It will not go well with a nation drenched in blood. And no one president or politician can keep God's hand from dispensing justice.

Returning to the text: Notice, Hosea 4:1 says that God had a "*controversy*" with Israel. That word is *riyb* meaning "a contest, strife." The *Theological Wordbook of the Old Testament* goes even farther and says *riyb* is strongly associated with "legal-judicial overtones." It's a picture of God pleading with Israel to shape up before He legally must act. I believe that's what God is saying to us today. We need to "wake up" and "shape up" by returning to the Lord and His statutes.

God warned Israel that the penalty for their apostacy would be the "*languishing*" of the land, people, animals, and even fish. Languish (*amal*) means "to droop, be sick, to mourn." The *Theological Wordbook of the Old Testament* said it also "expresses the state into which the objects of God's punishment and discipline come." This is a picture of it not going well with the nation that sheds innocent blood and practices habitual evil. Israel would now mourn. Its land would mourn and fail to produce. Its animals would be scarce. Its population weak and exhausted from the rigors of life.

Continuing with the text:

"Yet let no man strive, nor reprove another: for thy people are as they that strive with the priest. Therefore shalt thou fall in the day, and the prophet also shall fall with thee in the night, and I will destroy thy mother. My people are destroyed for lack of knowledge: because thou hast rejected knowledge, I will also reject thee, that thou shalt

be no priest to me: seeing thou hast forgotten the law of thy God, I will also forget thy children." Hosea 4:4-6

God cautioned the people not to point fingers. The nation's downfall was everyone's fault, including the priests. As guardians of God's Word, the Law, they failed miserably. They not only sinned themselves but led others into sin. In addition, Israel's prophets were false, further causing the kingdom to stumble and fall. Designated by God to be His priestly nation, His light in the world, Israel instead had become a covenant breaking nation full of darkness and sin. As a result, the nation ("*thy mother*") would be destroyed. Knowledge is again mentioned. Because the people rejected the knowledge of God and have become fools, God would now reject them.

Continuing with the text:

"As they were increased, so they sinned against me: therefore will I change their glory into shame. They eat up the sin of my people, and they set their heart on their iniquity. And there shall be, like people, like priest: and I will punish them for their ways, and reward them their doings. For they shall eat, and not have enough: they shall commit whoredom, and shall not increase: because they have left off to take heed to the LORD. Whoredom and wine and new wine take away the heart." Hosea 4:7-11

The more Israel increased in population, power, and affluence, the more they forgot God, and the more they sinned. This is a common pattern. Throughout the Church Age, it's no accident that persecution strengthened it, while wealth and power diminished it. The last day's Laodicean church is an example. Jesus had harsh words for it in Revelation 3:17, *"Because thou sayest,* ***I am rich, and increased with goods, and have need of***

nothing*; and knowest not that thou are wretched, and miserable, and poor, and blind, and naked."*

And Laodicea is everywhere. Rich and self-righteous, it dishes out pablum rather than the whole counsel of God. It's afraid to offend anyone yet not afraid to offend God. It's a church that Jesus threatens to "*spue*" out of His mouth, (Revelation 3:16). No wonder renowned American evangelist and paster R.A. Torrey (1856-1928) said, "I frankly confess I am afraid of luxury—not as afraid of it as I am of sin, but it comes next as an object of dread. It is a very subtle but a very potent enemy of power."

We should fear it, too, for it can make us self-satisfied and spiritually lazy, unwilling to lay our life, plans, or desires down before the Lord.

In Hosea, these priests *"eat up the sin of my people."* A portion of the sin offerings were given to the priests for their use. Therefore, they were enriched by these offerings. Instead of instructing the people in righteousness, the priests failed to restrain them, thus ensuring the continuation of their "gravy train."

Then God, in Hosea, said that Israel was going to reap what she had sowed. Because she had left the Lord, He would leave her. No longer honored and protected, she would experience shame and privation, a privation even her false gods couldn't reverse. Their idolatry, which included intoxication, had perverted their mind and understanding of the things of God.

Continuing with the text:

"My people ask counsel at their stocks, and their staff declareth unto them: for the spirit of whoredoms hath caused them to err, and they have gone a whoring from under their God. They sacrifice upon the tops of the mountains, and burn incense upon the hills, under oaks and poplars and elms, because the shadow thereof is good: therefore your daughters shall commit whoredom, and your spouses shall commit adultery. I will not punish your daughters when they commit whoredom, nor your spouses when they commit adultery: for themselves are separated with whores, they sacrifice with harlots: therefore the people that doth not understand shall fall." Hosea 4:12-14

Here, God again cited their idolatry. They had removed themselves from "*under*" God's authority and placed themselves under the authority of demon spirits. They inquired (*ask counsel*) of their wooden idols (*their stocks*) and thought their divining rods (*their staff*) could give them direction. They even burned incense to these demons.

Incense symbolizes not only sacrifices made to a deity, but also the prayers of that deity's followers. David, in Psalm 141:2, asked Yahweh to, *"Let my prayer be set forth before thee as **incense**; and the lifting up of my hands as the evening sacrifice."* And Revelation 5:8 says, *"And when he* (Jesus) *had taken the book* (the seven-sealed scroll), *the four beasts and four and twenty elders fell down before the Lamb, having every one of them harps, and golden vials full of odours, which are the **prayers of saints**."* Israel was to offer their prayers to Yahweh like incense. Instead, they offered them to demons.

They worshiped these spirits on mountaintops and hills, and under trees *"because the shadow thereof is good."* Shadow (*tsel)* means "shade," as well as "defense." On a superficial level, it means the people gathered under shade trees to perform perverted rituals in worship of their fertility gods. But on a deeper level, the people were seeking the shadow or defense of these entities rather than Yahweh. He was to be their source of protection. David understood this when he said in Psalm 17:8, *"Keep me as the apple of the eye, hide me under the* ***shadow*** *of thy wings."* And in Psalm 121:5 he said, *"The LORD is thy keeper: the LORD is thy* ***shade*** *upon thy right hand* (of power)."

Then God said He would not punish the *kallah,* meaning the brides or daughters-in-law, because the husbands and fathers were doing the same thing. Their lack of understanding made them unable to distinguish between Yahweh, the one true God, and idols. And because of this, they would be thrust down (*fall*) as Proverbs 10:8 warns. *"The wise in heart will receive commandments: but a prating fool shall* ***fall****."* Because the people of Israel had spurned God and His commandments, they had become prating fools.

Continuing with the text:

"Though thou, Israel, play the harlot, yet let not Judah offend; and come not ye unto Gilgal, neither go ye up to Bethaven, nor swear, the LORD liveth. For Israel slideth back as a backsliding heifer: now the LORD will feed them as a lamb in a large place. Ephraim is joined to idols: let him alone. Their drink is sour: they have committed whoredom continually: her rulers with shame do love, Give ye. The wind hath bound her up in her wings, and they shall be ashamed because of their sacrifices." Hosea 4:15-19

Israel was doomed. She had apostatized and left the God Who formed her as a nation and protected her in favor of worthless idols. Now, she would be judged. But God also warned Judah not to follow in Israel's footsteps, to stay away from her so as not to be tainted. Go not *"unto Gilgal."* Gilgal means "a wheel, circular, a whirlwind." Micah 6:5, Amos 4:4, and Hosea 12:11 all mention Gilgal's idolatry.

But there is also an added message here. Because Israel had toyed with the "whirlwind" of idolatry, they would now encounter the whirlwind of God's anger. Proverbs 10:25 says, *"As the **whirlwind** passeth, so is the wicked no more: but the righteous is an everlasting foundation."* Isaiah 66:15 says, *"For behold, the LORD will come with fire, and with his chariots like a **whirlwind**, to render his anger with fury, and his rebuke with flames of fire."* Jeremiah 23:19 and 30:23 also speak of God's whirlwind of anger. Even Hosea 8:7 mentions that Israel has *"sown the wind, and they shall reap the **whirlwind*** (of God's anger). But Nahum 1:3 says it best: *"The LORD is slow to anger, and great in power, and will not at all acquit the wicked: the LORD hath his way in the **whirlwind** and in the storm, and the clouds are the dust of his feet."* Sooner or later, unrepentant sinners will reap the whirlwind.

God also instructed Judah not to go to Bethaven. That word "Bethaven" means "house of evil, house of vanity." It is a deliberate perversion of Bethel, which means "house of God."

During Solomon's time, his many elaborate building projects created a tax burden on the people, either in substance or forced labor. After he died, his son, Rehoboam, refused to ease the burden, causing the people to revolt and the nation to split in two. Rehoboam ruled the southern kingdom, which consisted of the tribes of Judah and Benjamin, and was called Judah. The northern kingdom, called Israel, consisted of the remaining ten tribes with Jeroboam I becoming its first king.

Jeroboam was from the tribe of Ephraim, not from the ruling house of Judah. Aside from being an illegitimate king, he soon violated Exodus 20:4 regarding the making of graven images. To keep his people from returning to Jerusalem during the three compulsory festivals, Passover, Pentecost, and Tabernacles, Jeroboam commissioned the crafting of two golden calves. He installed one in Dan, the other in Bethel, causing God to refer to Bethel as Bethhaven.

Jeroboam then replaced the Levite priests with his own and made Bethel the worship center of his kingdom. To make matters worse, he also endorsed idolatrous worship at various high places. Because of all this, Jeroboam's twenty-two-year reign left Israel riddled with idolatry. Now, here, in Hosea 4, God was telling Judah to stay away from Bethel or Bethaven, and that worship there of the golden calf did not please Him.

But was Bethaven as the "house of vanity" also significant? Yes. Solomon, in Ecclesiastes 1:2 said, *"Vanity of vanities, saith the Preacher, vanity of vanities; all is vanity."* That word "vanity" is *hebel* and means "emptiness, unsatisfactory." After a lifetime of gratifying every carnal desire, Solomon concluded it was all vanity, emptiness. It didn't satisfy. He then determined that the entire purpose of life was to *"Fear God, and keep his commandments,"* (Ecclesiastes 12:13). This was the only thing that had lasting value.

A life filled with selfish pursuits is indeed empty and unsatisfying. As seen in Hosea chapter two, there is a part of us that only God can fill. He purposely made us that way. We are to be His enjoyment, and He is to be ours. But the choice is ours to live either a God-centered life or a self-centered one.

It's interesting to note that many of the people I've met who have chosen self are the very ones who try to demonstrate their virtue or moral superiority. They see nothing inconsistent in fighting to save the whales on one hand and on the other, fight for the right to kill babies in the womb. It's called virtue signaling. It's a form of self-righteousness rather than Christ's righteousness. The truth is, we are all sinners in need of Jesus our Savior. None of us can claim a high level of morality because, due to our sin nature, our moral compass is broken.

In Hosea, God not only warned Judah against committing idolatry but against swearing *"the LORD liveth."* Jews used that verbiage when making oaths. By them, they invoked God as witness that the words of their oath were true. But the Israelites were swearing these oaths while worshiping idols. Their oaths were not only meaningless but blasphemous. And God was telling Judah, "Don't do it!"

In addition, because Israel was like a rebellious and stubborn heifer, they should not expect God to *"feed them as a* (compliant) *lamb in a **large** place."* God wanted to be their Shepherd. They were to be His sheep, His lambs. Instead, they had become like unruly cows, easy to stampede in all directions. God had vowed to bring His people into the Promised Land. Exodus 3:8 calls it "large." *"And I* (God) *am come down to deliver them out of the hand of the Egyptians, and to bring them up out of that land unto a good land and a **large**, unto a land flowing with milk and honey; unto the place of the Canaanites, and the Hittites, and the Amorites, and the Perizzites, and the Hivites, and the Jebusites."* But the people could hardly expect God's continued protection and provision after turning their back on Him.

"Ephraim is joined to idols: let him alone." Ephriam means "double fruitful." It was not only the largest, most prosperous and powerful tribe, but for almost 200 years, the northern kingdom was often referred to as Ephraim.

"Their drink is sour: they have committed whoredom continually." As part of their pagan rituals, the Israelites became drunk and engaged in ritual sex. God was saying that her rulers love these shameful activities more than God's shekinah glory. In other words, *"her rulers with shame do love."*

That word "rulers" (*magen*) means "shield, buckler." While God was to be their shield and buckler, He also expected Israel's rulers to be their nation's as well. Psalm 18:30 says, *"As for God, his way is perfect: the word of the LORD is tried: he is a* ***buckler*** *to all those that trust in him."* And Psalm 91:4 says, *"He* (God) *shall cover thee with his feathers, and under his wings shalt thou trust: his truth shall be thy* ***shield*** *and* ***buckler****."*

Instead of acting as God's protecting arms around His people, these rulers became a different kind of shield and buckler, entrapping the people in idolatry to such an extent that there was no way to escape God's judgment. And that judgment comes on the wings of the wind or whirlwind. Instead of being protected under the shadow of God's wings as Psalm 91:4 suggests, Israel was bound up in the wings of the wind, or the whirlwind of God's wrath. Furthermore, due to Israel's idolatry, that nation must now be left (*let him alone*) to face the consequence.

What a tragic ending for the northern kingdom! How sad that they are empty, unsatisfied, unprotected, and forced to face the wind of judgment. That's not at all what God had intended. David understood this when he prayed, *"Keep me as the apple of the eye, hide me under the* ***shadow*** *of thy* ***wings****."* And Psalm 36:7 says, *"How excellent is thy lovingkindness, O God! therefore the children of men put their trust under the* ***shadow*** *of thy* ***wings****."*

And that is exactly where we are to put our trust. Beneath the shadow of God's wings there is safety and healing. It was so for Israel when they followed Yahweh, and it's so for us now if we follow Jesus. Malachi 4:2, promised this: *"But unto you that fear my* (God's) *name shall the Sun of righteousness arise with **healing** in his **wings**; and ye shall go forth, and grow up as calves of the stall."* (Not as unruly heifers as described in Hosea.)

The Sun of righteousness is just another title for the Messiah. A Jewish prayer shawl is called a *tallit* with fringe on the corner edges called *tzitzit*. And as a Jew, Jesus wore *tzitzit* or tassels, fringe that could be seen. These were often referred to as "wings." The Jews knew of the prophecy of the Messiah Who would have *"healing in his wings,"* therefore it is reason-able to conclude that the widow, with the issue of blood in Matthew 9:20, who touched the *"hem of his* (Jesus') *garment,"* actually touched his *tzitzit*. Indeed, that word "hem" in this verse is *kraspedon* and means, "fringe or tassel."

Again, in Matthew 14:35-36, when Jesus was in *"the land of Gennesaret"* the crowd brought their sick to Him *"And besought him that they might only touch the **hem** of his garment: and as many as touched were made **perfectly whole**."* That word "hem" again is *kraspedon*, fringe or tassel. By touching Jesus' tassels, they were not only hoping to be healed but were acknowledging He was the Messiah. Because of that, they were made *"perfectly whole"* in both spirit and body.

Speaking of wings, Jesus also referred to them in Matthew 23:37. Heartbroken over the Jews' rejection, and foreseeing the ensuing destruction of Jerusalem, He said: *"O Jerusalem, Jerusalem, thou that killest the prophets, and stonest them which are sent unto thee, how often would I have gathered thy children together, even as a hen gathereth her chickens under her **wings**, and* *ye would not!"* Here, the word "wings" is *pterux* and literally means, "feathers or wings." Jesus was using symbolism, comparing Himself to a mother hen who wanted to protect her young by gathering them under her feathery wings.

And oh, how He wants everyone to come under His wings today, just as He wanted Israel to do.

Chapter 5

"Hear ye this, O priests; and hearken ye house of Israel; and give ye ear, O house of the king; for judgment is toward you, because ye have been a snare on Mizpah, and a net spread upon Tabor. And the revolters are profound to make slaughter, though I have been a rebuker of them all. I know Ephraim, and Israel is not hid from me: for now, O Ephraim, thou committest whoredom, and Israel is defiled. They will not frame their doings to turn unto their God: for the spirit of whoredoms is in the midst of them, and they have not known the LORD." Hosea 5:1-4

Notice, when referring to the northern kingdom, God used both the names of Ephraim and Israel. Also, Ephraim was mentioned before Israel. But further down in verse 5, we see this reversed and Israel is mentioned first. Happenstance? No. As previously stated, Ephraim was the largest and most powerful and influential of the ten northern tribes. Therefore, God was rebuking them for failing to influence their kingdom for good. In verse five, when Israel is mentioned first, God was rebuking the entire northern kingdom for their sins.

Then notice, three groups are addressed: priests, people, rulers. God left no one out. His grievance was against the entire ten northern tribes for being *"a snare on Mizpah, and a net spread upon Tabor."* That word "snare" means "a trap." It also means "metal plate." Why is that important? Because Mizpah means "watchtower," a place where lookouts stood, scanning for danger. And these "watchmen" were to sound the alarm at the first sign of it. But spiritual "watchmen" were also set over the people to alert them to the dangers of apostasy and sin.

I've covered this subject in Book One of this series and will repeat a portion now.

In Ezekiel 3:17, God set a spiritual watchman over his people. *"Son of man,* (God is speaking to Ezekiel) *I have made thee a **watchman** unto the house of Israel: therefore hear the word at my mouth, and give them warning from me."* Isaiah 62:6 says, *"I* (God) *have set **watchmen** upon thy walls, O Jerusalem, which shall never hold their peace day nor night: ye that make mention of the LORD, keep not silence."*

If a watchman did not obey and warn the people of God's coming judgment, it carried a serious penalty. God considered that watchman guilty of the blood of those whom he did not warn. Ezekiel 33:2-6 details this. *"Son of man* (Ezekiel), *speak to the children of thy people, and say unto them, When I bring the sword upon a land, if the people of the land take a man of their coasts, and set him for their **watchman**: If when he seeth the sword come upon the land, he blow the trumpet, and warn the people; Then whosoever heareth the sound of the trumpet, and taketh not warning; if the sword come, and take him away, his blood shall be upon his own head. He heard the sound of the trumpet, and took not warning; his blood shall be upon him. But he that taketh warning shall deliver his soul. But if the **watchman** see the sword come, and blow not the trumpet, and the people be not warned; if the sword come, and take any person from among them, he is taken away in his iniquity; but his blood will I require at the **watchman's** hand."*

This warning also applied to spiritual watchmen (priests, prophets, and rulers). If they didn't warn people that their sins and apostasy would bring God's judgment, God would hold them accountable as well. Jeremiah 6:17-19 makes that clear. *"Also I* (God) *set* ***watchmen*** *over you, saying, Hearken to the sound of the trumpet. But they said, We will not hearken. Therefore hear, ye nations, and know, O congregation, what is among them. Hear, O earth: behold, I will bring evil upon this people, even the fruit of their thoughts, because they have not hearkened unto my words, nor to my law, but rejected it."*

In Isaiah 56:10-11, God talked about blind watchmen and corrupt shepherds. *"His* ***watchmen*** *are blind: they are all ignorant, they are all dumb dogs, they cannot bark; sleeping, lying down, loving to slumber. Yea, they are greedy dogs which can never have enough, and they are* ***shepherds*** *that cannot understand: they all look to their own way, every one for his gain, from his quarter."* Clearly, Isreal's watchmen failed them. Because they were more interested in enriching themselves than being godly stewards, they not only turned a blind eye to their own sins but encouraged others in theirs.

Because of their blindness, their watchtowers figuratively became clad in metal plates or sheathing (*snare on Mizpah*), obscuring their view of the coming danger. Their ignorance and greed caused them to become like "dumb dogs" that couldn't bark (warn). Thus, Israel continued unabated in their crimes against God.

God also pointed to their spreading a net *"upon Tabor."* Tabor means "a broken region, to be fragile." And "net" is a snare or trap. It infers that those "fragile" or "broken" in Israel were trapped by this idolatry and immorality sanctioned by both priests and elites. The *Theological Wordbook of the Old Testament* says net "metaphorically describes people being trapped by their enemies." The *Wordbook* also claims "net" can mean, "the wicked spreading nets to overcome the righteous." Once immorality and idolatry took hold in Israel, those who tried to live righteously were persecuted and looked down upon until they became a "broken" and "fragile" group.

"And the revolters are profound to make slaughter." Slaughter here refers to animal sacrifices. These rebels made sacrifices to false gods. And they were *"profound"* in doing so. That means they were deep into their debauchery and committed vile acts in their rituals. And they did this even while God continued to rebuke them (*though I have been a rebuker of them all*).

"Rebuker" (*muwcar*) means "chastisement, reproof, warn." Though God had continually warned them against these practices, had chastised them as a loving father would his erring child, they refused to turn. "Rebuker" reflects God's love and care for His people, and how much He wanted to avoid judgment. Proverbs 3:11-12 says, *"My son, despise not the chastening of the LORD; neither be weary of his correction: For whom the LORD* ***loveth*** *he correcteth; even as a father the son in whom he delighteth."* God had delighted in Israel. He had tried to keep them on the straight and narrow. Because they refused to listen, He was now legally obligated to render judgment.

Why was God legally obligated? Because He has set up immutable laws in His kingdom, one being that the wages of sin is death unless paid for by innocent blood. Because Israel had been sacrificing to false gods, their sins were not covered. And after years of warning them, God, as a just Judge, finally had to act. To go on endlessly threatening punishment without action would make His statutes meaningless.

God went on to say, *"I know Ephraim, and Israel is not hid from me."* God knew the depth of Ephraim's sins, every secret thing they had done. Omniscient Yahweh had seen it all, their whoredoms, the many ways they defiled themselves. Their idolatry was in the *"midst of them,"* meaning their "inner parts, their center." They were doing this with their whole being, fully engaged, fully committed.

Sometimes a person's outer façade looks good, but inside his thoughts, beliefs, what he holds dear, are anything but. And God sees it all. The danger is that evil thoughts can quickly become evil deeds. That's why David, in Psalm 51:10, prayed, *"Create in me a clean heart, O God; and renew a right spirit within me."*

In the end, Israel's elites refused to curtail their thoughts and desires, their evil fantasies that seduced them into serving other gods, thus destroying their relationship with Yahweh. And their evil filtered down to the people, creating an environment for sin to flourish.

Continuing with the text:

"And the pride of Israel doth testify to his face: therefore shall Israel and Ephraim fall in their iniquity; Judah also shall fall with them. They shall go with their flocks and with their herds to seek the LORD; but they shall not find him; he hath withdrawn himself from them. They have dealt treacherously against the LORD: for they have begotten strange children: now shall a month devour them with their portions." Hosea 5:5-7

Israel's pride was their undoing. They thought they didn't need the God Who delivered them from bondage and birthed them as a nation. Prosperous and powerful, they believed they could go their own way, make their own rules. Now, their ruin testified to their arrogance. Their *"iniquity"* had caused them to fall. That word "iniquity" is *avon* and means "perversity, evil." The *Theological Wordbook of the Old Testament* says it "denotes both the deed and its consequences, the misdeed and its punishment." In other words, what they did carried an automatic punishment, a punishment they couldn't escape.

But God also prophesied that Judah, too, would fall. That happened 135 years later in 587 B.C. when they were conquered by Babylon.

Then God said that though Israel would seek Him, they wouldn't find Him. He was withdrawing. That word "seek" is *baqash* and means "to search, specifically in worship or prayer." Because of their treachery and because they had *"begotten strange children,"* God, for a time, would not answer their prayers or accept their worship. We know their treachery was going after other gods. But what does *"strange children"* mean?

That word "strange" (*zuwr*) denotes "turning aside, be a foreigner, profane, to commit adultery." Because the Israelites failed to train up their children, these children didn't follow God, either. They, too, shunned their spiritual heritage and profaned themselves with idolatry.

Again, that was not what God had intended. Exodus 19:5-6 lays out God's desire for His people. *"Now therefore, if ye will obey my* (God's) *voice indeed, and keep my covenant, then ye shall be a* ***peculiar treasure*** *unto me above all people: for all the earth is mine: And ye shall be unto me a* ***kingdom of priests****, and an* ***holy nation****."* They were to be a peculiar treasure, a kingdom of priests, a holy nation. Instead, they became "strange."

It's worth noting that Jesus, through His sacrifice on the cross, made a way for Gentiles to become the very things God had desired for Israel. 1 Peter 2:9 says, *"But ye* (born again believers) *are a chosen generation, a* ***royal priesthood****, an* ***holy nation****, a* ***peculiar people****; that ye should shew forth the praises of him who hath called you out of darkness into his marvellous light."*

Oh, how merciful and loving God is! And what great lengths He has gone to not only bring people to Himself but elevate them to a wonderful position!

Verse four ends by God saying Israel's portions would be devoured during a month. That word "devour" (*akal*) means "to eat, burn up." Portions (*cheleq*) means "territory, an allotment, share in an inheritance." Does this mean their monthly food allotment won't even last a month? Uncertain. It could also point to the temporary loss of their inheritance as the "apple of God's eye," His "treasure, priests, and holy nation."

Continuing with the text:

"Blow ye the cornet in Gibeah, and the trumpet in Ramah: cry aloud at Bethaven, after thee, O Benjamin. Ephraim shall be desolate in the day of rebuke: among the tribes of Israel have I made known that which shall surely be. The princes of Judah were like them that remove the bound: therefore I will pour out my wrath upon them like water." Hosea 5:8-10

A cornet (*shofar*) was typically a ram's horn used to announce the beginning of the Sabbath, a new moon, the year of Jubilee, to express praise, warn of danger, and to convey military signals in battle. A trumpet (*chatsotserah*), on the other hand, was made of silver, the symbol of redemption. The historian

Josephus describes it as "a little short of a cubit (18-22 inches) . . . a narrow tube . . . slightly thicker than a flute." It was used by priests to summon the elders or their tribes, to break camp, to announce festivals or sacrifices to Yahweh, and as a call to arms during danger or war.

The blowing of the cornet in Hosea signals the destruction of Israel, the ten northern tribes. It's a done deal. They have exhausted God's mercy and grace. But here, God instructed that both the shofar and silver trumpet be blown to warn Benjamin, one of the tribes of the southern kingdom. Though danger lies ahead for them, redemption is available if repentance is forthcoming.

Gibeah and Ramah are mentioned. And both indicate height. Gibeah means "hill" while Ramah means "a height as a seat of idolatry, to rise, haughty." Thus, it can be a play on words with God instructing the alarm to be sounded upon a high place, enabling the sound to carry. It also suggests that this alarm is necessary because of the haughtiness, the heights or magnitude of Israel's sin. And it's a warning to Judah.

"Among the tribes of Israel have I made known that which shall surely be." God always gives advance warning of what He's about to do. Amos 3:7 says, *"Surely the Lord God will do nothing, but he revealeth his secret unto his servants the prophets."* That's God's kindness. He never springs anything on His people. And God had been warning Israel of the coming judgment for years. Now, He was warning the southern kingdom of Benjamin and Judah. He was telling His prophet Hosea to *"cry aloud at Bethhaven."* That phrase *"cry aloud"* (*ruwa*) means "to shout, raise an alarm." And we've already seen that Bethhaven (house of evil) is a perversion of Bethel (house of God). God

again warns the southern kingdom not to follow Israel by turning God's house into a house of evil and idolatry.

Now, God accused Judah's leaders and princes of removing the *"bound,"* a territorial marker. Perhaps this refers to how the leaders mistreated the poor, stole their property, etcetera. But according to the *Theological Wordbook of the Old Testament*, it can figuratively mean "a territory of darkness." And "remove" means "to retreat, departing away, turn away." Thus, we get a picture of Judah figuratively turning away from their original position as God's light and oracle in the world, to a "territory of darkness." The Amplified Bible says it more clearly: *"The princes of Judah are like those who remove the landmark, the barrier between right and wrong."* And because of that, God's wrath would be poured out like *"water."* It would be like a raging river, demolishing everything in its path, a path directed solely by God.

Continuing with the text:

"Ephraim is oppressed and broken in judgment, because he willingly walked after the commandment. Therefore will I be unto Ephraim as a moth, and to the house of Judah as rottenness. When Ephraim saw his sickness, and Judah saw his wound, then went Ephraim to the Assyrian, and sent to king Jareb: yet could he not heal you, nor cure you of your wound. For I will be unto Ephraim as a lion, and as a young lion to the house of Judah: I, even I, will tear and go away; I will take away, and none shall rescue him. I will go and return to my place, till they acknowledge their offence, and seek my face: in their affliction they will seek me early." Hosea 5:11-15

God's punishment for Israel's sins would break them. They would be a ruined nation. They had *"willingly"* yielded to the dictates of the elites by following in their footsteps and committing idolatry. That word "willingly" (*yaal*) means "weakness, to yield, foolish, become fools, show wicked folly." They had become the epitome of Psalm 14:1-3: *"The **fool** hath said in his heart, There is no God. They are corrupt, they have done abominable works, there is none that doeth good. The LORD looked down from heaven upon the children of men, to see if there were any that did understand, and seek God. They are all gone aside, they are all together become filthy: there is none that doeth good, no, not one."*

In return, God said He would be like a "*moth*" to Ephraim and "*rottenness*" to Judah. He was telling Ephraim that in the same way a moth destroys insidiously and often unnoticed, so will He destroy them. David, regarding God's chastisement and judgment for sins said this in Psalm 39:10-11: *"Remove thy stroke away from me: I am consumed by the blow of thine hand.* ***When thou with rebukes dost correct man for iniquity, thou makest his beauty to consume away like a moth:*** *surely every man is vanity."* God would consume Israel's beauty and leave them crushed and broken.

He then told Judah that because their nation, too, would eventually decay morally, He would be rottenness to them. Dry rot destroys the internal foundations of a structure. First, God would allow them to be destroyed from within. Then, He would allow Babylon to do the rest.

When Israel realized how worn and weak (*"saw his sickness"*) he was, the rulers went to Assyria's king Jareb for help. That name "Jareb" means "he will contend." Most scholars believe Jareb is a nickname for Sargon II because of his contentious nature. But Jareb can also mean "great king." Sargon, son of Tiglath-pileser III, who ruled Assyria from 721 B.C. to 705 B.C., was considered a great king of the Neo-Assyrian Empire.

For three years, Sargon's predecessor, Shalmaneser V, had been laying siege to Samaria (Israel's capital). Finally, in 722 B.C., Sargon completed the job, thus causing the downfall of the northern kingdom. He then deported thousands of Jews, scattering them throughout his empire. Afterward, he brought Syrian and Babylonian settlers to Samaria, along with their gods, to interbreed with the remaining inhabitants and utterly destroy them as a cohesive nation. Their descendants became the Samaritans and were looked down upon by Jews as inferior mongrels.

Unfortunately, history repeated itself. Rather than looking to God for protection, Judah, in weakness, also sought Assyria's help. Fearing Israel and Syria would invade, Judah made an alliance with Tiglath-pileser III, then ended up becoming his vassal and paying a heavy yearly tribute. In addition, this alliance opened Judah's door to Assyrian idolatry which seeped into the Jerusalem Temple itself.

In spite of Israel and Judah looking elsewhere for support, nothing could nor would turn God's hand from dispensing His judgment. No outside source would rescue them.

"I will be unto Ephraim as a lion, and as a young lion to the house of Judah: I, even I, will tear and go away; I will take away, and none shall rescue him." That word "lion" is *shachal*, and means "to roar, a lion from his characteristics." "Young lion" (*kephiyr*) means "a young lion, as covered with a mane." Lions were considered one of the most ferocious in the animal kingdom. Thus, this evokes both power and brutality. Additionally, God threaten-ed to "tear" Israel and Judah. It creates a picture of a lion devouring its prey. Indeed, the *Theological Wordbook of the Old Testament* says the primary meaning of "tear" is "to seize a creature with predaciousness (predatory behavior), tear the

flesh, and consume it." A frightening picture! It is a picture of God Whose patience had been exhausted, Who was about to bring down severe judgment on His people, a judgment that would leave Israel utterly decimated. Though Judah had more than a century before her bones would be picked, she, too, would not escape.

When our loving God becomes a roaring Lion, it's terrifying. The Bible contains many Scriptures of God as a lion. Job 10:16 refers to Him as a *"fierce **lion**."* Proverbs 19:12 talks about how *"The king's wrath* (both an earthly king and our heavenly king) *is as the roaring of a **lion**."* And Amos, a contemporary of Hosea, describes what God's judgment against Israel looks like. *"Thus saith the LORD; As the shepherd taketh out of the mouth of the **lion** two legs, or a piece of an ear; so shall the children of Israel be taken out that dwell in Samaria in the corner of a bed, and in Damascus in a couch,"* (Amos 3:12).

While God is likened to a lion and Jesus is called the *"lion of the tribe of Judah"* (Revelation 5:5), it doesn't mean God does the actual "tearing." Rather, God allows that other "lion," Satan, to do it through his proxies. First, Assyria destroyed Israel, then Babylon destroyed Judah. It's interesting to note that Sargon of Assyria was often depicted as a lion, and the Babylonian Empire was represented by a winged lion.

It is well to remember that when God removes His hand of protection from a nation or individual, they become easy prey for Satan, who seeks those he can devour, (1 Peter 5:8).

God ended by saying, *"I will go and return to my place, till they acknowledge their offence, and seek my face: in their affliction they will seek me early."* This is an end-times prophecy. And since it carries over into Hosea chapter 6, I will address it then.

Chapter 6

"Come, and let us return unto the LORD: for he hath torn, and he will heal us; he hath smitten, and he will bind us up. After two days will he revive us: in the third day he will raise us up, and we shall live in his sight. Then shall we know, if we follow on to know the LORD: his going forth is prepared as the morning; and he shall come unto us as the rain, as the latter and former rain unto the earth." Hosea 6:1-3

Bible chapters and verses are not original to the text but were added later as references and to easily locate Scripture passages. But they can also cause problems. That's why a prophecy found in Hosea 5:15 can bleed over into Hosea 6:1-3.

At the end of Hosea chapter 5, God said, *"I will go and return to **my place*** (heaven), *till they acknowledge **their offence**, and seek my face: in their affliction they will seek me early."* Because God said He would return to heaven it means He had previously left it. He also said He would stay there until Israel (both northern and southern kingdoms) repents. This points to how, in the future, Jesus will leave His place in heaven and come to earth as our Kinsman Redeemer. He did this when He was born in Bethlehem. Then thirty-three years later, He was rejected, crucified, died, rose from the dead, and ascended into heaven (His *place*). Some scholars vary on the timeline of this event, but most believe He lived from 4 B.C. to 30 A.D. No matter which dates are correct, it changed the world forever.

But what was Israel's "*offence*"? Since Jesus died for the sins of the whole world, Jews as well as Gentiles, this offense was not their rejection of His sacrificial crucifixion in Jerusalem. Rather, it was the rejection of Jesus as Messiah by the Jewish priests and leaders.

There are several indications in Scripture that these leaders knew exactly who Jesus was. The miracles, the ones the rabbis claimed only the Messiah could do, were all performed by Jesus. No evidence exists that anyone else, either prior to Jesus' time or since, has ever performed them. In addition, early on, rabbis gleaned from Scripture that there would be two Messiahs: Messiah ben Joseph, the Suffering Servant, (Genesis 49:22-26, Zechariah 9:9-10, Isaiah 53, Psalm 22) and Messiah ben David, the King (Daniel 7, Isaiah 9, and others). Thus, Jesus' first coming and the nature of His ministry could hardly come as a surprise.

Then there was Jesus' knowledge of Scripture. His in-depth understanding blew the leaders away, infuriated them, and provoked jealousy. His resurrection from the dead caused them to concoct a lie and bribe others to keep the truth hidden. Their lust for power, respect, and influence left no room for a Messiah or a Messianic Kingdom. They were only interested in building their own kingdom. Their great sin was not only their willful and knowing rejection of the Messiah, but their deliberate attempt to deceive others. They did everything to silence Jesus and keep their nation from knowing His identity.

However, even those who did recognize Jesus as Messiah, saw Him in the wrong light. In Matthew 21:1-11, Jesus rode a donkey into Jerusalem. The crowd went wild, waving palm branches and placing others along His path. Their voices swelled in unison, *"Hosanna to the son of David: Blessed is he that cometh in the name of the Lord; Hosanna in the highest."* All Israel knew that the Messiah would come from the line of David. And the phrase *"son of David"* was a direct reference to the Messiah. In John 12:13, the people call Jesus, *"the King of Israel,"* again referring to the Messiah. But this did not refer to Messiah ben Joseph, the suffering servant, but Messiah ben David, the King. They didn't want the Suffering Servant. Rather, they wanted a powerful ruler who would rescue them from the heel of Rome. They didn't understand that the rescue Jesus offered was far far greater.

No wonder Jesus, when talking about the end times, said in Matthew 23:37-39, *"O Jerusalem, Jerusalem, thou that killest the prophets, and stonest them which are sent unto thee, how often would I have gathered thy children together, even as a hen gathereth her chickens under her wings, and ye would not! Behold, your house is left unto you desolate. For I say unto you, Ye shall not see me henceforth till ye shall say, Blessed is he that cometh in the name of the Lord."*

In Hosea chapter 5 and now chapter 6, God was speaking to the nation of Israel and her leaders. Thus, the nation, as well as her leaders, will have to cry out to Jesus in repentance and faith and finally acknowledge Him as Messiah before He returns.

The wonderful thing is that Romans 11:25-32 tells us that all Israel will be saved. *"For I would not, brethren, that ye should be ignorant of this mystery, lest ye should be wise in your own conceits; that blindness in part is happened to Israel, until the fulness of the*

Gentiles be come in. ***And so all Israel shall be saved:*** *as it is written, There shall come out of Sion the Deliverer, and shall turn away ungodliness from Jacob:* ***For this is my covenant unto them, when I shall take away their sins****. As concerning the gospel, they are enemies for your sakes: but as touching the election, they are beloved for the fathers' sakes.* ***For the gifts and calling of God are without repentance.*** *For as ye in times past have not believed God, yet have now obtained mercy through their unbelief: Even so have these also now not believed, that through your mercy they also may obtain mercy. For God hath concluded them all in unbelief, that he might have mercy upon all."*

Zechariah 12:10 says that when Israel finally realizes who Jesus is, they will mourn. *"And I* (God) *will pour upon the house of David, and upon the inhabitants of Jerusalem, the spirit of grace and of supplications: and they shall look upon me whom they have pierced, and* ***they shall mourn for him, as one mourneth for his only son, and shall be in bitterness for him, as one that is in bitterness for his firstborn."***

A time is coming when Israel will repent and acknowledge Him. That's when God will heal and bind them up. And according to Hosea 5:15, it will happen during their *"affliction."* Again, this prophetically points to the end times, during the Tribulation or "Jacob's Trouble," (Jeremiah 30:7).

Zechariah 13:7-9 talks about the death of Messiah and the punishment of Israel for their rejection of Him. Referring to the end times or Jacob's Trouble, it tells us that two-thirds of the Jews will die. ***"Awake, O sword, against my shepherd*** (Jesus), *and against the man that is my fellow, saith the LORD of hosts:* ***smite the shepherd, and the sheep shall be scattered****: and I will turn mine hand upon the little ones. And it shall come to pass, that in all the land, saith the LORD,* ***two parts therein shall be cut off***

and die*; but the third shall be left therein. And I will bring the third part through the fire* (of the Tribulation), *and will refine them as silver is refined, and will try them as gold is tried:* ***they shall call on my name****, and I will hear them: I will say, It is my people: and they shall say, The LORD is my God."* What a happy thought that Israel will eventually be saved! But how sad to know it will come at such a heavy price!

After the last supper, when Jesus and His disciples went to the Mount of Olives, He, connecting Himself to Zechariah's prophecy, said, , *"All ye shall be offended because of me this night: for it is written, I will* ***smite the shepherd, and the sheep of the flock shall be scattered abroad,"*** (Matthew 26:31).

A side note: It is important to realize that in Zechariah it is God the Father who sends the sword against the Shepherd, Jesus, in order to fulfill His redemption plan; a plan Jesus willingly accepted. *"Looking unto Jesus the author and finisher of our faith;* ***who for the joy that was set before him endured the cross,*** *despising the shame, and is set down at the right hand of the throne of God,"* (Hebrews 12:2).

But the good news is this: though pain, suffering, and judgment are still to come upon Israel and the world, at its end, God will fulfill His covenant promise. Not only will He be Israel's God, Messiah, and King, He will be ours and rule the entire world in justice and peace. Throughout Israel's ups and downs, their cycles of sin, apostasy, repentance, and return, God never forgot His covenant. Through it all, He displayed His goodness by continually promising there would be restoration for His people. And He did this even while they were steeped in gross idolatry. Though God distanced Himself or withdrew at times, His covenant with Israel has always been in effect, is currently in effect, and will continue to be in effect into the Kingdom Age.

The next question is: When will all this happen?

"After two days will he revive us." First, let's look at that word "revive." It's *chayah* and means "to live, to revive, be quickened." The *Theological Wordbook of the Old Testament* adds, "In the OT, life is decided by a right relationship to the righteous standards of the word of God. . .. By cleaving to God, the righteous have life."

It's obvious this word implies that their "reviving" comes only after their repentance and once again having a righteous relationship with God. After that, He lovingly restores them. Then restoration implies a return to the original form, condition, position, all of which God does for Israel. During the end times, they will again become the apple of His eye, His treasure, priests, and holy nation.

God has been setting the stage for centuries, rescuing and supporting His people, keeping them from total annihilation. As mentioned, we saw the beginning of Israel's restoration in 1948 when she miraculously became a nation. In 1967, she recaptured Jerusalem. Following that, Jews all over the world began making *Aliyah* (returning to the land). All this has been orchestrated by God. But it is only part of His plan for their full reinstatement.

But what does *"after two days"* mean? I believe it represents two thousand years. We see this equation in 2 Peter 3:8. *"But, beloved, be not ignorant of this one thing, that* ***one day is with the Lord as a thousand years, and a thousand years as one day****."*

We also see this same equation in Genesis when God created the world in six days. Why six days? Why not one or fifteen? God could have taken as few or as many days as He wanted. And yes, I believe God created it all in literally six days just as Scripture indicates. But the creation timeline is also a template for human history, which is to last six thousand years or six days. The seventh day, the Sabbath, the day God rested, represents the seventh thousand-year period when God will rule on earth, tabernacle with His people, and give the planet and mankind rest from war, sickness, strife, and demonic influence. It will truly be a Sabbath Rest.

Because I believe a day represents one thousand years, I believe *"two days"* speak of two thousand years following Jesus' death and resurrection. We are currently in that time-frame. That means the "third day" will be Jesus' thousand year earthly reign. That's when Israel will be "raised" up as the head of nations and physically *"live in his sight."* That means we are close to the end of the Church Age, the Rapture, Tribulation, and beginning of the millennial Kingdom.

In the meantime, there must be a former and latter rain, a symbolic reference to the outpouring of the Holy Spirit. The former rain (*yowreh yarah*) means "the first rain, sprinkling, to flow as water." This spiritual sprinkling first occurred at Pentecost when the Holy Spirit came upon the disciples in the upper room. Acts 2:1-4 describes the event. *"And when the day of Pentecost was fully come, they were all with one accord in one place. And suddenly there came a sound from heaven as of a rushing mighty wind, and it filled all the house where they were sitting. And there appeared unto them cloven tongues like as of fire, and it sat upon each of them. And they were all filled with the Holy Ghost, and began to speak with other tongues, as the Spirit gave them utterance."*

When the disciples left the upper room to preach on the street, they were so full of the Holy Spirit people thought they were drunk. Peter, in Acts 2:16-18, had to explain what happened. *"But this is that which was spoken by the prophet Joel; And it shall come to pass in the* ***last days****, saith God, I will pour out of my Spirit upon all flesh: and your sons and your daughters shall prophesy, and your young men shall see visions, and your old men shall dream dreams: And on my servants and on my handmaidens I will pour out in those days of my Spirit; and they shall prophesy."*

Thus, we can conclude we have been in the last days since Pentecost. The former rains or early rains in Israel usually occur around October and November, the time of preparing the soil. The latter rains or spring rains occur in March and April around the time of harvest. For two thousand years, God has been pouring out the "former rain," producing numerous "revivals" and planting seeds for His kingdom. It's called the Church Age. When it ends, the latter rain will come to bring in the final harvest. I believe this will happen during the Tribulation when God unleashes the 144,000 Jewish evangelists, the two witnesses from heaven, and the flying angel who proclaims the gospel throughout the world.

Both Joel and James spoke of these events. *"Be glad then, ye children of Zion, and rejoice in the LORD your God: for he hath given you the former rain moderately, and he will cause to come down for you the rain,* ***the former rain, and the latter rain*** *in the first month,"* (Joel 2:23). And *"Be patient therefore, brethren, unto the coming of the Lord* (Jesus' second coming). *Behold, the husbandman waiteth for the precious fruit of the earth, and hath long patience for it, until he receive* ***the early and latter rain,****"* (James 5:7).

While earth has been experiencing the former outpouring of the Holy Spirit, it will soon experience His latter outpouring, and multiple millions will be saved. Oh, the matchless love and mercy of our God!

Continuing with the text:

"O Ephraim, what shall I do unto thee? O Judah, what shall I do unto thee? for your goodness is as a morning cloud, and as the early dew it goeth away. Therefore have I hewed them by the prophets; I have slain them by the words of my mouth: and thy judgments are as the light that goeth forth. For I desire mercy, and not sacrifice, and the knowledge of God more than burnt offerings." Hosea 6:4-6

I hear both God's love and frustration in the above. Like a loving but frustrated father who has patiently corrected his child over and over again for the same offense, so I hear God's exasperation when He speaks to Israel. Also, like a loving father who really doesn't want to punish his child but must because it is necessary, so God must punish Ephraim and Judah. Their obedience to Him, their loyalty, their love has been as fleeting and temporary as the drifting clouds and morning dew.

And they are without excuse. God's commandments given to Moses laid out His statutes and laws. It was to be the blueprint by which they lived. Following that, numerous prophets repeatedly issued God's warnings regarding the penalty for disobedience. Now, these warnings have risen as a testimony against Israel and legally must be followed by judgment. Though God has been faithful, patient, longsuffering, and merciful toward Israel, they failed to respond in kind. Their hearts were far from Him, and their superficial acts of sacrifice were just that, superficial.

Continuing with the text:

"But they like men have transgressed the covenant: there have they dealt treacherously against me. Gilead is a city of them that work iniquity, and is polluted with blood. And as troops of robbers wait for a man, so the company of priests murder in the way by consent: for they commit lewdness. I have seen an horrible thing in the house of Israel: there is the whoredom of Ephraim, Israel is defiled. Also, O Judah, he hath set an harvest for thee, when I returned the captivity of my people." Hosea 6:7-11

"They like men have transgressed the covenant." Here, God not only indicted Israel, but all mankind. As previously mentioned, Psalms 14:1-3 says, *"The fool hath said in his heart, There is no God. They are corrupt, they have done abominable works,* ***there is none that doeth good****. The LORD looked down from heaven upon the children of men, to see if there were any that did understand, and seek God. They are all gone aside, they are all together become filthy:* ***there is none that doeth good, no, not one****."* Romans 3:10 confirms this: *"****There is none righteous, no, not one****."* Romans 3:23 goes on to say, *"****For all have sinned****, and come short of the glory of God."* Because "all" have done this, "all" have *"dealt treacherously"* against God. And there is a penalty attached. Romans 6:23 tells us what it is: *"For the wages of sin is death; but the gift of God is eternal life through Jesus Christ our Lord."*

This is an immutable law and cannot be rescinded. Therefore, all mankind is under a death sentence. That's why God had to make a way of escape. In the Old Testament He did so by instituting animal sacrifices where the blood of an innocent animal was man's sin covering. But Israel's offerings were no longer sincere, therefore unacceptable to God. The filthiness of the priests, their lewdness and evil deeds, as well as their national sins, would now force God to act. In this same way, He will be forced to act against all those who have not obtained *"the gift of God . . . through Jesus Christ,"* the perfect sin atonement.

God highlighted the city of Gilead, calling it *"polluted with blood."* He called its people, workers of *"iniquity."* The city, once the habitation of the idolatrous Moabites and Amorites, had also been ruled by King Sihon, the giant half human, half angelic Nephilim hybrid. After Gilead was conquered by Joshua, it was allotted to the tribe of Manasseh. Later, when tensions arose between Benjamin and Ephraim, Gilead became their battleground where many were killed. It was, in every respect, a blood-soaked land.

Gilead was also the name given to the large central region of the northern kingdom. It, along with Megiddo and Dor, were three cities already controlled by the Assyrian king, Tiglath-pileser III. In addition to becoming the scene of violence and bloodshed, it was permeated with Assyrian paganism. To God, Gilead typified Israel's morally impoverished condition.

God went on to call Israel *"defiled."* He witnessed a *"horrible thing"* meaning He saw the magnitude of their idolatry and lewdness. That word "lewdness (*zimmah*) means "wickedness, heinous crime." But Judah was not far behind. God again prophesized that she, too, would experience His judgment for her own sins. Hosea 6:11 in the Amplified says it so well. *"Also, O Judah, there is a harvest of divine judgment appointed for you; when I would return My people from their captivity in which they are slaves to the misery brought on by their own sins."*

The above repeats the familiar theme that if no repentance occurs either in a sinful nation or sinful individual, sooner or later there will come a day of reckoning.

Chapter 7

*"When I would have healed Israel, then the iniquity of Ephraim was discovered, and the wickedness of Samaria: for they commit falsehood; and the thief cometh in, and the troop of robbers spoileth without. And they consider not in their hearts that I remember all their wickedness: now their own doings have beset them about; they are before my face. They make the king glad with their wickedness, and the princes with their lies. They are all adulterers, as **an oven heated by the baker**, who ceaseth from raising after he hath kneaded the dough, until it be leavened. In the day of our king the princes have made him sick with bottles of wine; he strethched out his hand with scorners. For they have made ready their heart like an **oven**, whiles they lie in wait: their baker sleepeth all the night; in the morning it **burneth** as a flaming fire. They are all **hot** as an **oven**, and devoured their judges; all their kings are fallen: there is none among them that called unto me."* Hosea 7:1-7

Again, we see God's desire to heal Israel. But their iniquity, constantly flaunted in His face, could no longer be ignored.

God specifically mentioned Samaria. That name means "watch-station, to hedge about." Fifty years after Israel split into north and south, the north's king, Omri, moved his capital from Tirzah to Samaria. Omri died before completing everything, so it fell to his son and successor, Ahab, to finish the project. The palace, called an "ivory house" due to the amount of ivory inlayed furnishings, was opulent.

Ahab had married the infamous Jezebel, pagan daughter of the Phoenician king. To please her, in Samaria, he built a temple to her god, Baal. In no time, Baal worship spread throughout the north, with Samaria becoming its center. This idolatry spearheaded all manner of wickedness. Instead of being a "watch-station" or "hedge" protecting God's people through godly leadership, Samaria became the center of spiritual pollution and a stench in His nostrils.

Though God may not react immediately to unconfessed, continuous sin, He never excuses or forgets it. That's where Israel made their mistake (*They consider not in their hearts that I remember all their wickedness)*. Because their blatant idolatry and immorality wasn't instantly met with judgment, the people thought God hadn't seen them or was overlooking them. They were wrong. God saw everything, every act committed from the king and rulers, down to the lowliest plebian.

In the above verses, God made three references to an oven. He painted a picture of unattended bread that becomes burnt and therefore useless. In the same way, Israel had become useless to Him. Their sin and idolatry made them unable to feed the Gentile world with His truth. Also, *"an oven heated by the baker"* is a Hebrew idiom referring to strong passion. God called them "adulterers" whose "heat," whose passion for Baal and other false gods have ruined them. As a result, these evil lusts have consumed judges, kings, and populace alike.

They had become like leavened dough. Leaven is a picture of sin. And dough is leavened or swollen by fermentation. The bakers, the ones who should have been watching (the rulers, priests, prophets) failed to properly care for the dough (Israel) and left it unattended, allowing it to become swollen with sin and thus kindling God's hot anger.

Also note, God connected *"bottles of wine"* to the kings and princes. This refers to a drunken state, a state where one's wisdom escapes him. It's also a picture of the northern kingdom, which, for decades, reeled with deceit, intrigue, and murder like a drunkard. Ahab was killed in 852 B.C. while fighting Assyria in the battle at Ramath-gilead. After him, five of the twelve successive northern kings would be assassinated by the time of the final Assyrian conquest in 722 B.C.

God also mentioned that the king *"strethched out his hand with scorners."* That word "scorners" (*latsats*) means to "deride, scorn." While "stretched" is *mashak* and means to "draw, to sow, to march, to develop." The king was sowing his loyalty and resources among scorners (Israel's backsliding elites and the hostile pagan nations). Considering all the palace intrigues and assassinations, he obviously wanted to keep the elites on his side. He was also willing to bribe pagan nations to act as friends and protectors. Instead of aligning himself with God, the king aligned himself with scorners.

The Bible has much to say about scorners. Here are just a few verses:

- Proverbs 13:1, *"A wise son heareth his father's instruction: but a* ***scorner*** *heareth not rebuke."*
- Proverbs 14:6, 9, *"A* ***scorner*** *seeketh wisdom, and findeth it not: but knowledge is easy unto him that understandeth. . .. Fools make a mock at sin: but among the righteous there is favour."*

- Proverbs 15:12, *"A **scorner** loveth not one that reproveth him: neither will he go unto the wise."*
- Proverbs 22:10, *"Cast out the **scorner**, and contention shall go out; yea, strife and reproach shall cease."*

So, scorners lack wisdom and don't take sin seriously. They look for others to accept and indulge their folly. They are contentious and quarrelsome, stirring up trouble and conflict wherever they go. In short, they are fools. And the Bible does not speak kindly of fools or scorners. Proverbs 3:33-35 says, *"The **curse** of the LORD is in the house of the wicked: but he blesseth the habitation of the just. Surely **he scorneth the scorners**: but he giveth grace unto the lowly. The wise shall inherit glory: but shame shall be the promotion of **fools**."* And Proverbs 19:29 tells us that, *"Judgments are prepared for **scorners**, and stripes for the back of **fools**."* Thus, we see that God's curse is on scorners and fools, as well as His contempt. And these types of people will only garner shame and judgment.

Continuing with the text:

"Ephraim, he hath mixed himself among the people; Ephraim is a cake not turned. Strangers have devoured his strength, and he knoweth it not: yea, gray hairs are here and there upon him, yet he knoweth not. And the pride of Israel testifieth to his face: and they do not return to the LORD their God, nor seek him for all this. Ephraim also is like a silly dove without heart: they call to Egypt, they go to Assyria. When they shall go, I will spread my net upon them; I will bring them down as the fowls of the heaven; I will chastise them, as their congregation hath heard." Hosea 7:8-12

Ephraim/Israel had *"mixed himself among the people."* That word "mixed" is *balal* and means "to mix, mingle." The *Theological Wordbook of the Old Testament* adds to it by saying mixed not only means to "mix, confuse, confound" but is "a ritualistic term used of mixing oil into the flour or meal of the cereal offering until every particle of flour was mingled or anointed with oil."

Israel was to be a separated nation, God's chosen people, one consecrated to Him (thoroughly mingled with His will and anointed with oil as His holy offering). But instead of being His living sacrifice, they so mingled or mixed themselves with the surrounding heathens they were no longer acceptable to Yahweh. God called them half baked (*a cake not turned*), over-cooked on the bottom, undercooked on top, making them good for nothing.

Israel's many years of paying tribute to Assyria had weakened the nation (*Strangers have devoured his strength*) sapping Israel of wealth and power, and causing it to become prematurely worn out and depleted (*gray hairs are here and there*). But though the *"pride of Israel testified to his face,"* Israel failed to see or acknowledge it because conceding it meant having to admit how far from God it had strayed.

But what is the *"pride of Israel"*? That word "pride" is *gaown* meaning "arrogancy, pride, swelling." Like leaven swelling dough, they had become swollen with their own importance. They were proud of being the "apple of God's eye." They were proud of their Temple. They were proud that their laws were written by the finger of God. They were proud of their system of sacrificial offerings as well as their priesthood. They were proud of their status among the nations, forgetting it was God Who had elevated them. The very things they were proud of testified to their apostasy, immorality, and spiritual decline. Their swollen pride had led them to become swollen with sin. Yet, despite all this, they refused to return to Yahweh.

As a result, Israel became like a *"silly dove without heart."* In ancient times, domesticated doves were raised for food and ritual sacrifices. "Silly" is *pathah* and means "open, roomy, simple, delude, deceive, flatter." And *"without heart"* indicates lack of understanding. Putting it all together, Israel had been deceived, deluded, and flattered into thinking that other nations would support and protect him. Instead of looking to God, he turned to Egypt and Assyria. He was like one that lacked understanding, not knowing where to turn, and flying here, there, and everywhere except to the One Who had always protected and supported him.

"I will spread my net upon them. I will bring them down as the fowls of the heaven." Fowlers use nets to snare birds. God was likening Himself to a fowler, a hunter. He was making it clear that although He was using Egypt and Assyria as His net to take down Israel, it was all His doing. It was His hand of chastisement, a chastisement the prophets had been warning about for years.

While Jesus' warning in Matthew 13:15 was meant for the Pharisees and Israel's rulers, I believe, as we enter these last of the last days, it can also apply to us. *"For this people's heart is waxed gross, and their ears are dull of hearing, and their eyes they have closed; lest at any time they should see with their eyes, and hear with their ears, and should understand with their heart, and should be converted, and I should heal them."*

Continuing with the text:

"Woe unto them! for they have fled from me: destruction unto them! because they have transgressed against me: though I have redeemed them, yet they have spoken lies against me. And they have not cried unto me with their heart, when they ***howled*** *upon their beds: they*

assemble themselves for corn and wine, and they rebel against me. Though I have bound and strengthened their arms, yet do they imagine mischief against me. They return, but not to the most High: they are like a deceitful bow: their princes shall fall by the sword for the rage of their tongue: this shall be their derision in the land of Egypt." Hosea 7:13-16

God again warned Israel. They would be destroyed. Their hearts had turned to other gods. Their actions, their disrespect, their gross idolatry make destruction necessary. Because this judgment causes crop failure and privation, they cry and howl, not for God, but for their comfort to be restored. That word "howled" (*yalal*) means "to howl with wailing." The *Theological Wordbook of the Old Testament* says it also "points to a relationship with anxiety, sorrow and distress," as well as to mourn because of "death or destruction." This indicates Israel's great distress. They are impoverished and hungry. They have seen friends and relatives die. Their homes have been destroyed. Many have been ripped from the land they love and forced to relocate among hostile pagans. They have seen and experienced all this and more, and still won't repent or return to God.

It reminds me of when the fourth seal of judgment is opened during the Tribulation, resulting in the death of one-fourth of the world's population through war and famine. Still, many people refuse to repent. Instead, Revelation 6:15-17 tells us that *"The kings of the earth, and the great men, and the rich men, and the chief captains, and the mighty men, and every bondman, and every free man, hid themselves in the dens and in the rocks of the mountains; And said to the mountains and rocks, Fall on us, and hide us from the face of him that setteth on the throne, and from the wrath of the Lamb: For the great day of his wrath is come; and who shall be able to stand?"*

Let's look again at Hosea 7:13, 15: "*Though I have redeemed them, yet they have spoken lies against me. . .. Though I have bound and strengthened their arms, yet do they imagine mischief against me.*"

Although this can refer to God redeeming Israel from the slave pits of Egypt and strengthening them as a nation, I believe it also points to their Kinsman Redeemer, Jesus, and Israel's rejection of Him. Not only did they reject Him, but the Pharisees and Sadducees lied about Him. They called Him a law breaker (Matthew 12:1-21) and claimed He cast out demons by the power of Satan (Matthew 12:24). They stood before Pilate and accused Jesus "*of many things,*" (Mark 15:3). They called Jesus a malefactor (a *kakopoios*, a criminal, an evil doer). "*Pilate then went out unto them* (the priests and temple guards), *and said, What accusation bring ye against this man? They answered and said unto him, If he* (Jesus) *were not a **malefactor**, we would not have delivered him up unto thee. Then said Pilate unto them, Take ye him, and judge him according to your law. The Jews therefore said unto him, It is not lawful for us to put any man to death,*" (John 18:29-31). And their ultimate "mischief" was to plot his murder.

I don't see any other way or time when man could do "mischief" to God. Yes, we can break God's heart by our rejection of Him, and do. But this is talking about "imagining mischief." "Imagine" (*chashab*) means "to plan, fabricate." And "mischief" is *ra* meaning, "evil, bad." The *Theological Wordbook of the Old Testament* also says it implies "a malicious glee or a threatening excitement." That pretty much describes Israel's religious leaders and their evil, fabricated, covert plans to rid themselves of Jesus. They didn't want their reign to end. Their desire to hold onto their exalted position, authority, and prosperity, made them maliciously and gleefully conspire against their Messiah, the One Who could change all that.

It's important to note here that Jesus died for the sins of the world, not just Israel's sins. And He did not die because Israel's religious leaders willed it. As already mentioned, it was God's plan all along. Thus, it was due to **all** of mankind's sins that made Jesus' crucifixion necessary. And He did it willingly. In John 10:17-18, Jesus said, *"Therefore doth my Father love me, because I lay down my life, that I might take it again.* ***No man taketh it from me****, but I lay it down of myself. I have power to lay it down, and I have power to take it again. This commandment have I received of my Father."*

Returning to Hosea: God called Israel *"a deceitful bow"* meaning they kept missing the mark. That's another way of saying they sinned. But they not only kept missing God's mark, His statutes, will, commands etcetera, they were deceitful and treacherous. Their actions were purposeful and willful. And the leaders (princes) encouraged them. They blasphemed God with their tongue and raged against Him when He chastised them.

The Bible has so much to say about the tongue that it would fill a chapter. So, I'll only include a few verses. First, God commands us in Psalm 34:13 to, *"Keep thy* ***tongue*** *from evil, and thy lips from speaking guile."*

Let's see what Scripture says about the tongue of the righteous.

- Psalm 37:30, *"The mouth of the righteous speaketh wisdom, and his* ***tongue*** *talketh of judgment."*
- Psalm 39:1 speaks of king David's desire to keep his tongue from speaking evil. *"I will take heed to my ways, that I sin not with my* ***tongue****: I will keep my mouth with a bridle, while the wicked is before me."*
- Proverbs 10:20, *"The* ***tongue*** *of the just is as choice silver: the heart of the wicked is little worth."*

- Proverbs 10:31, *"The mouth of the just bringeth forth wisdom: but the forward **tongue** shall be cut out."*

The Scriptures below deal with evil tongues.

- Psalm 5:9, *"For there is no faithfulness in their mouth; their inward part is very wickedness; their throat is an open sepulchre; they flatter* (divide, mince words, i.e. lie) *with their **tongue**."*
- Psalm 10:7, *"His mouth is full of cursing and deceit and fraud: under this **tongue** is mischief and vanity."*
- Psalm 50:19, *"Thou givest thy mouth* (the mouth of the wicked) *to evil, and thy **tongue** frameth deceit."*
- Psalm 52:2, *"Thy **tongue** deviseth mischiefs; like a sharp razor, working deceitfully."* Although this is a reference to David's betrayer, Doeg, the Edomite, it can apply to evil doers in general.

In the end, *"The LORD shall **cut off** all flattering lips, and the **tongue** that speaketh proud things,"* (Psalm 12:3).

And that's just what happened. In Hosea, Israel's rejection of God caused them to be dispersed into the world (Egypt). Then later, Israel's rejection of Messiah Jesus again caused them to be dispersed into the world.

Chapter 8

"Set the trumpet to thy mouth. He shall come as an eagle against the house of the LORD, because they have transgressed my covenant, and trespassed against my law. Israel shall cry unto me, My God, we know thee. Israel hath cast off the thing that is good: the enemy shall pursue him. They have set up kings, but not by me: they have made princes, and I knew it not: of their silver and their gold have they made them idols, that they may be cut off. Thy calf, O Samaria, hath cast thee off; mine anger is kindled against them: how long will it be ere they attain to innocency? For from Israel was it also: the workman made it; therefore it is not God: but the calf of Samaria shall be broken in pieces." Hosea 8:1-6

Here, God ordered the blowing of the trumpet, the *showphar* or ram's horn. As mentioned, the ram's horn was used to call the tribes to assembly, announce the Sabbath and new moon (*Rosh Chodesh*), and in battle signals. It was also blown on Rosh Hashanah (the beginning of the new year) as a call to repentance. And according to MyJewishLearning.com, it announced the anointing of a new king, thus, its blowing foreshadows the coming of Messiah.

And all of this can apply to the verses above. God was calling His people to assembly in order to hear His proclamation. A battle was coming *(He shall come as an eagle against the house of the LORD)*. Because of Israel's rebellion and gross sins, God was going to allow Assyria to destroy her. It was symbolically their Rosh Hashanah, their time for repentance. And prophetically speaking, only true repentance will cause the Messiah to come after the Tribulation of the last days.

The eagle implies strength and swiftness. In 743 B.C., Israel's northern king, Menahem, occupied the throne after assassinating the sitting king, Shallum. He believed becoming Assyria's vassal would solidify his power and position. And for a time, it did. But it caused discontentment and rebellion among his people. It also caused the assassination of his three successors and Israel's eventual demise in 722 B.C. As mentioned, when Isreal's last king, Hoshea, got tired of paying tribute to Assyria, Shalmaneser V, the son of Assyrian's king Tiglath-pileser III, began a three-year-long siege against Samaria which ended in the eradication of the northern kingdom as a nation.

From the beginning of their national birth, God had been their eagle. Exodus 19:4 says, *"Ye have seen what I did unto the Egyptians, and how I bare you on **eagles' wings**, and brought you unto myself."* And Deuteronomy 32:11-13 describes how God acted as their eagle. *"As an **eagle** stirreth up her nest, fluttereth over her young, spreadeth abroad her wings, taketh them, beareth them on her wings: So the LORD **alone** did lead him (*Israel*), and there was no strange god with him. He made him ride on the high places of the earth, that he might eat the increase of the fields; and he made him to suck honey out of the rock, and oil out of the flinty rock."*

Notice, it was God alone Who protected and provided for them. Because Israel had looked elsewhere, God allowed another eagle to come in, an eagle of destruction.

Prior to the final destruction of Judah by Babylon in 587 B.C., the prophet Habakkuk lamented her gross sins. The circumstances and events of her resulting judgment are similar to those of Israel's 135 years earlier. *"For, lo, I rise up the Chaldeans, that bitter and hasty nation, which shall march through the breath of the land, to possess the dwelling places that are not theirs. They are terrible and dreadful: their judgment and their dignity shall proceed of themselves. Their horses also are swifter than the leopards, and are more fierce than the evening wolves: and their horsemen shall spread themselves, and their horsemen shall come from far;* ***they shall fly as the eagle*** *that hasteth to eat. They shall come all for violence: their faces shall sup up as the east wind, and they shall gather the captivity as the sand. And they shall scoff at the kings, and the princes shall be a scorn unto them: they shall deride every strong hold; for they shall heap dust, and take it,"* (Habakkuk 1:6-10). The destruction of Judah by Babylon was just as brutal as Assyria's destruction of Israel. It was history repeating itself.

God again enumerated the reasons for Israel's judgment. *"They have transgressed my covenant, and trespassed against my law."* God had made an unbreakable covenant with Abraham, Isaac, and Jacob. He would be their God. They would be His people. He had also given them specific laws to follow. But they disobeyed. Instead of being His people, they had made themselves aliens and rebels. But though they had broken covenant with Him, and the needed punishment was coming, He had not broken with them. God would still keep His promise to their forefathers.

But there is reason for caution. If God didn't spare His own people, the very apple of His eye, why would He spare any other idolatrous nation? He wouldn't. Someday, God will put all the nations of earth on trial (Isaiah 2:4). Matthew 25:31-32 says, *"When the Son of man shall come in his glory, and all the holy angels with him, then shall he sit upon the throne of his glory: And before him shall be gathered all nations: and he shall separate them one from another, as a shepherd divideth his sheep from the goats."*

He will especially scrutinize their treatment of Israel. Matthew 25:34-46 clearly infers that their treatment of Jesus' "brethren," the Jews, is the measuring rod. In addition, Joel 3:2 says, *"I will also gather all nations, and will bring them down into the valley of Jehoshaphat, and will plead with them there for my people and for* ***my heritage Israel, whom they have scattered among the nations, and parted their land.****"* To the list in Matthew 25, Joel adds that the nations must also answer for scattering His people and parting their land. Those who think a two-state solution for Israel and the Palestinians is a good idea should think again. Parting God's land comes with a heavy penalty.

God goes on to say in Hosea, that Israel had set up kings and princes on their own. When the nation was united, kings were chosen by God and anointed by His prophet. This was true of Saul, David, and Solomon. After the kingdom split, the north began choosing their own kings. Thus, Jeroboam I was an unanointed Ephrathite and a former servant of Solomon who had functioned as taskmaster over the forced labor crews of both Ephriam and Manasseh. Ahijah, the prophet, predicted that the ten northern tribes would fall under Jeroboam's rule. Though the tearing of the kingdom was God's direct response to the nation's idolatry (their worship of Ashtoreth, Chemosh, and Milcom), there is no indication that Jeroboam's kingship was blessed or approved by Him. Rather, Scripture implies it was only God's permissive will.

Still, God was merciful. He promised Jeroboam that if he followed His commandments and did right as king David had done, He would establish Jeroboam's line on the throne.

Jeroboam went on to rule for twenty-two years. But because he did evil in God's sight, his son, Nadab, ruled only two years before being assassinated by his successor, Baasha.

Of the nineteen kings who ruled the northern kingdom, beginning with Jeroboam I and ending with Hoshea, all but one were considered evil in the sight of God. Jehu, the exception, was considered both good and evil. During Jehu's twenty-eight years of rule, he failed to fully eradicate idolatry as he had promised. He also failed to enact some of his promised civil reforms. Also, in an attempt to gain favor with Assyria's king, Shalmaneser III, Jehu paid him tribute, thus beginning an unholy alliance that would ultimately destroy the nation.

The entire 208 years of Israel's reigning kings (930 B.C. to 722 B.C.) was marred by idolatry. *"Of their silver and their gold have* ***they*** *made them idols, that* ***they*** *may be cut off."* Those words "cut off" is *karath* and means "to cut off, destroy, consume." The *Theological Wordbook of the Old Testament* adds this to the meaning: "cut off a part of the body, head, hand, foreskin, cut down trees, idols, eliminate, kill, cut a covenant."

But who are the "they" to be cut off? They are those who made the idols and those who worshipped them. Instead of cutting the foreskin of their heart, symbolizing their covenant with God, they would now be cut off. And instead of enjoying God's blessings, they would have to endure His judgment. It's interesting that Jesus tells us in Matthew 5:30 and Mark 9:43 to cut off our hand if it causes us to sin rather than go to hell. It's not meant to be taken literally. Rather, it's a Hebraic idiom indicating the seriousness of eternal hell and the symbolic lengths we should go in order to avoid it. Had Israel cut off their idolatry, God would not have had to cut them off.

As mentioned, this idolatry began with their first king, Jeroboam. *"Thy calf, O Samaria, hath cast thee off."* 1 Kings 12:27-28 tells us why he did this. *"If this people go up to do sacrifice in the house of the LORD at Jerusalem, then shall the heart of this people turn again unto their lord, even unto Rehoboam king of Judah, and they shall kill me, and go again to Rehoboam king of Judah. Whereupon the king took counsel, and made* ***two calves of gold,*** *and said unto them, It is too much for you to go up to Jerusalem:* ***behold thy gods, O Israel,*** *which brought thee up out of the land of Egypt."*

Zondervan's *Pictorial Encyclopedia of the Bible* lists Jeroboam's other failings. "He promoted worship at the high places, appointed non-Levites as priests, and changed the date of the feast of Tabernacles."

Because Israel's sixth king, Omri, made Samaria the capital of Israel, God signaled it out as Israel's power center, i.e., its leaders. He was telling them that their golden calves were of no help or use now. And the very things Israel looked to for help and protection would be *"broken in pieces."* She would come to see firsthand the utter impotence of her gods. In addition, it was pointless for her to keep pretending she was innocent (*how long will it be ere they attain to innocency?*). God had seen it all.

Continuing with the text:

"For they have sown the wind, and they shall reap the whirlwind: it hath no stalk: the bud shall yield no meal: if so be it yield, the strangers shall swallow it up. Israel is swallowed up: now shall they be among the Gentiles as a vessel wherein is no pleasure. For they are gone up to Assyria, a wild ass alone by himself: Ephraim hath hired lovers. Yea, though they have hired among the nations, now will I

gather them, and they shall sorrow a little for the burden of the king of princes (Assyria). *Because Ephraim hath made many altars to sin, altars shall be unto him to sin."* Hosea 8:7-11

For years, Israel had been sowing to the wind by worshipping other gods and paying *"lovers"* (other nations) for protection. As an untameable *"wild ass"* they threw off the Lord's restraint, then in unbridled fashion, pursued their own wanton desires. Now, Assyria, the very nation that had been receiving the bulk of Israel's tribute, would be the very whirlwind which destroyed them. No longer a useful vessel for God, Israel's labor, land, produce, resources, and posterity, would be used by Gentiles. Their future was to be one of sorrow and pain.

After years of playing the harlot, Israel would now reap the consequences of those sins. The law of sowing and reaping is a spiritual law. It applies to all and works whether one believes in it or not. Galatians 6:7 is clear. *"Be not deceived; God is not mocked: for whatsoever a man soweth, that shall he also reap."* Israel's sowing and reaping had come full circle.

Continuing with the text:

"I have written to him the great things of my law, but they were counted as a strange thing. They sacrifice flesh for the sacrifices of mine offerings, and eat it; but the LORD accepteth them not; now will he remember their iniquity, and visit their sins: they shall return to Egypt. For Israel hath forgotten his Maker, and buildeth temples; and Judah hath multiplied fenced cities: but I will send a fire upon his cities, and it shall devour the palaces thereof." Hosea 8:12-14

God gave Israel His 613 statutes in the Torah. Instead of adhering to them, Israel not only disobeyed but counted them as unimportant (*"they were counted as a strange thing"*). The king, priests, and people went through the motions, offering the required sacrifices. But it was done without heart, therefore unacceptable to God.

Because their hearts were far from Yahweh, they were easily seduced into worshipping other gods which led to gross immorality. Now, payment was due. God would symbolically return them to Egyptian bondage, symbol of the sinful world. Refusing to be God's bondservants, they would now become Assyria's.

God again mentioned Judah's future judgment because he was following in his sister's footsteps, (*I will send a **fire** upon his cities*). Jerusalem was indeed destroyed when Babylon torched it in 587 B.C. Recently, archaeologists analyzed the charred remains of a building burned during this Babylonian siege. Using advanced techniques of fire debris analysis, they discovered it was destroyed "in an intense inferno." God means what He says and says what He means.

Note, God said this fire that He sends upon both Israel and Judah *"shall devour the palaces thereof."* Both palaces, Israel's in Samaria and Judah's in Jerusalem were utterly destroyed. Nothing was spared. Only rubble remained.

Chapter 9

"Rejoice not, O Israel, for joy, as other people: for thou hast gone a whoring from thy God, thou hast loved a reward upon every cornfloor. The floor and the winepress shall not feed them, and the new wine shall fail in her. They shall not dwell in the LORD'S land; but Ephraim shall return to Egypt, and they shall eat unclean things in Assyria. They shall not offer wine offerings to the LORD, neither shall they be pleasing unto him: their sacrifices shall be unto them as the bread of mourners; all that eat thereof shall be polluted: for their bread for their soul shall not come into the house of the LORD." Hosea 9:1-4

God graphically exposed Israel's sins. They had gone *"a whoring,"* and *"loved a reward upon every cornfloor."* This refers to Israel's vile pagan practices as revealed in the words "reward" (*ethnan*) and "cornfloor." "Reward" means "hire, reward, a gift as the price of harlotry, the hire of a prostitute." "Cornfloor" or threshing floor was where grain was threshed after a harvest. It was also where paid cult prostitutes engaged in ritual sex in honor of their fertility gods. By engaging in acts of human procreation, they were physically demonstrating their request to their gods, namely that of producing a bountiful harvest.

Now, God told them they had wasted their time and money. Their abominations weren't going to ensure the fertility of the land or produce copious crops. Instead, they would experience famine. To make matters worse, they would also become captives and bondservants of the world, during which time they would eat "unclean" food in order to survive.

In addition, their sacrifices were no longer pleasing or acceptable to God. "Pleasing" (*arab*) means "to become surety, mortgage, engage, barter, pledges." In other words, God would not accept their sacrifices as sin offerings. They could not use them to "barter" away their offenses. This meant losing their means of atonement. The expression, *"their sacrifices shall be unto them as the bread of mourners,"* also confirms this. Mourning is a time of ritual impurity and separation from God. It refers to food eaten while mourning the death of one's friend or relative. God was calling both them and their sacrifices, ritually unclean.

Even at their best, their bread, their sin offerings, were only temporary measures, a foreshadowing of the real thing. God, in His mercy, had set up a system of Levitical sacrifices until the true "Bread," Jesus, came as the perfect sin offering. Even the place of His birth, Bethlehem, means "house of bread."

In John 6:31-33, Jesus made that connection. *"Our fathers did eat manna in the desert; as it is written, He gave them bread from heaven to eat. Then Jesus said unto them, Verily, verily, I say unto you, Moses gave you not that **bread** from heaven; but my Father giveth you the true **bread** from heaven. For the **bread** of God is he which cometh down from heaven, and giveth life unto the world."* Jesus went on to say in verse 35, *"I am the **bread** of life; he that cometh to me shall never hunger."* He repeated this in John 6:48. Verses 50-51 added, *"This is the **bread** which cometh down from heaven,* *that a man may eat thereof, and not die. I am the living* ***bread*** *which came down from heaven: if any man eat of this* ***bread****, he shall live for ever: and the* ***bread*** *that I will give is my flesh, which I will give for the life of the world."* In verse 58 He said, *"This is that* ***bread*** *which came down from heaven: not as your fathers did eat manna, and are dead: he that eateth of this* ***bread*** *shall live fore ever."*

In Matthew 26:17-30, Jesus was celebrating the Passover with His disciples. Verses 26-28 say, *"And as they were eating, Jesus took* ***bread****, and blessed it, and brake it, and gave it to the disciples and said, Take, eat, this is my body. And he took the cup, and gave thanks, and gave it to them, saying, Drink ye all of it; For this is my blood of the new testament, which is shed for many for the remission of sins."*

We know God's requirement was that innocent blood had to be shed for the remission of sins, a requirement He established in the Garden of Eden. This was clearly confirmed throughout both the Old and New Testament. In fact, Hebrews 9:22, in the New Testament, says, *"And almost all things are by the law purged with blood; and without shedding of blood is no remission* (of sins)*."*

But what no one could imagine was that it would be ***God's*** blood. And Jesus, the God-man, gave it all. Before He died, He said, "IT IS FINISHED." That word in Greek is *teleo* and means completed, **paid in full**. And because He completely satisfied God's sin penalty, He has the right to say, *"I am* ***the*** *way,* ***the*** *truth and* ***the*** *life, no man cometh unto the Father but by me"* (John 14:6). There are not many ways to God. There is only one. And that way is Jesus.

But as the One and Only holy and perfect sacrifice, Jesus had to become man (bread). He is still that bread today. Psalm 34:8 says, *"Oh taste and see that the Lord is good."* How do we taste and see Jesus' goodness? Since He is the very Word made flesh (John 1:14), we come to know and understand His goodness by studying His Word. By ingesting it. By making it part of us, part of our lives.

Continuing with the text:

"What will ye do in the solemn day, and in the day of the feast of the LORD? For, lo, they are gone because of destruction: Egypt shall gather them up, Memphis shall bury them: the pleasant places for their silver, nettles shall possess them: thorns shall be in their tabernacles. The days of visitation are come, the days of recompence are come; Israel shall know it: the prophet is a fool, the spiritual man is mad, for the multitude of thine iniquity, and the great hatred. The watchman of Ephraim was with my God: but the prophet is a snare of a fowler in all his ways, and hatred in the house of his God. They have deeply corrupted themselves as in the days of Gibeah: therefore he will remember their iniquity, he will visit their sins."
Hosea 9:5-9

The people of Israel would no longer be able to celebrate the Feasts of the Lord because they were going into Assyrian captivity (referred to here as Egypt, symbolizing the world). To discourage further rebellion, Assyria usually scattered their captives, especially the elite, educated, and skilled, throughout their empire. And Assyria's empire was vast, incorporating much of that known world. Zondervan's *Pictorial Encyclopedia of the Bible* states this empire "included Babylon, Elam, Media, Syria, Palestine, and Arabia, along with South Antolia, Cilicia and Egypt."

"Memphis shall bury them." Memphis was the ancient capital of unified Egypt. Even after it was replaced by Tanis and Thebes, it was still the site of a royal palace as well as the center of gross

idolatry. Again, the mention of Memphis further confirms that Israel would be scattered, and her people would die throughout the capitals of the world.

"Nettles shall possess them: thorns shall be in their tabernacles." God warned of this when He instructed them to drive the pagans from the Promised Land and to destroy their idols. *"But if ye will not drive out the inhabitants of the land from before you; then it shall come to pass, that those which ye let remain of them shall be pricks in your eyes, and* ***thorns*** *in your sides, and shall vex you in the land wherein ye dwell,"* (Numbers 33:55). And Proverbs 24:30-31 says, *"I went by the field of the slothful, and by the vineyard of the man void of understanding; And, lo, it was all grown over with* ***thorns****, and* ***nettles*** *had covered the face thereof, and the stone wall thereof was broken down."*

Instead of driving out all the nations, Israel only conquered some and made alliances with others. As a result, her spiritual beliefs became mixed with those of the pagans. She became "slothful" towards the things of God, and void of godly understanding. Now, her prosperity (her silver, etcetera) would be taken by others. All that her people had labored for and held dear would become nothing more than thorns and thistles.

Thorns were also in their tabernacles (*ohel*), which means their "dwelling place, tabernacle, tent, covering." Their tabernacles, their Temple or place where sin was covered through animal sacrifices were filled with spiritual thorns and unacceptable to God. This again illustrates they had no sin covering. It also depicted them individually as unacceptable living sacrifices to Yahweh. In addition, thorns and nettles symbolize their life in captivity as one of privation and servitude.

They only had themselves to blame. For decades, Israel disrespected and persecuted God's prophets for exposing their sins, preferring instead to listen to those who said what they wanted to hear. Followers of Yahweh and His prophets were considered madmen and were also persecuted. No longer God's watchmen over the people, Israel's leaders became corrupt, and in turn, corrupted their nation.

Gibeah is again associated with depravity, as mentioned in Hosea chapter five. Hosea again refers to Gibeah in chapter ten. Zondervan's *Pictorial Encyclopedia of the Bible* calls Gibeah the "very paradigm of evil." This illustrates God's view of them. *"They have deeply corrupted themselves as in the days of Gibeah."*

Continuing with the text:

"I found Israel like grapes in the wilderness; I saw your fathers as the firstripe in the fig tree at her first time: but they went to Baalpeor, and separated themselves unto that shame; and their abominations were according as they loved. As for Ephraim, their glory shall fly away like a bird, from the birth, and from the womb, and from the conception. Though they bring up their children, yet will I bereave them, that there shall not be a man left: yea, woe also to them when I depart from them! Ephraim, as I saw Tyrus, is planted in a pleasant place: but Ephraim shall bring forth his children to the murderer. Give them, O LORD: what wilt thou give? give them a miscarrying womb and dry breasts. All their wickedness is in Gilgal: for there I hated them: for the wickedness of their doings I will drive them out of mine house, I will love them no more: all their princes are revolters. Ephraim is smitten, their root is dried up, they shall bear no fruit: yea, though they bring forth, yet will I slay even the beloved fruit of their womb. My God will cast them away, because they did not

hearken unto him: and they shall be wanderers among the nations." Hosea 9:10-17

What heartbreaking words! First, "found" (*matsa*) means "to come forth, appear, exist, or attain." *The Theological Wordbook of the Old Testament* adds that it describes "a result following a time of seeking." Thus, we get a picture of God seeking the "wilderness" of the world for a people to call His own. Once chosen, He began forging them into a nation. "Grapes" (*enab*) means "to bear fruit, a grape." These people were to bear fruit for Him. They were to be His harvest.

To fully understand this, we must go to Genesis 11:6-8, to the tower of Babel where God scattered the people by confounding their language. *"And the LORD said, Behold, the people is one, and they have all one language; and this they begin to do: and now nothing will be restrained from them, which they have imagined to do. Go to, let us go down, and there confound their language, that they may not understand one another's speech. So the LORD scattered them abroad thence upon the face of all the earth: and they left off to build the city."*

Deuteronomy 32:8-10 gives us further insight. The King James version says, *"When the Most High divided to the nations their inheritance, when he separated the sons of Adam, he set the bounds of the people according to the number of the children of Israel. For the LORD'S portion is his people; Jacob is the lot of his inheritance. He found him in a desert land, and in the waste howling wilderness; he led him about, he instructed him, he kept him as the apple of his eye."*

Though this ties into Hosea 9:10, it doesn't give the complete picture. It omits a critical clue found in *The Septuagint*, the Old Testament Scriptures used prior and during Jesus' time. It is slightly different and says, *"When the Most High divided the nations, when he separated the sons of Adam, he set the bounds of the nations* ***according to the number of the angels of God****. And his people Jacob became the portion of the Lord, Israel was the line of his inheritance. He maintained him in the wilderness, in burning thirst and a dry land: he led him about and instructed him, and kept him as the apple of an eye."*

The *"number of the angels of God"* refers to angelic beings. Here we see that the number of nations was determined by the number of God's angels. According to the Jewish Midrash, God allowed seventy angels to disrupt man's speech, then scattered the people in order to form seventy nations. This number corresponds to the Table of Nations spoken of in Genesis 10, which lists the seventy nations springing from Noah and his descendants.

But who are these angels? Many scholars believe they were fallen angels. Nimrod and his followers were building a tower to heaven in an attempt to open a portal through which they could once again interact with fallen angels just as their ancestors had done prior to the flood. These fallen angels gave their fathers forbidden knowledge and power. Nimrod, who had set himself up in opposition to God (*"He was a mighty hunter before the LORD,"* Genesis 10:9) wanted this connection, this knowledge and power in order to secure his rulership.

By the time God scattered the people, they were already interacting with fallen angels which they began seeing as gods. Psalm 82 describes the evil practices of these angels and God's condemnation of them. *"God standeth in the congregation of the mighty; he judgeth among the gods* (angels). (Note: *The Septuagint* begins Psalm 82 this way: *"God stands in the assembly of gods: and in the midst of them will judge gods."*) *How long will ye judge unjustly, and accept the persons of the wicked? Selah. Defend the poor and fatherless: do justice to the afflicted and needy. Deliver the poor and needy; rid them out of the hand of the wicked. They know not, neither will they understand; they walk on in darkness: all the foundations of the earth are out of course. I have said, Ye are gods; and all of you are children of the most High. But ye shall die like men, and fall like one of the princes. Arise, O God, judge the earth: for thou shalt inherit all nations."*

Many Bible scholars believe this Psalm is directed to earthly judges who are to act on God's behalf and judge fairly and wisely. I won't dispute that. But because Scripture is often multilayered, I believe it is also a rebuke to the "gods," to the fallen angels who influence and control the nations unjustly and unwisely.

That's why God was telling the people of Babel after He confounded their language: You can have your gods and all the misery and sorrow they will bring. Thus, these angels became the controlling entities over the seventy nations.

We get a glimpse of spiritual warfare between these ruling fallen angels and God's ministering angels in Daniel 10:12-13. Daniel waited twenty-one days before God's angelic messenger, along with Michael the archangel, could break through the prince of Persia's opposition and deliver God's answer to Daniel's prayers.

So, while the seventy nations happily accepted angelic beings as their overlords, God claimed Shem as His lot. Israel would be His inheritance. And Michael, the archangel, would be Israel's protector.

For centuries, this was the understanding of many rabbis and Jewish scholars. In their Midrash, they believe lots were drawn with the lot of Abraham's ancestor, Shem, falling to God while the other nations fell to the seventy angels. Eventually, these nations split into many others. According to worldometer.info and worldatlas.com, the U.N. considers there to be 195 nations while the U.S. lists 197.

Does this mean that only seventy spirit beings control all the nations or have other fallen angels joined them? Uncertain. Either way, it means that every nation, except the nation of Israel, has an evil entity influencing them. Is it any wonder why Israel is so hated by the world?

Paul, in Ephesians 6:12 alludes to this demonic influence. *"For we wrestle not against flesh and blood, but against principalities, against powers, against the rulers of the darkness of this world, against spiritual wickedness in high places."* Notice the hierarchy. It goes from lowest to highest. I think the *"rulers of the darkness of this world"* refers to the rulers over nations, while *"spiritual wickedness in high places"* refers to Satan. Whatever the case, evil spiritual entities are real and oppose God, nations, and us.

But why did the KJV omit such important information? Because this is part of the Genesis 6 narrative when fallen angels cohabitated with women to create monstrous hybrids called Nephilim. *"And it came to pass, when men began to multiply on the face of the earth, and daughters were born unto them, That the sons of God saw the daughters of men that they were fair; and they took them wives of all which they chose. . .. There were giants in the earth in those days; and also after that, when the sons of God came in unto the daughters of men, and they bare children to them, the same became mighty men which were of old, men of renown,"* (Genesis 6:1-2, 4). These Nephilim became the Titans of Greek and other mythologies.

By the time the KJV was drafted, which incorporated several different compilations of Scripture, the church had completely buried this part of history. In the 5th Century A.D., the church even came up with the silly Sethite theory that claimed the sons of god were really the godly sons of Seth (third son of Adam and Eve). And the daughters of men were the evil daughters of Cain (slayer of Abel). And all this without the slightest Scriptural support.

In addition, scholars and priests wanted the KJV to be widely accepted throughout the English-speaking world. Therefore, one must conclude that this omission occurred either through ignorance or as a deliberate attempt to obfuscate the historical angelic comingling with man. For more on the Nephilim, see my book, *The Coming Deception*.

The Septuagint version shows the importance of Israel to God and the deep ramifications of their rebellion. Israel was to be God's nation, His sign and wonder, His oracle, His voice to the fallen world, the means by which fallen man could come to know and love Him. Israel was to be His *"firstripe,"* His first fruits from a fig tree meant to "feed" the rest of the world.

But even in the face of His grace and mercy, Israel constantly disappointed God. She also disappointed Jesus when He came. Because the fig tree symbolizes Israel, we can understand why Jesus cursed it in Matthew 21:19-21 when it bore only leaves and no fruit. After decades of God's mercy, Jesus was looking for a godly harvest.

Though God chose Jacob (symbolic of the twelve tribes of Israel) it didn't take them long to apostatize. Soon after entering the Promised Land, they began worshipping Baalpeor (the Baal of Peor, a mountain in Moab). This was the god Balaam lured Israel into worshipping by having the Moabite women sexually seduce Israel's men, then turn them to Baal. (Deuteronomy 4:3).

Hosea again mentioned Gilgal. *"All their wickedness is in Gilgal."* It's association with gross idolatry and evil has already been covered.

Hosea went on to say that as a result of their sins, Israel would no longer carry the glory of God. Once, they were like Tyrus (Tyre) known for their wealth and prosperity. Now, they would be impoverished, ravaged, and slain. Their numbers would become few, their women, barren, and those who got pregnant would miscarry. In short, God would diminish them as a people group. And this has been fulfilled in a staggering way. Compared to other nations, the number of Jews in the world is miniscule. According to worldpopulationreview.com, there were only about 17.2 million Jews worldwide in 2026, which represents a little over 0.2% of the entire global population of 8.3 billion.

"They shall be wanderers among the nations." Beginning with the first Assyrian conquest and exile of Jews in 740 B.C. under king Pul until now, Jews have been dispersed throughout the world. That means millions upon millions have wandered the globe for centuries, just as Hosea predicted. But praise God, at the end of the seven-year Tribulation, the fig tree *will* finally produce fruit.

Chapter 10

"Israel is an empty vine, he bringeth forth fruit unto himself: according to the multitude of his fruit he hath increased the altars; according to the goodness of his land they have made goodly images. Their heart is divided; now shall they be found faulty: he shall break down their altars, he shall spoil their images. For now they shall say, We have no king, because we feared not the LORD; what then should a king do to us? They have spoken words, swearing falsely in making a covenant: thus judgment springeth up as hemlock in the furrows of the field." Hosea 10:1-4

Hosea is full of repetition, with agricultural references being one of them. These repeating themes are meant to illustrate the gravity of Israel's sins and their coming judgment. God does not mince words. He obviously wants His message clearly understood. Thus, He speaks to an agrarian society in terms they understand.

To begin with, "empty" (*baqaq*) means "to pour out, to empty." Once Israel was prosperous, having an abundance of everything including produce. But because she credited this abundance to pagan gods and built altars to them, she was now an *"empty vine."*

"He bringeth forth fruit unto himself." "Forth" (*shavah*) means "to level, resemble, agree with, become like." It's a play on words. Israel's good harvests and subsequent belief that pagan idols were responsible, made him produce fruit resembling them. Instead of fruit pleasing to God, Israel became as perverse as the false gods he worshipped.

"Their heart is divided." Israel often mingled the worship of Yahweh with the worship of idols, taking from each those elements they liked. James 1:8 tells us that *"A double minded man is unstable in all his ways."* Mixing religions, taking something from one and something else from another like morsels from a smorgasbord, is unacceptable to God. Isaiah 42:8 makes that clear: *"I am the LORD: that is my name: and my glory will I not give to another, neither my praise to graven images."*

We see this mingling today. The message that there are many roads to God is prevalent. The New Age mixes Eastern religions with Christianity and the occult. Christian churches mix their beliefs with Islam to form Chrislam. The previous Catholic pope, Frances, even declared that atheists will go to heaven. This potpourri of beliefs is preparing the way for the religion of the antichrist, a religion that will lack meaning because it stands for nothing. Alexander Hamilton and others said, "If you don't stand for something, you'll fall for anything." Without the moral clarity of God's Word, the Bible, it will be easy to fall for the latest deception and lie.

"Thus judgment springeth up as hemlock in the furrows of the field." "Hemlock" (*rosh*) means "a poisonous plant, the poppy, gall, venom, poison." But it's more commonly known as "wormwood." Aside from having no king, their idolatrous altars would be torn down and judgment, like poison, would cover their land.

When Israel entered into a covenant with God, this warning was given in Deuteronomy 29:16-18: *"For ye know how we have dwelt in the land of Egypt; and how we came through the nations which ye passed by; And ye have seen their abominations, and their idols, wood and stone, silver and gold, which were among them: Lest there should be among you man, or woman, or family, or tribe, whose heart turneth away this day from the LORD our God, to go and serve the gods of these nations; lest there should be among you a root that beareth* ***gall*** *and* ***wormwood****."* Their idolatry had indeed produced a root of gall and wormwood (hemlock) and would now cover and destroy them.

Years later, when Judah, the southern kingdom, was judged for their sins, Jeremiah 9:15 said something similar. *"Therefore thus saith the LORD of hosts, the God of Israel; Behold, I will feed them, even this people, with* ***wormwood****, and give them water of* ***gall*** *to drink."*

Following after other gods such as the idols of success, power, riches, etcetera, will always bring bitterness because it separates us from the true God. And like Israel and Judah, we will come to learn that it is indeed a bitter thing to be God's enemy.

Continuing with the text:

"The inhabitants of Samaria shall fear because of the calves of Bethhaven: for the people thereof shall mourn over it, and the priests thereof that rejoiced on it, for the glory thereof, because it is departed from it. It shall be also carried unto Assyria for a present to king Jareb: Ephraim shall receive shame, and Israel shall be ashamed of his own counsel. As for Samaria, her king is cut off as the foam upon the water. The high places also of Aven, the sin of Israel, shall be destroyed: the thorn and the thistle shall come up on their altars; and they shall say to the mountains, Cover us; and to the hills, Fall on us.

O Israel, thou hast sinned from the days of Gibeah: there they stood: the battle in Gibeah against the children of iniquity did not overtake them. It is in my desire that I should chastise them; and the people shall be gathered against them, when they shall bind themselves in their two furrows." Hosea 10:5-10

As mentioned, Samaria became the capital of the northern kingdom of Israel under Omri, father of king Ahab. But because it's symbolic of that nation's rule and authority, Samaria also speaks of its first king, Jeroboam I, who instituted calf worship. Now, the very calves they worshipped and sacrificed to would become sacrifices themselves. Israel's shameful idolatry would bring shame upon her people. She, along with her calves, would be taken to Assyria as captives and spoils.

"As for Samaria, her king is cut off as the foam upon the water." As mentioned, two years before Assyria's final conquest, Israel's nineteenth and last king, Hoshea, was removed from the throne, leaving her without a king.

"The high places also of Aven, the sin of Israel, shall be destroyed." Aven means "wickedness, emptiness, trouble." The *Theological Wordbook of the Old Testament* says Aven also "designates mourning in association with death." Israel's sins would be dealt with; their idolatry, their calf worship, put to death. Nothing but useless thorns and thistles would be left. The phrase *"The thorn and the thistle shall come up on their altars,"* is a Jewish idiom meaning their altars would be abandoned. It's a picture of something forsaken and overgrown.

"And they shall say to the mountains, Cover us; and to the hills, Fall on us." This denotes extreme distress and fear produced by God's judgment. It is also a prophecy of things to come,

pointing to Jacob's Trouble or the seven-year Tribulation. When talking about this time, Isaiah 2:19 says, *"And they* (the rebels against God) *shall go into the holes of the rocks, and into the caves of the earth, for fear of the LORD, and for the glory of his majesty, when he ariseth to shake terribly the earth."*

Jesus also prophesized of this. When He was on the way to Golgotha to be crucified, Luke 23:27-30 tells us, *"And there followed him* (Jesus) *a great company of people, and of women, which also bewailed and lamented him. But Jesus turning unto them said, Daughters of Jerusalem, weep not for me, but weep for yourselves, and for your children. For, behold, the days are coming, in which they shall say, Blessed are the barren, and the wombs that never bare, and the paps which never gave suck.* ***Then shall they begin to say to the mountains, Fall on us; and to hills, Cover us.****"*

And then there's Revelation 6 which describes the early horrors of the Tribulation. Jesus has opened six of the seven seals causing the earth to reel. Verses 15-17 describe the reaction of the surviving rebels and idolators. *"And the kings of the earth, and the great men, and the rich men, and the chief captains, and the mighty men, and every bondman, and every free man, hid themselves in the dens and in the rocks of the mountains; And said to the mountains and rocks,* ***Fall on us, and hide us*** *from the face of him that setteth on the throne, and from the wrath of the Lamb: For the great day of his wrath is come; and who shall be able to stand?"* When this happens, these people will be utterly terrified. But they haven't seen anything yet. They still have seven trumpet and seven vial judgments to face.

The horrors of the Tribulation cannot be overstated. Jesus Himself said, *"For then shall be great tribulation, such as was not since the beginning of the world to this time, no, nor ever shall be,"* (Matthew 24:21). It will be so terrible that nothing in history compares with it. No wonder Johnathan Edwards said it was a fearful thing for a sinner to fall into the hands of an angry God. Though God is love itself, He is also holy and must deal with unrepented sin.

"O Israel, thou hast sinned from the days of Gibeah: there they stood: the battle in Gibeah against the children of iniquity did not overtake them." Gibeah is again referenced here. As previously noted, it was considered a place of great evil. It was also the place where Ephraim almost annihilated the entire tribe of Benjamin. After a Levite from Ephraim rested from his journey by spending the night at Gibeah of Benjamin, the men of that city surrounded the house and demanded he come out so they could have sex with him. Instead of complying, the Levite gave them his concubine, which they abused all night, resulting in her death. When the Levite returned to Ephraim with his dead concubine, he cut her into twelve pieces, then sent one piece to each of the twelve tribes. This resulted in the tribes coming against Benjamin in retaliation for their gross deed.

It's obvious this story closely resembles what the males of Sodom wanted to do to Lot's two angelic visitors, indicating the utter depravity of the Benjaminite's. For this reason, God allowed Israel to prevail against them. *"The battle in Gibeah against the children of iniquity did not overtake them."* But though the Israelites prevailed, there were heavy casualties on both sides.

"It is in my desire that I should chastise them; and the people shall be gathered against them, when they shall bind themselves in their two furrows." Furrows are made when land is plowed. Israel had plowed her land in rebellion and idolatry. Thus, she would be chastised. God used Israel to chastise Benjamin for their sin at

Gibeah. Now, He was saying He would chastise Israel for hers and also use others to do it.

Continuing with the text:

"And Ephraim is as an heifer that is taught, and loveth to tread out the corn; but I passed over upon her fair neck: I will make Ephraim to ride; Judah shall plow, and Jacob shall break his clods. Sow to yourselves in righteousness, reap in mercy; break up your fallow ground: for it is time to seek the LORD, till he come and rain righteousness upon you. Ye have plowed wickedness, ye have reaped iniquity; ye have eaten the fruit of lies: because thou didst trust in thy way, in the multitude of thy mighty men. Therefore shall a tumult arise among thy people, and all thy fortresses shall be spoiled, as Shalman spoiled Betharbel in the day of battle: the mother was dashed in pieces upon her children. So shall Bethel do unto you because of your great wickedness: in a morning shall the king of Israel utterly be cut off." Hosea 10:11-15

For generations, God had been training Israel in His ways and statutes. During it, God's burden had been light. His goodness and provision made it easy for the nation to prosper. But all that was about to change. Through conquest, hardship, and trials, God would make Israel/Ephraim ride His way. He would force the nation into compliance, all in preparation for that future day (after the seven-year Tribulation) when Judah will once again praise the Lord (plow) and Jacob (all twelve tribes, thus the whole nation of Israel) shall break their clods of sin and rebellion. It will be a time when, once again, Israel will seek God and His righteousness.

If Israel had remained faithful to God, their current suffering would have been avoided. Instead, their continual wickedness made judgment necessary. And it would come by the hand of Shalman (Assyria's king Shalmaneser V).

Betharbel means "house of God's ambush," implying that Samaria was where He planned His ambush or judgment of Ephraim. War is always brutal. But in those days, it was especially so. Men, women, and children were slain without mercy. The phrase *"the mother was dashed in pieces upon her children,"* is an illustration of Assyria's propensity for cruelty and carnage.

"In a morning shall the king of Israel utterly be cut off." Israel's king, Hosea, was cut off when he was imprisoned by Assyria, leaving the nation without a king during most of Shalmaneser's siege.

Though God prefers repentance to judgment, when it's not forthcoming, judgment must fall.

Chapter 11

"When Israel was a child, then I loved him, and called my son out of Egypt. As they called them, so they went from them: they sacrificed unto Baalim, and burned incense to graven images. I taught Ephraim also to go, taking them by their arms; but they knew not that I healed them. I drew them with cords of a man, with bands of love: and I was to them as they that take off the yoke on their jaws, and I laid meat unto them." Hosea 11:1-4

God loves Israel. Out of all the nations of the world, He picked him for His own, redeemed him from the slave pits of Egypt, and called him His son. Before Moses stood in front of Pharaoh demanding he let the Hebrews go, God told him what to say in Exodus 4:22-23, *"And thou shalt say unto Pharoah, Thus saith the LORD, Israel is my* ***son, even my firstborn****: And I say unto thee, Let my* ***son*** *go, that he may serve me: and if thou refuse to let him go, behold, I will slay thy son, even thy firstborn."*

Thus, it references Israel's historic deliverance and his exalted position as God's son. But it's also prophetic and points to another Son, to Israel's Messiah Jesus, the Son of God. We see this allusion in Matthew 2:12-15. God instructed Joseph to take Mary and baby Jesus to Egypt to escape Herod's assassination order. Verse 15 tells us they remained there *"until the death of*

Herod: that it might be fulfilled which was spoken of the Lord by the prophet, saying, Out of Egypt have I called my ***son****."*

But while Jesus, the God-man, is the perfect Son, Israel is the prodigal. Though God delivered him from Egyptian bondage, took the yoke off his neck, taught him to walk in His ways by giving him laws and statutes, provided, protected, and loved him, Israel disrespected God, rebelled, and credited false gods for the very blessings Yahweh had bestowed.

Yet, God still loves Israel. In this same way, He loves those who become sons through a new birth in Christ even though they often fail Him, too. This is illustrated in Luke 15:11-32. A well-loved but selfish and self-indulgent son takes his inheritance, leaves home, then squanders all he has. Finding himself destitute, starving, and working with pigs (unclean animals), he decides to return home. Never expecting his father to accept him back as a son, his hope was just to be accepted as a servant. To his surprise, when in sight of his home, the prodigal saw his father running toward him with open arms. *"But when he was yet a great way off, his father saw him, and had compassion, and ran, and fell on his neck, and kissed him. And the son said unto him, Father, I have sinned against heaven, and in thy sight, and am no more worthy to be called thy son. But the father said to his servants, Bring forth the best robe, and put it on him; and put a ring on his hand, and shoes on his feet: And bring hither the fatted calf, and kill it; and let us eat, and be merry: For this my son was dead, and is alive again; he was lost, and is found. And they began to be merry."* (verses 20-24)

This is God's heart not only toward Israel but toward Gentiles. When Israel repents as a nation during the seven-year Tribulation, God will once again call them His son and envelope them in open arms. In the same way, God will accept anyone who repents and comes to Jesus as Savior. And those He will also call "sons" (child/joint heirs).

John 1:12 says, *"But as many as received him* (Jesus)*, to them gave he power to become the* ***sons of God****, even to them that believe on his name."* And Romans 8:14-17 says, *"For as many as are led by the Spirit of God, they are* ***the sons of God.*** *For ye have not received the spirit of bondage again to fear; but ye have received the Spirit of adoption, whereby we cry, Abba, Father. The Spirit itself beareth witness with our spirit, that* ***we are the children of God****: And if children, then heirs; heirs of God, and joint-heirs with Christ."*

Oh, the mercy, grace, and love of God! He is ever willing to forgive and receive us to Himself. No one needs to go through the Tribulation or White Throne judgment. All we have to do is repent and accept Him!

Continuing with the text:

"He shall not return into the land of Egypt, but the Assyrian shall be his king, because they refused to return. And the sword shall abide on his cities, and shall consume his branches, and devour them, because of their own counsels. And my people are bent to backsliding from me: though they called them to the most High, none at all would exalt him. How shall I give thee up, Ephraim? how shall I deliver thee, Israel? how shall I make thee as Admah? how shall I set thee as Zeboim? mine heart is turned within me, my repentings are kindled together. I will not execute the fierceness of mine anger, I will not return to destroy Ephraim: for I am God, and not man; the Holy One in the midst of thee: and I will not enter into the city."
Hosea 11:5-9

The fact that Assyria will conquer Israel in judgment is repeated. Israel will be slaughtered by the sword throughout their cities. Because they had gone their own way (*their own counsels*), their "branches," their children will be destroyed, cutting off their legacy.

In spite of Israel knowing and calling God the Most High, they did not honor Him as such, serving instead, lesser gods. Now, God pondered what to do with these rebels. He still loved them. And because of that and because of the covenant He made with their fathers, He determined not to utterly destroy them like He did Admah and Zeboim. Adman and Zeboim, both cities of the plain, were completely destroyed along with Sodom and Gomorrah (Genesis 14:8, 19:24-25, Deuteronomy 29:23). Thus, God tamped down His fierce anger and would only dispense a partial punishment.

Continuing with the text:

"They shall walk after the LORD: he shall ***roar like a lion****: when he shall roar, then the children shall tremble from the west. They shall tremble as a bird out of Egypt, and as a dove out of the land of Assyria: and I will place them in their houses, saith the LORD. Ephraim compassed me about with lies, and the house of Israel with deceit: but Judah yet ruleth with God, and is faithful with the saints."* Hosea 11:10-12

"They shall walk after the LORD: he shall roar like a lion." Again, this is prophetic, pointing to a future time when Israel will be restored and follow God. It also points to Jesus, the very Lion of the Tribe of Judah. God the Father and Jesus being pictured as a lion was covered in Hosea 5. Recall that "lion" is a symbol of strength. But it is a strength applied to protection as well as judgment. In Proverbs 19:12, Isaiah 5:29-30, and Amos 3:8-15, we see God as a lion of judgment. While in Isaiah 31:4-5 and

Joel 3:16-17, we see Him as the lion of protection, One Who fights for Israel.

Let's look at each.

The lion of judgment:

- Proverbs 19:12, *"The king's wrath is as the roaring of a* ***lion****."*
- Isaiah 5:29-30 talks about the wicked. Isaiah 5:20 says, *"Woe unto them that call evil good, and good evil."* Isaiah went on to say that judgment would come to these evil doers, and that God often used other lions to administer this judgment. Verses 29-30 say, *"Their roaring* (those nations, people, or instruments He used for judgment) *shall be like a* ***lion****, they shall roar like young lions: yea, they shall roar, and lay hold of the prey, and shall carry it away safe, and none shall deliver it. And in that day they shall roar against them like the roaring of the sea: and if one look unto the land, behold darkness and sorrow, and the light is darkened in the heavens thereof."*
- Amos, a contemporary of Hosea, did not live long enough to see Israel conquered by Assyria. Nevertheless, he prophesied about that coming event. *"Hear this word that the LORD hath spoken against you, O children of Israel, against the whole family which I brought up from the land of Egypt, saying,* ***You only have I known of all the families of the earth*** (Note again the reference to the fact that when the earth was split up by languages, Israel was the only people group God took for Himself. The rest fell under the control of fallen angels, those '*rulers of the darkness of this world*' mentioned in Ephesians 6:12.): *therefore I will punish you for all your iniquities. . .. The* ***lion*** *hath roared, who will not fear? the Lord GOD hath spoken, who can but prophesy? Publish in the palaces at Ashdod, and in the palaces in the land of Egypt, and say, Assemble yourselves upon the mountains of Samaria*

(God was calling these people to war against Israel*), and behold the great tumults in the midst thereof, and the oppressed in the midst thereof. For they know not to do right, saith the LORD, who store up violence and robbery in their palaces* (referring to the many assassinations of the Israelite kings and their evil deeds*). Therefore thus saith the Lord GOD; An adversary there shall be even round about the land; and he shall bring down thy strength from thee* (Israel's years of tribute to Assyria, and Assyria's constant incursions and hostility weakened Israel) *and thy palaces shall be spoiled. Thus saith the LORD; As the shepherd taketh out of the mouth of the lion two legs, or a piece of an ear; so shall the children of Israel be taken out that dwell in Samaria in the corner of a bed, and in Damascus in a couch. Hear ye, and testify in the house of Jacob, saith the Lord GOD, the God of hosts, That in the day that I shall visit the transgressions of Israel upon him I will also visit the altars of Bethel* (where they worshipped the calf): *and the horns of the altar shall be cut off, and fall to the ground. And I will smite the winter house with the summer house; and the houses of ivory* (Ahab's Samaritan palace was called the 'house of ivory') *shall perish, and the great houses shall have an end, saith the LORD."* Amos 3:1-2, 8-15

The lion of redemption:

- Isaiah 31:4-7 (Amplified), *"For the Lord has said to me, As the* ***lion*** *or the* ***young lion*** *growls over his prey—and though a large band of shepherds is called out against him, he will not be terrified at their voice or daunted at their noise—so the Lord of hosts will come down to fight upon Mount Zion and upon its hills. Like birds hovering, so will the Lord of hosts defend Jerusalem; He will protect and deliver it, He will pass over and spare and preserve it. Return, O children of Israel, to Him against Whom you have so deeply plunged into revolt. For in* *that day every man of you will cast away in contempt and disgust his idols of silver and his idols of gold, which your own hands have sinfully made for you."*

- Joel 3:16-17, *"The LORD also shall* ***roar*** *out of Zion, and utter his voice from Jerusalem; and the heavens and the earth shall shake: but the LORD will be the hope of his people, and the strength of the children of Israel. So shall ye know that I am the LORD your God dwelling in Zion, my holy mountain: then shall Jerusalem be holy, and there shall no strangers pass through her any more."*

It's interesting to note that Jesus is both the Lion of judgment and the Lion of redemption. As the Lamb of God, He spiritually redeemed the world with His blood. As the Lion of the tribe of Judah, He will physically judge the world during the Tribulation, then redeem it prior to His millennial reign.

Here, in Hosea 11:10-12, we see that in the future God will roar (call His people back to Him and support their return with the needed strength) and end Israel's diaspora.

The Jewish diaspora is a long history of sorrow and hardship. Some displacements were forced. Others were voluntary. In 250 B.C., *The Sibylline Oracles* claimed that "Every land and every sea is full of thee (Jews)." By Jesus' time, more Jews lived outside Israel than inside. The Assyrians, Babylonians, and Romans all took Jews as slaves and compelled millions of others to vacate their land.

By New Testament times, Egypt had the highest population of Jews, followed by Syria. Less populated, but also centers of Jewish migration, were Greece and Asia Minor. During the reign of Tiberius Caesar (14 A.D–37 A.D.) and Claudius Caesar (41 A.D.–54 A.D.), Jews were so numerous in Rome both

Caesars persecuted them, hoping to force their exodus. After the destruction of Jerusalem in 70 A.D. and the Kokhba rebellion of 135 A.D., Rome decimated Israel's Jewish population through slaughter, then scattered the rest as slaves throughout their empire.

Pogroms in the Middle Ages further scattered the Jews. By then, they had divided into two distinct groups: the Sephardic Jews of Portugal, Spain, Middle East, and North Africa; the Ashkenazi of Eastern and Northern Europe. In 1290 A.D., England was one of the first countries to expel their Jews. Spain followed in 1492. The harsh Russian pogroms of the eighteen and nineteen hundreds further dispersed the Jewish population. This heartache culminated in Hitler's "Final Solution," when millions of Jews were displaced and six million others were exterminated. Following that, Arabs expelled their Jews from 1948 to 1973.

"Ephraim compassed me about with lies, and the house of Israel with deceit: but Judah yet ruleth with God, and is faithful with the saints." God again lamented Israel's sins while still counting Judah as faithful. But in the not-too-distant future, this would change, and Judah would also be judged. The wonderful thing is that one day both Judah and Israel will again be called His people.

Chapter 12

"Ephraim feedeth on wind, and followeth after the east wind: he daily increaseth lies and desolation; and they do make a covenant with the Assyrians, and oil is carried into Egypt. The LORD hath also a controversy with Judah, and will punish Jacob according to his ways: according to his doings will he recompense him. He took his brother by the heel in the womb, and by his strength he had power with God: Yea, he had power over the angel, and prevailed: he wept, and made supplication unto him: he found him in Bethel, and there he spake with us; Even the LORD God of hosts; the LORD is his memorial." Hosea 12:1-5

Both phrases, *"Ephraim feedeth on wind, and followeth after the east wind,"* are Hebrew idioms. The first means Ephraim was unreasonable, uncontrolled, and foolish. The second means he was greatly deceived and misled. In short, Ephraim's rebellion against Yahweh and his pursuit of other gods made that nation live vain, empty, and spiritually unproductive. And their ungodliness only increased over time.

For years, Israel made covenants with idolatrous nations (Assyria and Egypt). To garner favor and ensure their protection, he paid them tribute. This caused Israel to drain his resources. His olive oil, especially, was a valuable commodity.

The pure, beaten form was used to light the giant gold menorah in Israel's temple. And Egypt prized Israel's olive oil because it was one of the twelve different oils used by Egypt to produce their perfumes and ointments.

"The LORD hath also a controversy with Judah." God now turned His attention to Judah. As previously mentioned, they were already following in Israel's footsteps. That's why God's punishment would eventually fall on them, resulting in the chastisement of all twelve tribes (represented by Jacob's twelve sons).

Jacob's history is then recapped. His name means "supplanter, heel catcher, deceiver, manipulator." It describes his character. Hosea pointed to the fact that Jacob, like all mankind, was flawed from the beginning. This is not only what God had to work with but was willing to work with. Why? Because unlike his brother, Esau, Jacob cared about the covenant God made with his forefathers, Abraham and Isaac. Esau, the first born, did not. Thus, God bypassed him. *"Jacob have I loved, but Esau have I hated,"* (Romans 9:13). This is also mentioned in Malachi 1:2-3. It's a Hebrew idiom and doesn't mean God hated Esau. Rather, it means that God chose Jacob over Esau for the reasons mentioned. The omniscient God already knew Esau's character and that he would have little regard for spiritual things or the covenant promises. And Esau proved it by selling his birthright to Jacob for a bowl of lentils (Genesis 25:30-34).

This transference of a firstborn male's privileges defied convention. It meant the Abrahamic Covenant would now pass to Jacob, and that he, during his lifetime, was expected to be a witness to the nations of that covenant and his great God. Yet, while Jacob esteemed it, desiring all God's blessings, protection, and support, I don't believe he made a full and personal commitment to Yahweh until his departure from Laban's house.

Let's dig into it.

The name Laban means "to become white, to make bricks." The ararim-publications.com website goes further and says it means "to become white in the sense of a blank slate," or "having all heart (emotion) and little rational sense." We know from Scripture that Laban was a manipulator, a schemer. Now the manipulator, the schemer Jacob, was going to meet his match. His time in Paddan-aram would prove to be like a blank slate, where he could rewrite his character and become a different man.

Laban's name, "To make bricks," is another clue. The people at the Tower of Babel made bricks (labored in the world) to build a great edifice in hopes of making a name for themselves (Genesis 11:3-4). The purpose of their tower was to open a heavenly portal in order to contact fallen angels, acquire forbidden knowledge, and become powerful and great. At Laban's, Jacob was also going to "make bricks," to labor for twenty years. While the people of the world make bricks, God desires that their lives be altars to Him, made of uncut, non-fashioned stone (Exodus 20:25).

Though Jacob, in Genesis 28:18-19, made a memorial to God on his way to Paddan-aram by pouring oil over a stone and calling the place Bethel, House of God, he didn't build an unhewn altar there until his return to Bethel.

After that, Jacob *"had power over the angel, and prevailed: he wept, and made supplication unto him."* I believe this is Jacob's turning point. I covered this in my book, *12 Questions New Christians Frequently Ask* and will include some of it now.

Although Jacob inherited the Abrahamic Covenant, I don't believe that initially he had a personal relationship with God. Rather, he saw how much God blessed his forefathers and knew these blessings were attached to that covenant. He seemed to want the perks without the commitment. A specific bloodline cannot make us righteous. Remember, Esau also came from Abraham's bloodline. Romans 2:28-29 says, *"For he is not a Jew, which is one outwardly; neither is that circumcision, which is outward in the flesh: But he is a Jew, which is one inwardly; and circumcision is that of the heart, in the spirit, and not in the letter; whose praise is not of men, but of God."* Scripture tells us that it was Abraham's **faith** that was counted as righteousness (Genesis 15:6, Romans 4:1-5, Galatians 3:6). It shows us that a person can't become a believer simply by being born into a Christian family. It's not by a physical birth but a spiritual one. For Jacob, this spiritual birth was a long time in coming.

Here's how it happened.

Years before, while fleeing from his brother, Esau, Jacob stopped in El overnight and had a dream of a ladder reaching heaven. Because this was where Jacob encountered God, he called the place Bethel, House of God, referring to the God of Abraham and Isaac. During this dream, Jacob received God's promise to protect him, be with him, and give him a land grant. His response is found in Genesis 28:20-21, *"**If** God will be with me, and will keep me in this way that I go, and will give me bread to eat, and raiment to put on, So that I come again to my father's house in peace; **then** shall the LORD be my God."* He's not making a true commitment to God. Rather, it's futuristic and almost cynical, one that hinges on God's performance. **If** God did everything

Jacob wanted, **then** Jacob would make Yahweh his God. That's why I think it was necessary for Jacob to leave Bethel, the House of God, for Laban's House of Bricks or house of worldly labor and striving. It was where Jacob's slate could be erased and made white, his character of deceit and manipulation expunged and rewritten by God.

Jacob finally revisited Bethel twenty years later. This journey began after God identified Himself as *"the **God of Beth-el**, where thou anointedst the pillar, and where thou vowedst a vow unto me: now arise, get thee out from this land, and return unto the land of thy kindred,* (Genesis 31:13)." It was time for Jacob to have his heart circumcised.

In Genesis 32, Jacob prepares to face his brother, Esau. He fears Esau still carries a grudge for being tricked out of his birthright and blessing. Would he kill Jacob and his family? Not wanting to take that chance, Jacob separates his wives, children, possessions, and servants into three groups. Hopefully, this will ensure the survival of some of them. After this, Genesis says, *"And Jacob was left alone.."*

Our decision to come to God must always be made by us. No one can do it for us. In that sense, we are alone. And it often involves wrestling with God before we surrender, just as Jacob, while alone, wrestled with God. This is when Jacob makes the transition. This is when he truly comes into God's family. God had performed the "**if**." Now Jacob had to fulfil his word of *"**then** shall the LORD be my God."* And it would take Jacob wrestling with God Himself!

We see this wrestling in Genesis 32:24-30. God has indeed protected Jacob, prospered him, given him bread and raiment, and was sending him back to his father's house, though peace was not assured. Now, it was time for Jacob to honor the words he spoke in Genesis 28. During the struggle, Jacob realized that his blessing must come from God not from the house of bricks. This is seen in Genesis 32:26, *"I will not let thee go, except thou bless me."* Then, in an act of supreme authority and power, God (pre-incarnate Jesus) touched Jacob's *thigh,* the seat of Jacob's power, future achievement, and fruit, then changed his name to Israel. No longer "Jacob" the supplanter, he was now "Israel," prince with God. Afterward, Jacob called the place of his struggle "Peniel" meaning "face of God." *"I have seen God face to face, and my life is preserved,"* (Genesis 32:30).

In Genesis 35:1, God gave Jacob additional instructions. *"And God said unto Jacob, Arise, go up to* ***Beth-el****, and dwell there: and make there an altar unto God, that appeared unto thee when thou fleddest from the face of Esau, thy brother."* Jacob had already built an important altar in Shalem, a city of Shechem, after the successful and congenial meeting with his brother, Esau. He called the altar El-e-lohe-Israel, meaning "God, the God of Israel." Jacob, now called Israel, was declaring that Yahweh was not just the God of Abraham and Isaac, but ***his*** God, verifying his transformation and commitment. This is also prophetic. Israel has an everlasting covenant with God, which they have broken over and over again. But God never has. Though most modern Jews are irreligious and still refuse to accept their Messiah, Jesus, God still honors His covenant with them. They are still His people. The land He granted them is still their land. Yet, most don't have a relationship with Him. They are still Jacob, striving in the house of bricks instead of in the house of God. But one day, they will again become Israel, prince with God.

After building the altar in Shalem, Jacob was nearly ready to make an unhewn altar to God in Bethel. But first he needed to take care of some business.

Laban and his sons were pagans. Before leaving Syria, Rachel, Jacob's wife, stole her father's idols, perhaps thinking they would provide protection and good fortune on the journey. So, prior to arriving at Bethel, Jacob purged his household by taking his wives' earrings (often worn as totems or in deference to a false god) and the idols Rachel stole, then buried them under an oak tree in Shechem. Like the future enslaved Israelites who would leave Egypt tainted by Egyptian beliefs, so Jacob's wives left Paddan-aram tainted by Laban's.

Jacob truly found God *"in Bethel, and there he spake with us; Even the LORD God of hosts; the LORD is his memorial."* His twenty-year-long journey had finally brought him to the house of God, not as a supplanter but in godly fellowship as a prince worthy to build an unhewn altar to his holy God. But he limped because of God's touch, changing forever the way he walked through life. This indicates a price must be paid. Jacob had to give up his power and surrender to God. Once we surrender to God, the way we walk will change, too. It may take time, but eventually, we will no longer walk like the people of the world.

Continuing with the text:

"Therefore turn thou to thy God: keep mercy and judgment, and wait on thy God continually. He is a merchant, the balances of deceit are in his hand: he loveth to oppress. And Ephraim said, Yet I am become rich, I have found me out substance: in all my labours they shall find none iniquity in me that were sin. And I that am the LORD thy God from the land of Egypt will yet make thee to dwell in tabernacle, as in the days of the solemn feast." Hosea 12:6-9

Israel had become as proud, faithless, greedy, and deceitful as the Canaanites. The Israelites believed they themselves or the lesser gods they served had brought about their prosperity and good fortune. Yet, they pretended to be blameless before Yahweh. As a result, God would have to discipline them. But that discipline would not be one of utter destruction. Furthermore, God promised that when they return to Him, He will again embrace them as His people. Then it will be like in the days when His Shekinah glory rested over the wilderness tent of meeting. This points to Jesus' millennial reign. After Israel acknowledges Jesus as their Messiah, they will become head of nations, and Jesus, in all His glory, will tabernacle in Jerusalem with His people.

Continuing with the text:

"I have also spoken by the prophets, and I have multiplied visions, and used similitudes, by the ministry of the prophets. Is there iniquity in Gilead? surely they are vanity: they sacrifice bullocks in Gilgal; yea, their altars are as heaps in the furrows of the fields. And Jacob fled into the country of Syria, and Israel served for a wife, and for a wife he kept sheep. And by a prophet the LORD brought Israel out of Egypt, and by a prophet was he preserved. Ephraim provoked him to anger most bitterly: therefore shall he leave his blood upon him, and his reproach shall his Lord return unto him."
Hosea 12:10-16

This is a recounting of history. Throughout it, God guided, instructed, and warned His people via prophets, visions, and similitudes (parables, stories, and physical enactments like Jeremiah wearing an ox's yoke prophesying Judah's coming subjugation to Babylon). Even with all that, they continually sinned. We've already seen that Gilead and Gilgal refer to evil places and practices, including sacrifices to idols. Here, Gilgal also seems to be a play on words. Gilgal means "a heap of stones, ruins." Hosea was describing Gilgal's pagan altars as *"heaps in the furrows of the fields,"* which referred to stones that are removed and dumped during the plowing of a field. It points to the future of these altars, altars that will be dumped like useless stones after God has plowed His land.

God's deliverance of Israel out of Egypt is mentioned. So is their preservation during their forty years of wandering. So is Jacob's journey to Laban in Paddan-aram and his gaining wives by serving Laban for fourteen years, seven for Leah, another seven for Rachel. It's a reminder of Israel's humble beginnings and the mighty role God played in it. All Israel knew this history. And they knew how much they owed God. Therefore, the blood shed during judgment for their sins would now be on their hands.

When God warns and warns and warns of coming judgment, those who fail to heed can blame no one but themselves when it finally arrives. Just as God continuously warned the twelve tribes, so He has warned the world of the coming seven-year Tribulation, the most devastating time the world will ever see, and still so few pay heed.

Chapter 13

"When Ephraim spake trembling, he exalted himself in Israel; but when he offended in Baal, he died (spiritually). *And now they sin more and more, and have made them molten images of their silver, and idols according to their own understanding, all of it the work of the craftsmen: they say of them, Let the men that sacrifice kiss the calves. Therefore they shall be as the morning cloud, and as the early dew that passeth away, as the chaff that is driven with the whirlwind out of the floor, and as the smoke out of the chimney. Yet I am the LORD thy God from the land of Egypt, and thou shalt know no god but me: for there is no saviour beside me."* Hosea 13:1-4

When Jacob was nearing death, he called his sons together and prophesied over each of them. Ephraim was Joseph's younger son; Manasseh, his eldest. Even so, Jacob gave Ephraim the blessing of a "first son" indicating Ephraim would be the more powerful of the two. And indeed, Ephraim became a great tribe. And when that tribe feared God (*spake trembling*), God prospered it. In fact, it was the most influential of the ten tribes that formed the northern kingdom. Thus, that kingdom was not only referred to as Israel but Ephraim.

"And now they sin more and more, and have made them molten images of their silver, and idols according to their own

understanding, all of it the work of the craftsmen: they say of them, Let the men that sacrifice kiss the calves." As mentioned, the northern kingdom's first ruler was Jeroboam I, an Ephraimite. To his shame, he hired craftsmen to fashion two golden calves, then installed one in Dan, the other in Bethel. This idolatry (*Let the men that sacrifice kiss the calves)* was the beginning of their downfall. Now, Israel/Ephraim would vanish like morning clouds, dew, and smoke. Again, note the mention of a whirlwind, referring to God's anger and coming judgement.

"Thou shalt know no god but me: for there is no saviour beside me." After Jeroboam installed the golden calves, he told his people, *"Behold thy gods,"* (1 Kings 12:28). Now, here in Hosea, God was telling them, behold, HE was their God, their only God and Savior!

Continuing with the text:

"I did know thee in the wilderness, in the land of great drought. According to their pasture, so were they filled; they were filled, and their heart was exalted; therefore have they forgotten me. Therefore I will be unto them as a lion: as a leopard by the way will I observe them: I will meet them as a bear that is bereaved of her whelps (indicating anguish and ferociousness), *and will rend the caul of their heart, and there will I devour them like a lion: the wild beast shall* ***tear*** *them."* Hosea 13:5-8

Throughout those long, hard years in the wilderness, God kept his people, providing them with food and water, even keeping their clothing and shoes from wearing out. Deuteronomy 29:5 (Amplified) says, *"I have led you forty years in the wilderness; your clothes have not worn out upon you, and your sandals have not worn off your feet."* God also gave them victory over many of the stronger pagan nations as they worked their way through the

Promised Land. Instead of gratitude, they became proud of their accomplishments, proud of their new position in the world.

It's easy to forget God when things go well. But how quickly we call on Him for help when things aren't! But God is not One to be used. He is more than our provider and protector. He is the very Creator of the Universe, an awesome, holy, and powerful God who deserves our love and worship.

Hosea states that in time the Israelites drifted from Yahweh toward lesser gods, breaking God's heart. Because they have rent God's heart, He would now rend theirs (*will rend the caul of their heart*). The caul of their heart is a picture of Israel's hardened heart toward God. It's a picture of a heart that has become closed to Him; a heart He must tear open. In a way, it's a forced circumcision. In Deuteronomy 10:16, Moses reminded his people that because God had chosen their forefathers they should *"**Circumcise** therefore the foreskin of your **heart**, and be no more stiffnecked."* Moses then told them they could either choose blessings or curses through how they lived. If they were faithful to Yahweh, then, *"the LORD thy God will bring thee into the land which thy fathers possessed, and thou shalt possess it; and he will do thee good, and multiply thee above thy fathers. And the LORD thy God will **circumcise thine heart**, and the heart of thy seed, to love the LORD thy God with all thine heart, and with all thy soul, that thou mayest live,"* (Deuteronomy 30:5-6).

God wanted their hearts, their love, their faithfulness, their loyalty, and devotion. We've already seen that Romans 2:29 says, *"But he is a Jew, which is one inwardly; and **circumcision is that of the heart**, in the spirit, and not in the letter; whose praise is not of men, but of God."* God didn't want their meaningless superficial worship, their lip service. He wanted ***them***. And someday, during the seven-year Tribulation, they will be totally His. Zechariah 12:10 speaks of that day. *"And I* (God) *will pour upon the house of David, and upon the inhabitants of Jerusalem, the spirit of grace and of supplications: and they shall look upon me whom they have pierced, and they shall mourn for him, as one mourneth for his only son, and shall be in bitterness for him, as one that is in bitterness for his firstborn."*

To accomplish this, Yahweh the Shepherd would become a predator to His flock. Symbols of a lion, leopard, and bear are used as prophetic warnings of Israel's coming afflictions by Gentile nations. First Israel, then Judah would go into exile and be subjugated.

Daniel chapter seven gives us further insight into who those nations are. The lion is Babylon, succeeded by the Medo-Persian empire (bear), followed by Greece (leopard). All three impacted the Jews. These were followed by the Roman Empire. By then, Israel was back in the land, though subject to Rome. Note that *"the wild beast shall tear them."* This is the last empire mentioned. I believe it signifies the antichrist, who, most scholars believe, will come out of the Holy Roman Empire. In Revelation 11:7, he is called *"the beast."* Webster defines "beast" as "an animal, or a person who is brutal, gross, vile, disgusting, stupid, etcetera." This is a good description of the antichrist. He is also described as a willful king in Daniel 11:36, one who will deceive Israel then seek to destroy her.

All this gives us a picture of the antichrist's character, one who acts like a beast and will *"tear"* Israel and her people. Jeremiah 30:7 describes this time. *"Alas! for that day is great, so that none is like it: it is even the time of Jacob's trouble; but he shall be saved out of it."* Yes, God will intervene and save the Jews but not, according to Zechariah 13:8, before two-thirds of them are killed. Unfortunately, this is what it will take to bring the heart of Israel back to God and to their Messiah, Jesus.

Continuing with the text:

"O Israel, thou hast destroyed thyself; but in me is thine help. ***I will be thine king****: where is any other that may save thee in all thy cities? and thy judges of whom thou saidist, Give me a king and princes? I gave thee a king in mine anger, and took him away in my wrath. The iniquity of Ephraim is bound up; his sin is hid. The sorrows of a travailing woman shall come upon him: he is* ***an unwise son****; for he should not stay long in the place of the breaking forth of children."* Hosea 13:9-13

I hear God's anguished heart in this. Israel has turned from the very One who was able to keep and save them. God, as helper, was a well-known theme in Scripture. King David acknowledged this in Psalm 54:4. *"Behold, God is mine* ***helper****: the Lord is with them that uphold my soul."* And again in Psalm 121:2, *"My* ***help*** *cometh from the LORD, which made heaven and earth."* Even Paul, in Hebrews 13:6, addressed this. After saying that God would never leave or forsake the believer, he said: *"So that we may boldly say, The Lord is my* ***helper****, and I will not fear what man shall do unto me."*

Where else but from the Creator of the Universe can true help come from? There is nothing too hard for Him. Like Israel, many people look to others or themselves for rescue, choosing to live apart from God. But sooner or later they discover that people fail them or that being the captain of their own ship has hung them up on a reef or driven them into rocks.

And that's just what Israel did. By rejecting God, they destroyed themselves. While they no longer have a king or other leaders to save them, God, ever merciful, stated ***He*** would be their King. He said this after their rejection, after Israel knew He was to be their king from the very beginning. I have covered this Kingship extensively in my book, *"Encountering Jesus Throughout the Bible"* and partially in Book One of this series but will include it here due to its aid in clarifying God's position.

Old Testament Scriptures acknowledge that Israel initially considered God to not only be their King, but King of the world and universe. Below are a few:

First, as King of Israel:

As mentioned, before Jacob died, he blessed his twelve sons. But along with his blessings came prophecies. In Genesis 49:9-10, Jacob called Judah a *"lion's welp,"* and prophesied that, *"The **sceptre** shall not depart from Judah, nor a **lawgiver** from between his feet, until **Shiloh** come; and unto him shall the gathering of the people be."*

This is profound. A scepter implies authority to rule. Jacob was prophesying that a lawgiver, a future ruler, would come from the tribe of Judah. This points to king David as well as their Messiah Jesus, for "Shiloh" means Messiah. So early on, the Jews began watching for their promised earthly king. In the meantime, God would be their King.

At first, Israel had no problem with that. After all, they were God's chosen people according to Deuteronomy 7:7-8: *"The LORD did not set his love upon you* (Israel*), nor **choose** you because ye were more in number than any people; for ye were the fewest of all people: But because the LORD loved you, and because he would keep the oath which he had sworn unto your fathers, hath the LORD* *brought you out with a mighty hand, and redeemed you out of the house of bondmen, from the house of Pharaoh king of Egypt."*

God's very presence, in the form of a cloud and fire, led Israel safely in the wilderness for forty years. All this contributed to Israel's awareness that He was their Ruler. The following Scriptures illustrate this:

Psalm 24:7-10, *"Lift up your heads, O ye gates; and be ye lift up, ye everlasting doors; and the* ***King*** *of glory shall come in. Who is this* ***King*** *of glory? The LORD strong and mighty, the LORD mighty in battle. Lift up your heads, O ye gates; even lift them up, ye everlasting doors; and the* ***King*** *of glory shall come in. Who is this* ***King*** *of glory? The LORD of hosts, he is the* ***King*** *of glory."*

Psalm 89:18, *"For the LORD is our defense; and the Holy One of Israel is our* ***king****."*

Israel, in Psalm 149:2, acknowledged that God was not only their King but their Creator. *"Let Israel rejoice in him (*God*) that made him (*Israel*); let the children of Zion be joyful in their* ***King****."*

Next, as King of the world and universe:

Israel understood that God's authority didn't end with them. He was also King of the world and universe.

Psalm 103:19, *"The LORD hath prepared his* ***throne*** *in the heavens; and his* ***kingdom ruleth over all****."* The phrase "over all" means the known and unknown world as well as the heavens where God is enthroned.

1 Chronicles 29:11, *"Thine, O LORD, is the greatness, and the power, and the glory, and the victory, and the majesty: for all that is*

in the ***heaven and in the earth is thine****; thine is the* ***kingdom****, O LORD, and* ***thou art exalted as head above all****."*

Psalm 47:2, 6-8 *"For the LORD most high is terrible; he is a great* ***King*** *over all the earth. . .. Sing praises to God, sing praises: sing praises unto our* ***King****, sing praises. For God is the* ***King of all the earth****: sing ye praises with understanding.* ***God reigneth over the heathen****: God sitteth upon the throne of his holiness."*

Jeremiah 10:7, 10, *"Who would not fear thee* (God)*, O* ***King of nations****? for to thee doth it appertain: forasmuch as among all the wise men of the nations, and in all their kingdoms, there is none like unto thee. . .. But the LORD is the true God, he is the living God, and an everlasting* ***king****: at his wrath the earth shall tremble, and the nations shall not be able to abide his indignation."*

Psalm 22:28, *"For the* ***kingdom*** *is the LORD'S: and he is the governor among the* ***nations****."* A governor is just another name for ruler. Israel clearly understood and believed that God's rule extended far beyond their nation.

Even when Israel was ruled by earthly kings, some of them, like David, personally acknowledged God as the true King. The following verses make that clear:

- Psalm 10:16, *"The LORD is* ***King*** *for ever and ever."*
- Psalm 29:10b, *"The LORD sitteth* ***King*** *for ever."*
- In Psalm 95:3, *"the LORD is a great God, and a great* ***King*** *above all gods."*
- Psalm 5:2, *"Hearken unto the voice of my cry, my* ***King****, and my God: for unto thee will I pray."*
- Psalm 145:1, *"I* (David) *will extol thee, my God, O* ***king****; and I will bless thy name for ever and ever."*

David was so overwhelmed by God's goodness and glory, and so sure others would be too, he said this in Psalm145:11, *"They* (the righteous) *shall speak of the glory of thy **kingdom**, and talk of thy power."* Though God had His own glorious heavenly kingdom, there was no doubt in David's mind that God was also Ruler over the kingdoms of the world, including his.

Hezekiah, in 2 Kings 19:15, also declared that God alone was God over *"all the kingdoms of the earth."*

Individuals acknowledged God as King:

When Isaiah saw God on His throne, he saw himself for what he was, a sinner, and God as utterly pure and holy. He said in Isaiah 6:5, *"Woe is me! for I am undone; because I am a man of unclean lips, and I dwell in the midst of a people of unclean lips: for mine eyes have seen the **King**, the LORD of hosts."* What an awesome sight that must have been! And how humbling! The great and powerful are nothing in light of the majesty, glory, and holiness of God.

Even Nebuchadnezzar, the pagan king of Babylon, had his moments. In 597 B.C., following his first attempt to conquer Jerusalem, he brought many Jewish prisoners back to his city. Daniel was one of them. At that time, the Babylonian kingdom was very powerful. But when king Nebuchadnezzar's pride became too great, God decided to whittle him down. He made him to become beast-like, eat grass, and live in the open fields for seven years (symbolic of the nature of the future antichrist). At the end of that time, Nebuchadnezzar's sanity was restored. He said this in Daniel 4:37, *"Now I Nebuchadnezzar praise and extol and honour the **King of heaven**, all whose works are truth, and his ways judgment: and those that walk in pride he is able to abase."* What a lesson to learn the hard way!

Temple musicians also acknowledged God as their King. This can be found in Psalms 44:4, 68:24 and 84:3 as well as in Psalm 74:12 when Maschil of Asaph said, *"For God is my* ***King*** *of old, working salvation in the midst of the earth."*

Then there was Gideon, who was notable in his declaration that God was King. Here's what happened:

The Midianites had been a thorn in Israel's side for years, invading their land, plundering their food and goods. Finally, God instructed Gideon to stop it. An interesting story revealing numerous spiritual truths, it culminates in Midian's defeat at the hands of Gideon and his army. After this great victory, the people wanted Gideon and his son to rule over them.

The promise of power can be heady. It's also dangerous. England's 1800's Lord Acton said it best, "Power tends to corrupt, and absolute power corrupts absolutely."

Was it difficult for Gideon to subdue his natural pride and ego? Perhaps. But in the end, he refused to allow his countrymen to thrust him into a position that he understood only God should occupy. He said this amazing thing in Judges 8:23, *"I will not rule over you, neither shall my son rule over you: the* ***LORD*** *shall* ***rule*** *over you."*

God Himself acknowledges that He is King:

In Isaiah 41:21, God chastised His people for worshipping idols, *"Produce your cause* (give a reason why you have chosen to worship idols*), saith the LORD; bring forth your strong reasons, saith the* ***King*** *of Jacob* (Israel)." God was making His position clear. **He** is King over Israel, and as King, He has the right to demand loyalty and obedience from His subjects or the reason why they weren't forthcoming.

Again, in Isaiah 43:15, God made His position clear. *"I am the LORD, your Holy One, the creator of Israel, your **King**."*

God's kingdom is an everlasting kingdom.

Psalm 45:6, *"Thy throne, O God, is for **ever and ever**: the sceptre of thy **kingdom** is a right sceptre."*

Daniel 4:3, *"How great are his* (God's) *signs! and how mighty are his wonders! his **kingdom** is an **everlasting kingdom**, and his dominion is from generation to generation."*

Psalm 93:2, "Thy (God's) ***throne*** *is established of old: thou art from **everlasting**."*

Psalm 145:11-13, *"They* (the righteous) *shall speak of the glory of thy **kingdom**, and talk of thy power; To make known to the sons of men his* (God's) *mighty acts, and the glorious majesty of his **kingdom.** Thy **kingdom** is an **everlasting kingdom**, and thy dominion endureth throughout all generations."*

God's kingship was not a new development. Long before He was Israel's King and even before the earth was created, He ruled over a vast heavenly empire.

Though many kings in Israel understood they were merely representing God to their people, and that their rule was temporary while God's was everlasting, the fact remained, Israel was never meant to have an earthly king.

Now, we go to Israel and her first king, Saul.

As mentioned, prior to Saul, Israel had no earthly king. God was King and ruled over them through the prophets and judges.

1 Samuel 8: 4-7 details how this all changed. *"Then all the elders of Israel gathered themselves together, and came to Samuel* (the prophet) *unto Ramah, And said unto him, Behold, thou art old, and thy sons walk not in thy ways: now make us a king to judge us* ***like all the nations****. But the thing displeased Samuel, when they said, Give us a king to judge us. And Samuel prayed unto the LORD. And the LORD said unto Samuel, Hearken unto the voice of the people in all that they say unto thee:* ***for they have not rejected thee, but they have rejected me, that I should not reign over them****."*

First, notice they wanted to be like other nations when God clearly didn't want that. They were to be His people, set apart in covenant relationship with Him. Deuteronomy 7:6: *"For thou* (Israel) *art an holy people unto the LORD thy God: the LORD thy God hath chosen thee to be a special people unto himself, above all people that are upon the face of the earth."* Even so, God gave Israel the same free will He gave Adam and Eve, the same free will He gives us all, and allowed them to have Saul as king.

Then notice the broken heart of God. His people had rejected Him when all He wanted as their King was to care for, protect, and provide for them. He also knew the suffering that was in store for Israel because of their decision, a decision which would have far reaching and dire consequences.

This request of the people showed there was already a spiritual decline in Israel. Leaders always reflect what's going on in their society. If you want to know the condition of a society, look at the caliber of its leaders. The people of Israel had already been reigning privately in their own lives, and this desire to be like all the other nations, to have a human king rather than God, was a manifestation of that condition.

Saul is a picture of King Self. Because he was king and not God, it only took him two years before blundering. What happened? He and his men were gathered in Gilgal, preparing to face the Philistines. The prophet Samuel was to come before the battle to offer sacrifices. When he didn't, many Israelites panicked. Some deserted. Fearing his whole army was going to abandon him, Saul took matters into his own hands and offered a burnt sacrifice to God, something only priests were permitted to do.

When Samuel finally arrived, he told Saul, *"Thou has done foolishly* (by offering the animal sacrifices)*: thou hast not kept the commandment of the LORD thy God, which he commanded thee: for now would the LORD have established thy kingdom upon Israel for ever.* ***But now thy kingdom shall not continue,"*** (1 Samuel 13:13-14). God was telling Saul his kingdom would be cut off, that he would be the last in his bloodline to wear the crown.

Saul's next blunder came soon after. In 1 Samuel 15:3, God commanded Saul to utterly destroy Amalek *"Now go and smite Amalek, and utterly destroy all that they have, and spare them not; but slay both man and woman, infant, and suckling, ox, and sheep, camel and ass."*

Again, Saul disobeyed. In addition to keeping Agag, the Amalek king, alive, he also spared the best animals out of fear his soldiers would resent not sharing the spoils of war, a common practice at the time. When Samuel rebuked him, Saul lied and said he had planned to use the animals as a sacrifice to God. Samuel responded in 1 Samuel 15:22, *"Behold, to obey is better than sacrifice."*

Why is obedience better than sacrifice? Because obedience is the relationship, the interaction between a subject and his king. Whoever we obey is the king. If we obey God's Word, He is King. If we obey our own dictates and desires, then Self is King.

God was not king over Israel or Saul, but Self was. Because Saul disobeyed God, his rightful King, he lost God's favor. After that, Saul's reign continued to go downhill. We see him years later, once again preparing to face the Philistines in battle. We find him worried and anxious because he is unable to hear from God. 1 Samuel 28:6 says, *"And when Saul enquired of the LORD, the LORD answered him not, neither by dreams, nor by U'rim, nor by prophets."* As King Self he was on his own, with only his counsel to lean on, and that terrified him.

What was he to do? Left to his own devices, Saul made the worst possible decision. He disguised himself and sought guidance from the witch of Endor. He asked her to conjure up the spirit of Samuel (1 Samuel 28:7-20). Verse 15 says, *"And Samuel said to Saul, Why hast thou disquieted me, to bring me up? And Saul answered, I'm sore distressed; for the Philistines make war against me, and* ***God is departed from me****, and answereth me no more, either by prophets, nor by dreams: therefore I have called thee, that thou mayest make known unto me what I shall do."*

What a pathetic picture of King Self! From ruling as God's representative, with God's anointing, guidance, and favor, Saul was now alone and careening into his final degradation by consulting a witch, a practice forbidden by God. Because Saul ruled as King Self, Satan had been able to torment him for years. 1 Samuel 16:14 says, *"But the Spirit of the LORD departed from Saul, and an evil spirit from the LORD troubled him."* While 1 Samuel 16:23 adds, *"And it came to pass, when the evil spirit from God was upon Saul, that David took an harp, and played with his hand: so Saul was refreshed, and was well, and the evil spirit departed from him."*

How miserable Saul must have been! As King Self he had come out from under God's protection and susceptible to the wiles of the devil. Thus, Saul reaped years of despair and sorrow. Now, with Saul's last act of foolishness, Satan was able to complete the takeover. And true to form, Satan, the destroyer, did just that. Saul died in the ensuing battle.

Because a king is the absolute ruler over a kingdom or territory, God must be King over all, over every aspect of our lives. When we accept Jesus as our Savior, it's the first step in setting up God's kingdom within us. After that, we need to make Him Lord. When we do, we make God part of both the big and little things in our lives. That means He is King over our attitudes, desires, ambition, money, family, relationships, time, our **everything**.

Jesus said in John 14:30, *"Hereafter I will not talk much with you: for the prince of this world cometh, and hath nothing in me."* Jesus was 100% man. When the temperature dropped, He was cold. When he went too long without food, He was hungry. He also had emotions that could prick His heart and make Him weep. And even though He was also 100% God, He surrendered kingship of His life to God the Father. He continually made statements like: *"I do only what the Father tells me to do. I do nothing without the Father,"* etcetera.

Because Jesus was totally submitted to the Father and obeyed Him in everything, Jesus the man could say that Satan had nothing in Him. All His fleshly and soulish territory were under submission. That's why Jesus told us to seek first the kingdom of God, and that the kingdom of God is within us, etcetera. That's why the apostle Paul could say everything was dung (manure) compared to Jesus. God was King over his life.

Since the only kingdom Satan can conquer is the kingdom of Self, obviously the smart thing would be to make God King over our lives. And as a King Who loves us, God has precious promises He wants us to inherit. He wants only the best for us; to enable us to stand in times of trouble and live the full life He has planned.

Now, encountering Jesus as King in the Old Testament:

In Genesis 14:18-20, we see the preincarnate Jesus, King of Righteousness and Peace, officiate as priest after the order of Melchisedec by offering Abraham bread and wine. We also saw this typology in the Song of Solomon where Jesus is depicted as both King and Bridegroom. But are there other places in the Old Testament which depict Jesus as King, either directly or through symbolism and prophecy?

Yes, many.

In 1 Chronicles 17:14, God promised David that his seed would have an eternal throne. This promise was speaking of Jesus, Messiah ben David, whose kingdom will never end. *"But I* (God) *will settle him in mine house and in my kingdom for ever: and his* ***throne*** *shall be established for* ***evermore."***

Isaiah 9:6 foretold the birth of Jesus and described Him this way: *"For unto us a child is born, unto us a* ***son*** *is given: and the* ***government*** *shall be upon his shoulder: and his name shall be called Wonderful, Counsellor, The* ***mighty God****, The everlasting Father, The Prince of Peace."* It's a comprehensive description. But for this study note the words "*son*" and "*mighty God.*" This tells us the coming One will be God Himself, the Son, the second Person of the Trinity. Then note the phrase, *"the government shall be upon his shoulder."* It indicates Jesus is Ruler. He will carry the government of the whole earth. It will be solely in His control.

Zechariah 9:9 prophetically spoke of Jesus. *"Rejoice greatly, O daughter of Zion; shout, O daughter of Jerusalem: behold, thy* ***King*** *cometh unto thee: he is just, and having salvation; lowly, and riding upon an ass, and upon a colt the foal of an ass."*

This prophecy was fulfilled by Jesus when he entered Jerusalem on a donkey. Jesus knew the end was near. Soon He would fulfill His role as the "Lamb of God" and sacrifice His life for all. But before He did, something interesting happened. In Luke 19:30-40, He told his disciples to get a certain donkey with its colt, and then He rode that donkey into Jerusalem. The crowd went wild. People waved palm branches and spread them, as well as their cloaks, on the ground before Him. Palm branches symbolized victory and waving them was meant to honor kings. These people were not only expressing their joy, but their belief that goodness and victory would finally come through Jesus, their new King. *"Hosanna,"* they shouted. *"Blessed be the* ***King*** *that cometh in the name of the Lord: peace in heaven, and glory in the highest,"* (Luke 19:38). *"Blessed be the kingdom of our father David, that cometh in the name of the Lord,"* they said in Mark 11:10. They were acknowledging that Jesus was Messiah ben David, the King of Israel. In addition, by riding a donkey into Jerusalem and accepting the people's praise, Jesus, too, acknowledged He was King.

Soon after, Jesus was indeed crowned King—with a crown of thorns. Matthew 27:28-29, *"And they* (the Roman soldiers) *stripped him (*Jesus*), and put on him a scarlet robe. And when they had plated a crown of thorns, they put it upon his head, and a reed in his right hand: and they bowed the knee before him, and mocked him, saying,* ***Hail King of the Jews****."*

Notice, in addition to having a crown, Jesus was draped with a scarlet robe. John 19:5 calls it a "purple robe," representing the color of the royal robe of a king. I want to stop here and drill down a bit on Jesus' scarlet robe as described in Matthew 27:28. That word scarlet is *kokkinos* in Greek and is an unusual word. It means "crimson or red." It's the color of blood. But it also means "a kernel of seed, corn, grain." John 7:42 reminds us that Jesus is the very **Seed** promised in Genesis 3:15 Who would crush Satan's head. He was also the **Seed** from the line of David.

In John 12:24 (Amplified), Jesus said, *"I assure you, most solemnly I tell you, Unless a* ***grain*** (a seed) *of wheat* ***falls into the earth and dies****, it remains (just one grain; it never becomes more but lives) by itself alone. But if it dies, it produces many others and yields a rich harvest."* Hidden in that word, scarlet, is the picture of Jesus, the Son of God, as the Seed, falling *"into the earth,"* shedding his blood and dying for us so that God the Father could have many sons and daughters. Jesus made it possible for a great harvest of believers to share His kingdom forever.

Now, back to Jesus being crowned king. The soldiers crowned Him with thorns, draped Him in a royal-colored robe, gave

Him a reed scepter, all to mock Him. They had no idea of the significance of what they were doing. But God did.

It was the month of Nisan. The first of Nisan was considered the New Year for Kings, the day when the calculation of a king's reign began. And Jesus was crowned on Passover, the 15th of Nisan, the very day Israel's kings were coronated. Coincidence? Hardly. Jesus, appearing before Pilate and the leaders of Israel as crowned and robed, then presented to the people, fulfilled every requirement of a legal coronation. Unbeknown to them, the soldiers, Pilate, and the elders of Israel were performing an official act.

At Jesus' public presentation as King, Pilate even said in John 19:14b, *"Behold your **King**."* And in John 19:19, Pilate had "JESUS OF NAZARETH THE KING OF THE JEWS" inscribed on a plaque which was nailed to the cross.

And it wasn't unusual for a king to ride a lowly animal like a donkey. Solomon did it in 1 Kings 1:33 when he rode a mule to Gihon to be anointed as king over Israel by the prophet, Nathan. It was a sign of humility but also a sign of peace. Kings rode such animals when coming in peace and rode war horses when going into battle.

Israel longed for the prophesied Davidic King to bring peace and righteousness to their land. They were not looking for, nor were they interested in, Messiah ben Joseph, the Suffering Servant. Though Jesus was indeed their King, He first came to suffer, and most of Israel didn't understand that. Even so, John 12:15 says, *"**Fear** not, daughter of Sion: behold thy **King** cometh, sitting on an ass's colt,"* indicating that though Jesus' earthly Kingdom wouldn't be realized now, the One sitting on the donkey was indeed their true King, and they could hope and rejoice in His future reign.

So, here we see a picture of Jesus, the King of kings, entering Jerusalem in peace; humble and meek and ready to die for each of us. What a picture of the heart and character of God! But there's another side. When Jesus returns, He'll not be riding a donkey. Revelation 19:11-16 tells us that He will be riding a white horse, a war horse, and His vestures will be dipped in blood, *"and on His thigh a name written, KING OF KINGS AND LORD OF LORDS."* He will not be a King of Peace, but a King coming to battle with the unsaved of the world. What a contrast to King Jesus in Matthew!

It is a cautionary tale. Let us submit ourselves to our meek, gentle King now, for if we don't, we will eventually be forced to submit to the King whose vesture is dipped in blood.

Psalm 2 talks about the reign of Jesus and how the kings of the earth will try to thwart His rule, but God has the last laugh. Verse 6 says, *"Yet **have** I set my **king** upon my holy hill of Zion."* Notice the word "have." It is past tense, meaning it is done. It is settled in the spiritual realm. And when the time is right, nothing can stop it from manifesting physically.

Psalm 45 is all about Jesus' kingdom. Verses 1, 11, and 14 say, *"My heart is inditing a good matter: I speak of the things which I have made touching the **king*** (Jesus)*: my tongue is the pen of a ready writer. . .. So shall the **king*** (Jesus) *greatly desire thy beauty* (the beauty of believers)*: for he is thy Lord; and worship thou him. . .. She* (the church, the bride of Christ) *shall be brought unto the **king** in raiment of needlework: the virgins her companions that follow her shall be brought unto thee."*

This is talking about the time when Jesus will officiate as both God and King, for not only is He to rule but He is to be worshipped. He loves His believers and considers them beautiful because they are clothed in His righteousness. And when the Rapture occurs, His Church, His bride, will be brought to Him and then He will take her to the bridal chamber in heaven. It is a glorious passage, full of promises for those who love Him.

Psalm 48:2 goes on to tell us where Jesus will rule. *"Beautiful for situation, the joy of the whole earth, is mount Zion, on the sides of the north, the city of the great* ***King****."* Jesus, the great King, will rule from Jerusalem, fulfilling the promise God made to David concerning an everlasting throne and kingdom. God always keeps His promises.

Jeremiah 23:5-6 continues the theme of Jesus coming from the line of David. *"Behold, the days come, saith the LORD, that I will raise unto David a righteous Branch, and a* ***King*** *shall reign and prosper, and shall execute judgment and justice in the earth. In his days, Judah shall be saved, and Israel shall dwell safely: and this is his name whereby he shall be called, THE LORD OUR RIGHTEOUSNESS."* It is repeated in Jeremiah 33:15. Both Scriptures specifically refer to the end times when Jesus will sit on His throne in Jerusalem.

Isaiah 11:1-5 supports this and gives more details. *"And there shall come forth a rod out of the* ***stem of Jesse*** (David's father*) and a* ***Branch*** (Jesus) *shall grow out of his roots: And the spirit of the LORD shall rest upon him, the spirit of wisdom and understanding, the spirit of counsel and might, the spirit of knowledge and of the fear of the LORD. And shall make him of quick understanding in the fear of the LORD; and he shall not judge after the sight of his eyes, neither reprove after the hearing of his ears: But with righteousness shall he* *judge the poor, and reprove with equity for the meek of the earth: and* ***he shall smite the earth with the rod of his mouth,*** *and with the breath of his lips shall he slay the wicked."*

Zechariah 3:8b also mentions the "branch." God is speaking about the Messiah and says, *"I will bring forth my servant the* ***BRANCH.****"* God again affirms this in Zechariah 6:12-13.

Notice, it continues the theme that the Messiah and King will come from the line of David. Also notice that Isaiah 11:5 mentions how this king will smite the earth with the rod of his mouth. That alludes to Revelation 1:16 and 2:16, the *"sword of his* (Jesus') *mouth,"* and Revelation 19:15-16 which says, *"And* ***out of his*** (Jesus') ***mouth goeth a sharp sword****, that with it he should smite the nations: and he shall rule them with a* ***rod of iron****: and he treadeth the winepress of the fierceness and wrath of Almighty God. And he hath on his vesture and on his thigh a name written, KING OF KINGS, AND LORD OF LORDS."*

And here's a warning in Isaiah 60:12: *"For the nation and kingdom that will not serve thee* (Jesus) *shall perish; yea those nations shall be utterly wasted."* Scripture explains Scripture. There will come a time when the bill is due. And it will be terrifying for those who don't know the Lord and have fought against Him. That's why it's so important to come to Jesus while there is still time.

Psalm 2:12 refers to this by saying, *"Kiss the Son, lest he be angry, and ye* ***perish from the way****, when his wrath is kindled but a little. Blessed are all they that put their trust in him."* That word, "kiss" is *nashaq* and means, "to attach, to fasten together." It refers to the custom of kissing a king's foot to show respect, homage, and obedience. By kissing the foot of a king, one fastened or attached himself to that king's rule. The action suggested that person would be a willing and obedient subject. In the same way, we are to attach ourselves to Jesus, acknowledging that He is our King and Ruler before we *"perish from the way."*

It's interesting to note that in Luke 7:37-38, when the woman with the alabaster jar came and anointed Jesus' feet, she also kissed them. That word "kissed" means, "kiss earnestly." It also means, "that which is joined." It's impossible to know if she was kissing Jesus as King. But it is possible to understand that through her actions, she was joining or attaching herself to Him.

And for those who attach themselves to Jesus, a wonderful future awaits. Daniel 7:18 says, *"But the* ***saints*** *of the most High shall take the kingdom, and possess the kingdom for ever, even for ever and ever."* And Daniel 7:27 says, *"And the kingdom and dominion, and the greatness of the kingdom under the whole heaven, shall be given to the people of the* ***saints*** *of the most High, whose kingdom is an everlasting kingdom, and all dominions shall serve and obey him* (King Jesus)*."*

It couldn't be clearer. Only the saints of God, both Jew and Gentile who have accepted Jesus, will inherit the kingdom. Oh, how sad for those left out and consigned to hell for all eternity when God made it so easy to be reconciled to Him through Christ!

Encountering Jesus as King in the New Testament:

Although I've already covered some of the New Testament references to Jesus as King when covering references in the Old Testament because they overlap, there is still much to see in the New Testament regarding this.

First, when the angel Gabriel appeared to Mary and told her she was going to have a son, he went on to name and describe Him in Luke 1:31-32, *"And, behold, thou* (Mary) *shalt conceive in thy womb, and bring forth a son, and shalt call his name JESUS. He shall be great, and shall be called the Son of the Highest: and the Lord God shall give unto him the* ***throne of his father David****."* So, even before Jesus arrived on earth, He was declared King.

Then, Jesus was born in Bethlehem, the City of David, again foreshadowing His arrival as the future King of Israel. It's a fulfilment of Micah 5:2. *"But thou,* ***Bethlehem Ephratah****, though thou be little among the thousands of Judah, yet out of thee shall he come forth unto me that is to be* ***ruler*** *of Israel; whose goings forth have been from of old, from everlasting."*

Remember, according to Jacob's prophecy in Genesis 49:10, the eternal ruler was to come from the tribe of Judah. And that's exactly from where Jesus came. Revelation 5:5 also confirms this when describing the apostle John weeping in heaven because no one was found worthy to open the seven-seal scroll, *"And one of the elders saith unto me* (John), *Weep not: behold the* ***Lion of the tribe of Juda, the Root of David****, hath prevailed to open the book, and to loose the seven seals thereof."*

After Jesus was born, He was visited by magi. Mathew 2:1-2 says, *"Now when Jesus was born in Bethlehem of Judea in the days of Herod the king, behold, there came* ***wise men*** *from the east to Jerusalem, Saying, Where is he that is born* ***King of the Jews****? For we have seen his star in the east, and are come to* ***worship*** *him."*

Who were these wise men, these magi? And why was their coming to Bethlehem significant? Tradition tells us there were three of them who followed a star to Bethlehem, then presented Jesus with gifts. For the most part it's correct, except the

Bible doesn't tell us the number. I suspect the tradition of "three" came about because the Bible mentions they brought three gifts, all costly, all prophetic.

So, were these just "smart" men who happened to see something unusual in the sky and decided to investigate? No and no. The magi were elite members of a governing class in Persia (Iran). They were powerful, educated, and extremely wealthy. They knew astronomy and prophecy, even Bible prophecy. They were from a special caste called *Magoi,* from whence the name magi comes, with no connection to magic. But because of their knowledge of astronomy and prophecy, they were considered a mystical priesthood probably with occult powers. They worshipped the elements: fire, water, earth, and air, rather than multiple gods which was more typical of that time. They had great political power that continued throughout several successive empires: Babylon, Medo-Persian, Greek, and Parthian. The *Megistanes,* comprising their upper council, were the kingmakers of the ancient world. Their decisions, even in matters of state, were considered final and binding. No one became king without their approval.

It was during the Babylonian era that the magi became acquainted with the prophet Daniel, Nebuchadnezzar's Jewish captive who served more than seventy years in their court. Daniel was widely respected and wielded great power. During his servitude, the magi were exposed to the Jewish Scriptures. In time, their religious manifestations began to heavily reflect aspects of Judaism. Since they were well acquainted with Daniel's prophecy of the birth of a Messiah and great King, they continually studied the stars looking for signs of His coming. And when they saw it, they traveled countless miles to lay their treasures before this "promised one" and declare Him "King."

Matthew 2:3 says that Herod and all Jerusalem were troubled by their arrival. And no wonder. These were not just three nicely dressed men all alone on camels. Rather, the delegation of the *Magistanes* could have included up to a hundred magi, a large servant staff, and a vast army to protect them. They would have traveled in grandeur and style, necessitating numerous conveyances to carry it all. The sight of this large caravan would have inspired not only awe but fear. There was no way Herod dared lay a finger on them.

These wisemen from the east, these kingmakers, came in great pomp and ceremony to declare Jesus, KING. And their spiritual insight was sufficient that when they saw Jesus, in his humble home as a toddler, they weren't fooled. They still recognized Him for Who He was, then gave Him gifts. Matthew 2:11, *"And when they* (the magi) *were come into the house, they saw the young child with Mary his mother, and fell down, and* ***worshipped*** *him: and when they had opened their treasures, they presented unto him gifts;* ***gold, and frankincense, and myrrh****."*

Note the order the gifts are listed. First gold, which represents royalty, then frankincense which was used in sacrificial cleansing, and finally, myrrh, a spice used to anoint a body for burial. The gifts say Jesus is King. But they also say He would become a sacrifice and die.

Since Jesus was born in Bethlehem, the place where the lambs for the Temple sacrifices were bred and raised, did the magi understand that King Jesus would first be the sacrificial Lamb of God? Uncertain. But they did understand and acknowledge that here was a great king, and their presence was a declaration of that fact. Though it's doubtful that Rome recognized their authority, Herod and all Jerusalem would have acknowledged their exalted position as kingmakers throughout parts of the world. Also notice, the magi **worshipped** Jesus.

We know Jesus didn't need the magi to make Him King. He already was/is/will be. But isn't it just like God to confirm His plan and purpose? To use the natural to confirm the spiritual? It was a sign to us, a sign to help us understand Who Jesus really is. That is just part of God's goodness and mercy.

In Matthew 3:2, John the Baptist declared that *"the **kingdom** of heaven is at hand."* It was at hand because the Messiah and Israel's King had come.

Jesus also declared that the *"**kingdom** of heaven is at hand"* in Matthew 4:17. And according to Matthew 4:23, *"Jesus went about all Galilee, teaching in their synagogues, and preaching the **gospel of the kingdom**, and healing all manner of sickness and all manner of disease among the people."* Then in the Lord's prayer, Jesus said, in Matthew 6:10, *"Thy **kingdom** come,"* referring to the kingdom of heaven. As mentioned, God has a heavenly kingdom, and He wants it to be manifested on earth. Someday, Jesus will return and set up that kingdom. In the meantime, believers in Jesus can experience God's kingdom within them. Jesus said in Luke 17:21b, *"the **kingdom** of God is within you."* It is a kingdom of joy, peace, love, and bright hope.

Remember how Jesus, in Matthew 6:33, counsels us to "seek" the kingdom of God, desire it, make it our priority? Why? Because if we do, *"All these things* (the things we need and sometimes the things we want) *shall be added unto you."* How marvelous! We don't need to strive and strain. We just need to put God first, be obedient to His Word, and allow His Holy Spirit to change and direct us. That should be a comfort to everyone.

Jesus shared the mysteries of the kingdom of heaven through eight parables in Matthew 13. That's relevant since eight is the number of new beginnings. And that's exactly what Jesus did. He gave us a new beginning, a new opportunity to have peace with God, to have a relationship with Him, as well as the promise of a wonderful eternity in heaven. I encourage you to read the chapter yourself. I will only list the topics here:

- parable of the sower
- parable of the tares and wheat
- parable of the grain of mustard seed
- parable of leaven
- parable of treasure in a field
- parable of a merchant seeking pearls
- parable of the fishing net
- parable of the householder

Jesus is a gracious King:

After Peter proclaimed Jesus was the Messiah and Son of God, Jesus promised He would give him, *"the keys of the **kingdom** of heaven."* Matthew 16:19 says, *"I will give unto thee* (Peter and the church) *the **keys of the kingdom of heaven**: and whatsoever thou shalt bind on earth shall be bound in heaven: and whatsoever thou shalt loose on earth shall be loosed in heaven."* This is talking about the authority of every believer, not just Peter's. When we take authority in Jesus' name, not even the gates of hell can prevail against us.

When Pilate asked Jesus if He was the king of the Jews, Jesus said He was, then added in John 18:36, *"My **kingdom** is not of this world."* What does it mean? We have already read how the kingdom was at hand, how it was within us, and that Jesus would give His followers the keys to it. It means that King

Jesus has yet to physically set up His earthly kingdom. That will come after the Tribulation. In the meantime, those who follow Him can experience His kingdom within them through the Holy Spirit. Romans 14:17 says, *"For the **kingdom** of God is not meat and drink; but righteousness, and peace, and joy in the Holy Ghost."*

Hebrews 12:28 says, *"Wherefore we receiving a **kingdom** which cannot be moved, let us have grace, whereby we may serve God acceptably with reverence and godly fear."*

And James 2:5 says, *"Hath not God chosen the poor of this world rich in faith, and heirs of the **kingdom** which he hath promised to them that love him?"* We don't have to be anyone of note. We don't have to be rich or famous or one of the elites to have a place in God's kingdom. How wonderful is that?

Jesus also said in Luke 22:29, *"I appoint unto you* (His disciples) *a **kingdom**, as my Father hath appointed unto me."* Yes, believers in Jesus will rule and reign with Him and He will give us something exciting to do.

In Matthew 16:28, Jesus prophesied that at least one of His disciples would *"not taste of death, till they see the Son of man coming in his **kingdom**."* How is that possible when all the original disciples have died, and the millennial kingdom has yet to come? Certainly, this prophecy wasn't fulfilled. Yes, it was. After a door was opened and the apostle John was translated to heaven (raptured) in Revelation 4:1, he was shown a series of future events. One of them was the glorious return to earth of Jesus as King of kings and Lord of lords. John was the disciple that didn't die until he saw the vision of Jesus coming in His kingdom.

Here's what John saw and heard in Revelation 11:15, *"And the seventh angel sounded; and there were great voices in heaven, saying, The kingdoms of this world are become the **kingdoms** of our Lord, and of his Christ; and he shall reign for ever and ever."* And again this in Revelation 12:10, *"And I* (John*) heard a loud voice saying in heaven, Now is come salvation, and strength, and the **kingdom** of our God, and the power of his Christ: for the accuser of our brethren* (Satan) *is cast down, which accused them before our God day and night."* Someday, God will say "ENOUGH," and put an end to Satan's wicked kingdom, then set up His own wonderful kingdom on earth.

Others who acknowledged Jesus as King:

Going back to Mary's visitation by the angel Gabriel, he not only described Who Jesus was, but also described His kingdom in Luke 1:33b, *"of his **kingdom** there shall be **no end**."* This is an everlasting kingdom. It will supplant all other kingdoms. No other kingdom will ever emerge again. This is final. It is finished. It is settled.

Nathanael, the apostle, called Jesus, Son of God and King of Israel in John 1:49.

In 1 Timothy 1:17, Paul said this about Jesus, *"Now unto the **King** eternal, immortal, invisible, the only wise God, be honour and glory for ever and ever. Amen."*

Then in 1 Timothy 6:14-15, Paul counseled Timothy to keep the gospel pure *"until the appearing of our Lord Jesus Christ: Which in his times he shall shew, who is the blessed and only Potentate, the **King of kings**, and Lord of lords."*

John, when he was in heaven, saw those who had died for Jesus during the Tribulation and said in Revelation 15:3, *"And they* (the martyrs*) sing the song of Moses the servant of God, and the song of the Lamb, saying, Great and marvellous are thy works, Lord God Almighty; just and true are thy ways, thou* ***King*** *of saints."* These martyred saints were singing to Jesus, their King.

Revelation 17:14 talks about Jesus overcoming the antichrist and other evil world rulers. *"These shall make war with the Lamb, and the Lamb shall overcome them: for he is Lord of lords, and* ***King of kings****: and they that are with him are called, the chosen, and faithful."*

And we've already seen that when Jesus returns to rule and reign *"He hath on his vesture and on his thigh a name written, KING OF KINGS, AND LORD OF LORDS,"* (Revelation 19:16). And according to Revelation 19:11, He will be riding a white horse. Remember, kings ride horses when going into battle. The next time Jesus comes, He will come as a warring king, ready to destroy His enemies and take control of His kingdom.

So, what should our reaction be to our King?

These Scriptures tell us:

- Psalm 97:1, *"The LORD reigneth; let the earth* ***rejoice****; let the multitude of isles* ***be glad*** *thereof."*
- Psalm 98:6, *"With trumpets and sound of cornet* ***make a joyful noise*** *before the LORD, the King."*
- Psalm 99:1-3, *"The LORD reigneth;* ***let the people tremble****: he sitteth between the cherubims;* ***let the earth be moved****. The LORD is great in Zion; and he is high above all the people. Let them* ***praise*** *thy great and terrible name; for it is holy."*

- Jeremiah 10:7, *"Who would not **fear** thee, O King of nations? For to thee doth it appertain; forasmuch as among all the wise men of the nations, and in all their kingdoms, there is none like unto thee."*

The above clearly indicates our rightful response to the King of all creation. It should be joyful, worshipful, reverentially-fear-inspiring, awe-inspiring, and full of praise. May that be our response to the promise of His coming.

Returning to Hosea:

Throughout Hosea, the central theme of judgment is repeated again and again. God's love is fierce (Song of Solomon 8:6, Psalm 136:26, Isaiah 54:10) but so is His wrath (Romans 1:18, Romans 2:5, Jeremiah 30:24, Isaiah 30:27).

I believe Hosea 13:13 is a prophetic reference to the end time's event known as Jacob's Trouble or the seven-year Tribulation. *"The sorrows of a travailing woman shall come upon him: he is an unwise son; for he should not stay long in the place of the breaking forth of children."* Jesus described this in Matthew 24 when He spoke of deception, wars, and rumors of wars, famine, pestilence, and earthquakes. In verse 8 He said, *"These are the beginning of **sorrows**."* "Sorrows" (*odin)* means "pangs of childbirth, travail, sorrow."

This is the time when God will fully deal with His people Israel. Though they will suffer greatly, a remnant will survive and return to the Lord and acknowledge Jesus as their Messiah. As mentioned, two-thirds of those "unwise" sons who go through the Tribulation will die. The "wise" sons will accept Jesus now and be spared the horrors of those seven years.

Continuing with the text:

"I will ransom them from the power of the grave; I will redeem them from death: O death, I will be thy plagues: O grave, I will be thy destruction: repentance shall be hid from mine eyes. Though he be fruitful among his brethren, an east wind shall come, the wind of the LORD shall come up from the wilderness, and his spring shall become dry, and his fountain shall be dried up: he shall spoil the treasure of all pleasant vessels. Samaria shall become desolate, for she hath rebelled against her God: they shall fall by the sword: their infants shall be dashed in pieces, and their women with child shall be ripped up." Hosea 13:14-16

First, God promised a future deliverance, *"I will* ***ransom*** *them from the power of the grave; I will* ***redeem*** *them from death: O death, I will be thy plagues: O grave, I will be thy destruction."* Like so much of Scripture, this is prophetic and points not only to God's rescue of Israel but His rescue of the whole world through the complete and perfect ransom made by Jesus. "Ransom" (*padah*) means "deliver, ransom, rescue." The word "grave" (*sheowl*) is "hades, the world of the dead, grave, hell pit." And "redeem" (*gaal*) "to redeem according to the Oriental law of kinship, to redeem as part of a kinsman." Jesus is our Kinsman Redeemer Who became man, our relative, so He could pay the penalty of our sins. He was the *"ransom for many,"* (Mark 10:45).

The Septuagint, the Greek translation of the Hebrew Scriptures used in Jesus' day, says it a bit differently. *"I will deliver them out of the power of Hades, and will redeem them from death: where is thy penalty, O death? O Hades, where is thy sting?"* When speaking about what Jesus had accomplished for mankind through His death and resurrection, Paul, the apostle, surely had to be thinking about Hosea, *"O death, where is thy sting? O grave, where is thy victory? The sting of death is sin; and the strength of sin is the law. But thanks be to God, which giveth us the victory through our Lord Jesus Christ,"* (1 Corinthians 15:55-57).

Thus, in Hosea, God was saying that just as He would keep the nation of Israel from total destruction, so He would make a way for mankind to escape eternal destruction in hell through Jesus. And this is settled. God will not change His mind. He will not repent of His promise (*repentance shall be hid from mine eyes)*.

After God promised Israel's destruction would not be total and that, in the future, they would be restored as a nation, He then pronounced judgment. As mentioned, Ephraim was the most powerful and largest of the ten northern tribes. But their strength would not save them now, or the rest of the kingdom. God would send an east wind, a *qadiym*. *The Wordbook of the Old Testament* defines east wind as "east, east wind, one that denotes the desert wind which brings feared destruction and is absolutely controlled by God." So here comes Assyria from the east to do God's bidding. They are His hand of punishment. And that punishment is severe because Assyria is a fierce and brutal nation, one that slaughters men, women, infants as well as those in the womb.

Israel's spring (*maqowr*), their "fountain or source of living water," would dry up. It not only speaks of what will happen physically, but metaphorically. The very source of what they believed necessary for life will dry up. That word "dry" is *buwah* and means "to be ashamed, be disappointed, put to shame." What Israel counted on, their power, strength, resources, alliances with pagan nations, their false gods will not bring salvation, only shame, ruin, and death. Forgetting their true source of life, they drank from poisoned waters.

In the same way, Jesus is our living water. In John 4:14 Jesus said, *"Whosoever drinketh of the water that I shall give him shall never thirst; but the water that I shall give him shall be in him a well of water springing up into everlasting life."* Again, in John 7:37-38, Jesus said, *"If any man thirst, let him come unto me, and drink. He that believeth on me, as the scripture hath said, out of his belly shall flow rivers of living water."* Those who drink from any other source than Jesus, drink poisoned water, and like Ephraim, will face judgment one day, a judgment ending in death.

But that's not God's desire. He wishes all to be His and live with Him forever. Jesus, in Matthew 5:6, said, *"Blessed are they which do hunger and* ***thirst*** *after righteousness: for they shall be filled."* If one wants to know God and His righteousness, all he has to do is come to Jesus and he will be satisfied. This invitation is again given in Revelation, the last book of the Bible. It's as though God wanted to be sure no one was left out; that the message was clear; and would resonate as one closed the Book. *"And the Spirit and the bride say, Come. And let him that heareth say, Come. And let him that is* ***athirst*** *come. And whosoever will, let him take the water of life freely,"* (Revelation 22:17).

Can God be anymore loving or merciful or generous?

Chapter 14

"O Israel, return unto the LORD thy God; for thou hast fallen by thine iniquity. Take with you words, and turn to the LORD: say unto him, Take away all iniquity, and receive us graciously: so will we render the calves of our lips. Asshur shall not save us; we will not ride upon horses: neither will we say any more to the work of our hands, Ye are our gods: for in thee the fatherless findeth mercy. I will heal their backsliding, I will love them freely: for mine anger is turned away from him. I will be as the dew unto Israel: he shall grow as the lily, and cast forth his roots as Lebanon. His branches shall spread, and his beauty shall be as the olive tree, and his smell as Lebanon." Hosea 14:1-6

Even though their gross sin had caused their calamity, God continued to implore Israel to return to Him. He promised if they repented, He would accept them again. Then He laid out His requirements. Their repentance must be sincere. They must turn from their idols. And He was not interested in superficial animal sacrifices but the sincere praises of their lips (*render the calves of our lips).* Instead of worshipping (kissing) the golden calves in Dan and Bethel, their lips were to render praise to Yahweh.

"Render" (*shalam*) means "be complete, sound," and indicates this sacrifice of praise had to spring from a truly circumcised (sound) heart of repentance and love. Hebrews 13:15 says, *"By him therefore let us offer* ***the sacrifice of praise*** *to God continually, that is, the fruit of our lips giving thanks to his name."* This is what God wanted from the lips of His people, Israel.

In addition, they were to acknowledge that Asshur wouldn't save them. According to Zondervan's *Pictorial Encyclopedia of the Bible,* Asshur was the "patron deity . . . and capital city of Assyria." For decades, Israel pinned their hopes of protection and prosperity on Egypt and Assyria, both symbols of the world's systems. Instead, God wanted Israel to realize He, not the world, was their true protector and provider.

Neither were they to ride horses, thinking their protection was dependent upon them. Horses were owned by kings and elites, and used in battle. God, in Deuteronomy 17:16 forbade Israel's rulers to own them. *"But he* (the ruler) *shall not multiply horses to himself, nor cause the people to return to Egypt, to the end that he should multiply horses: forasmuch as the LORD hath said unto you, Ye shall henceforth return no more that way."*

Solomon disobeyed by purchasing thousands from Egypt, a land known for their horses. According to 2 Chronicles 9:25, he had *"four thousand stalls for horses and chariots."*

Because of Solomon's disobedience, Israel came to believe that horses and chariots were essential in winning the wars that occurred with their neighbors. They forgot Deuteronomy 20:1, *"When thou* (Israel) *goest out to battle against thine enemies, and seest* ***horses, and chariots****, and a people more than thou, be not afraid of them: for the LORD thy God is with thee, which brought thee up out of the land of Egypt."* God wanted His people to trust in Him, not in anything else. David understood this when he said in Psalm 20:7, *"**Some trust in chariots, and some in horses**: but we will remember the name of the LORD our God."* David was saying that when Israel faced their enemies, they needed to remember all that the Lord had done for them and by doing so, would realize He'd do it again. In other words, they could trust Him.

God knew that by *"multiplying horses,"* the people would be tempted to look at them as their source of victory. But God also foreknew that horses, because of their strength and power, would be equated with sacred things and even dedicated to the sun. That's why, Judah's godly king, Josiah, had to eliminate those horses devoted to worship when he came into power (2 Kings 23:11).

"Neither will we say any more to the work of our hands, Ye are our gods: for in thee the fatherless findeth mercy." After true repentance, Israel, collectively, will no longer look to their handmade idols as gods. They will also understand that because they had turned from Yahweh and become prodigal sons, they were now orphans. And only because of God's mercy would they be restored.

And that's what God was saying. Because He ***was*** merciful, Israel would not be fatherless forever. This is in stark contrast to Hosea 1:6 when God commanded Hosea to name his daughter, "Lo-ruhaman," meaning *"I will no more have mercy upon the house of Israel."* This was followed by the birth of Hosea's son which God named, "Lo-ammi," meaning *"You are not my people and I will not be your God."*

But as mentioned, God, at a future time, would bring Israel back into sonship, heal them, and treat them with loving kindness. He would be their covering of dew. Because Israel is arid, dew was an important supplement to rain and vital for agricultural success. Without it, crops could die or become stunted. In the same way, God would be their vital source of life, protection, and prosperity. He would ensure not only their survival but that they thrived.

We've already seen water as a metaphor for God's blessings. When blind Isaac, thinking it was Esau, gave Jacob the "first son's" blessings, he said in Genesis 27:28, *"Therefore God give thee of the* ***dew*** *of heaven, and the fatness of the earth, and plenty of corn and wine."* And when Moses blessed the twelve tribes and came around to Joseph, he said in Deuteronomy 33:13, *"Blessed of the LORD be his land, for the precious things of heaven, for the* ***dew****, and for the deep that coucheth beneath."* Job acknowledged also, that part of his success and wealth was attributed to the dew, (Job 29:19).

What a promise God laid out in Hosea! It's repeated in Micah 5. It's also repeated in Zechariah 8:7-8, 12, *"Thus saith the LORD of hosts; Behold, I will save my people from the east country, and from the west country; And I will bring them, and they shall dwell in the midst of Jerusalem: and they shall be my people, and I will be their God, in truth and in righteousness. . . . For the seed shall be prosperous; the vine shall give her fruit, and the ground shall give her increase, and the heavens shall give their* ***dew****; and I will cause the remnant of this people to possess all these things."*

What a loving and merciful God! Despite everything Israel had done to offend Him, He still loved them and promised them a wonderful future. Israel *"shall grow as the lily, and cast forth his roots as Lebanon."* White lilies were not only known for their beauty but symbolized purity. That word "grow" is *parach* and means to "break forth as a bud, bloom, sprout, break out, fly."

And Lebanon means "white mountain," and was known for its prolific vegetation, its strong towering trees, and fragrant scent. That's Israel's future. They will become a righteous nation, strong, sturdy, and deeply rooted not only in their own land but in their God. And as such, will become a pleasing fragrance to Him.

Continuing with the text:

"They that dwell under his shadow shall return; they shall revive as the corn, and grow as the vine: the scent thereof shall be as the wine of Lebanon. Ephraim shall say, What have I to do any more with idols? I have heard him, and observed him: I am like a green fir tree. From me is thy fruit found. Who is wise, and he shall understand these things? prudent, and he shall know them? for the ways of the LORD are right, and the just shall walk in them: but the transgressors shall fall therein." Hosea 14:7-9

The time of Israel's restoration will be marked by prosperity and total devotion to Yahweh. He and He alone will be their God. Idols will have no place in Israel because the remnant Jews will come to know that their God is the source of everything they could want or need. *(I* (God) *am like a green fir tree. From me is thy fruit found.)* Therefore, the only wise and prudent thing to do was to walk in God's ways. Those who don't, will fall.

That word "fall" is *kashal,* meaning "to stumble." It's a warning to those who don't follow the Lord.

But for those who choose to walk in God's ways, the Scriptures promise the following:

- Proverbs 3:23, *"Then shalt thou walk in thy way safely, and thy foot shall not stumble."*
- Proverbs 4:18, *"But the path of the just is as the shining light, that shineth more and more unto the perfect day."*
- Proverbs 6:23, *"For the commandment is a lamp, and the law is light; and reproofs of instruction are the way of life."*
- Psalm 119:105, *"Thy word is a lamp unto my feet, and a light unto my path."*

For those who choose the opposite, Scripture promises this:

- Proverbs 4:19, *"The way of the wicked is as darkness: they know not at what they stumble."*
- Isaiah 8:15, *"And many* (the wicked) *among them shall stumble, and fall, and be broken, and be snared, and be taken."*
- Isaiah 59:10, *"We* (sinners) *grope for the wall like the blind, and we grope as if we had no eyes: we stumble at noon day as in the night; we are in desolate places as dead men."*
- Jeremiah 13:16, *"Give glory to the LORD your God, before he cause darkness, and before your feet stumble upon the dark mountains, and while ye look for light, he turn it into the shadow of death, and make it gross darkness."*

What contrasting choices God has set before us! It's either life and light with Him, or death and darkness without Him. Jesus alluded to this when He said, *"I am the light of the world: he that followeth me shall not walk in darkness, but shall have the light of life,"* (John 8:12).

Conclusion:

Hosea is a story of unrequited love and God's heartbreak over His people's disrespect and rebellion. Its constant repetition lays out, in excruciating detail, Israel's many sins and resulting consequences. These consequences are gradual at first. It starts with their squandering of wealth and natural resources. Because they looked to other nations for protection, they ended up having to pay tribute, either as bribes or compulsory fees, resulting in the ultimate destruction of the northern kingdom.

Though God's love is more than evident throughout, the central theme is the necessity of judgment by a holy God. But the amazing thing is this: God's judgment is actually an offshoot of His love because it's always meant to bring the offending party back into right relationship with Him.

The lessons in Hosea go far beyond Israel. They apply to us today. God loves each of us and desires than none should perish. But because He is holy, He cannot let sin slide. That's why He made a remedy through Jesus' blood sacrifice. To understand why a blood sacrifice was necessary, see my book, *"Following the Blood Trail from Genesis to Revelation."*

The amazing truth is this: God is always willing to accept a repentant sinner into His family. All one need do is ask!

Lamentations

Chapter 1

Jeremiah is the author of Lamentations. In it, he details his grief over the destruction of Jerusalem, the Temple, and the kingdom of Judah. For years, he warned of this, calling His people to repentance. For his trouble, he was ignored, persecuted, and imprisoned because the people preferred to listen to their false prophets' declarations of "peace and safety." Finally, in 587 B.C., his warnings came true. Nebuchadnezzar sacked the southern kingdom of Judah.

Jeremiah lived during times of violence, chaos, and treachery. In 609 B.C., Judah's godly king Josiah was slain while battling Pharaoh Neco's army. He was succeeded by his son, Jehoahaz. Because Assyrian power was waning, Pharaoh Neco took control of the Syrian-Palestine area and replaced Jehoahaz with Jehoahaz's brother, Eliakim (which Neco renamed, Jehoiakim).

Not long after, Pharaoh Neco was himself defeated by Nebuchadnezzar, rendering Jehoiakim a Babylonian vassal around 605-604 B.C. During this time, sixteen-year-old Daniel, along with other nobles (the historian, Josephus, puts that number at three thousand), was taken to Babylon as tribute.

Three years later, Jehoiakim revolted, bringing the Babylonians back to Jerusalem. He died before Nebuchadnezzar reached the city gates leaving Jehoiakim's eighteen year old son, Jehoiachin, to rule in his place. His rule lasted only three months because his attempt to make an alliance with the Egyptians, as a means of thwarting Babylon, infuriated Nebuchadnezzar. So, after Jerusalem fell, he installed Mattaniah, Jehoiachin's twenty-one-year-old uncle, on the throne, then renamed him Zedekiah.

History soon repeated itself. Ignoring the prophet Jeremiah's warning, Zedekiah also revolted, causing Nebuchadnezzar to again raise an army against the Jews. After eighteen months of siege, and the betrayal by Egypt to send the promised reinforcements, Jerusalem fell.

Lamentations, meaning "mourning, groaning, sorrow," is appropriately named. Jeremiah, an eyewitness to Judah's destruction, describes the siege, famine and starvation, the cowardice of the rulers who ran away, the looting and burning of the Temple and palace, the eradication of the city walls, the extermination of the leaders, and the exile of the population.

But Lamentations is also poetry. According to Zondervan's *Pictorial Encyclopedia of the Bible*, not only is it written in poetic style, but the first four chapters in *The Septuagint* form an acrostic where every line begins with each successive letter of the Hebrew alphabet.

Before we get into the text, let's get to know more about Jeremiah. Who was he? What brought him to this point? How was he able to survive? And why was he not taken into Babylonian captivity with the others?

Jeremiah's father, Hilkiah, was a priest from the line of Abiathar (king David's high priest). But Jeremiah's path was to be different. In 627 B.C., at age twenty, he was called by God to be a prophet to both Judah and the nations. His was to be a hard life. Forbidden to marry and ordered to refrain from all normal enjoyments and amusements, his life of austerity and celibacy was to be a sign to Israel of their impending judgment.

He prophesied during the reign of several kings beginning with Josiah. Because king Josiah worked to spiritually restore Israel after the evil and idolatrous reign of Manasseh, Jeremiah experienced little persecution during Josiah's thirty-one-year rule. But after Josiah's death at Megiddo in 609 B.C., things changed. Under the next four kings (Jehoahaz, Jehoiakim, Jehoiachin, Zedekiah) he was constantly persecuted.

Jehoiakim, especially, was a reprobate. During his reign, he killed prophets and those who followed Josiah's reforms. He also persecuted Jeremiah. Many others also turned against Jeremiah, and instead listened to the false prophets. Due to this continuous rejection from the rulers and his own countrymen, Jeremiah often despaired, and even cursed his birth. But he never stopped prophesying because God's word was like a *"burning fire"* that couldn't be contained (Jeremiah 20:9).

During Zedekiah's rule, Jeremiah received death threats, was beaten, imprisoned, and even confined in a muddy cistern. Because the Babylonians learned that Jeremiah had predicted their conquest and had pleaded with his people to submit to Babylonian rule, he was well treated and allowed to choose whether to go to Babylon or remain in Jerusalem. He chose Jerusalem. But several months later, Jeremiah, under duress, was taken by the Jerusalem remnant to Egypt, where tradition says he lived out the remainder of his life. While there, he regularly corresponded with the Jews exiled in Babylon. Even so, most of his people continued to reject his message, claiming it was not their sin against Yahweh that cause their demise, but their failure to worship the queen of heaven.

Now let's go to the text:

*"How **doth** the city **sit** solitary, that was full of people! how is she become as a widow! she that was great among the nations, and princess among the provinces, how is she become tributary!"* Lamentations 1:1

As mentioned, Jeremiah witnessed Jerusalem's destruction firsthand. As an emotional and compassionate man, he could barely contain his grief. Both words "doth" and "sit" are the same word, *yashab,* meaning "to sit down, especially as judge." Jerusalem has been judged and was now solitary (*badad*) "alone, desolate, separate."

As a city (*iyr*) it should have been guarded by watchmen to alert the inhabitants of danger. More importantly, its spiritual watchmen (prophets and priests) should have warned the people of their moral deficiencies. Instead, they spoke of peace, safety, and prosperity. They stressed that God wasn't angry. Repentance was unnecessary. All was well. Now, they were forced to eat the fruit of their lies.

And Jerusalem, once a princess, a jewel among the nations, had become as desolate as a widow. This is a play on words. "Widow" (*almanah*) not only means a widow but "a desolate place," indicating that Jerusalem's disgrace was compounded. No longer God's wife, she was a widow who had been conquered and made a tributary (*mac*). Now, overseen by taskmasters and forced to pay tribute or labor, she had been stripped of both wealth and autonomy, making her desolate.

Contrast that to Jerusalem's former glory when king Solomon made gold and silver *"as plenteous as stones,"* (2 Chronicles 1:15); when his fleet of merchant ships brought Israel treasures from all the known world (1 Kings 9:26-28); and foreigners came to benefit from Solomon's wisdom, (1 Kings 10:1-13). Now, three hundred and forty-four years after Solomon's death, the southern kingdom of Judah was no more. A succession of evil kings saw to that. They scoffed at God's laws and brazenly led the nation into gross idolatry. Ironically, during his waning years as king, Solomon opened this door himself. By allowing his 700 wives and 300 concubines to set up altars and shrines to their false gods, he paved the way for an idolatrous invasion and set in motion the apparatus of Israel's destruction.

Continuing with the text:

"She weepeth sore in the night, and her tears are on her cheeks: among all her lovers she hath none to comfort her: all her friends have dealt treacherously with her, they are become her enemies." Lamentations 1:2

Jeremiah, called the weeping prophet, pictured Jerusalem as a weeping woman. That phrase *"all her lovers,"* is a Jewish idiom referring to those kings or nations with which Judah had made alliances. It must have come as a bitter shock when Egypt failed to fulfill its promise to support Judah against Babylon, making Judah ripe for takeover and turning her into a desolate weeping widow, alone in the world.

On another level, these "lovers" could also allude to Judah's idols. First introduced by Solomon and his women were *"Ashtoreth the goddess of the Zidonians"* and *"Milcom the abomination of the Ammonites"* (1 Kings 11:5).

Ashtoreth, also called queen of heaven and mother goddess, was associated with fertility. Her worship often involved sexual rituals. Ashtoreth morphed into other goddesses in various cultures and was known by different names including Diana. Nothing is known about Milcom or his worship. Some scholars equate him with Molech. Others claim they are separate entities.

Additional pagan deities worshipped by Israel were Tammuz, god of fertility and husbandry; Chemosh, the Moabite god of war and human sacrifices; Baal, also connected to agriculture as well as fertility; and Molech, specifically connected to child sacrifices; all detestable to God and all involving gross and depraved rituals.

In the face of Israel's vile idolatry and internal rot, it's hard to believe there were those like Daniel and his three friends (Shadrach, Meshack, and Abednego) still intensely and courageously faithful to Yahweh. While little is known about the three friends, Scripture tells us that Daniel remained faithful to God throughout all his years in Babylonian captivity.

Even though these false gods were usually depicted by lifeless, manmade statues, one must understand that demonic entities were behind them, just as they are behind all idols and occult symbols. Recall that Paul talked about this when he said in Ephesians 6:12 that we *"wrestle not against flesh and blood, but against principalities, against powers, against the rulers of the darkness of this world, against spiritual wickedness in high places."*

These entities still operate today. Most people have become too sophisticated to bow before statues, but they venerate and invite demons into their lives through tarot cards, Ouija boards, channeling familiar spirits, and mind-altering drugs, just to name a few. Even the spirit of Molech is alive and well, for it resides in the abortion industry. But idols can also be anything that one puts before or in place of God like money, power, fame, etcetera. And just as it led to Judah's demise, so it will lead to ours.

Continuing with the text:

"Judah is gone into captivity because of affliction, and because of ***great*** *servitude: she dwelleth among the heathen, she findeth no rest: all her persecutors overtook her between the straits. The ways of Zion do mourn, because none come to the solemn feasts: all her gates are desolate: her priests sigh, her virgins are afflicted, and she is in bitterness."* Lamentations 1:3-4

Note, Jeremiah specified that it was Judah that had gone into captivity. The northern kingdom of Israel had already been conquered 135 years earlier. Now, it was Judah's turn. God had finally had it with her idolatry and disrespect. Judah would experience Israel's fate. And their affliction would be great. That word "captivity" (*galab*) not only means "to exile," but "to denude, strip." Unlike Israel whose land was inhabited, albeit by foreigners, Judah would be stripped bare. Only a few poor and unskilled inhabitants would remain. Most of her population would be forced to dwell in Babylon among idol worshiping heathens (*gowy*). Heathens in Hebrew not only means "foreign nation, Gentile" but "a troop of animals or flight of locust." The inhabitants of Judah who abandoned God for their national and demonic "lovers," were now in the hands of people who would behave like animals or devouring locust.

And their captivity would be in ***great*** bondage. They would have no rest or peace. Their persecutors would be relentless. "Persecutors" (*radaph*) means to run after especially for the "purpose of making war or taking revenge." And "straits" (*metsar*) means "something tight, trouble, distress." Theirs would be a life of servitude and distress, a life controlled by vengeful and cruel captors.

Jeremiah also mourned that Jerusalem's "ways," meaning "a road, a course of life, mode of action," had been drastically altered. Zion (*Tsiyown*) the mountain of Jerusalem, can refer to Jerusalem, the city of David, the Temple, and the city of God "where Yahweh dwells." For Jews, it symbolized their nation's religious center. But they also believed it was the world's religious center as well. Surely, God would spare it.

How devastating to realize not even Zion would survive! No longer would priests prepare sacrifices or burn pleasing incense. The feasts, those seven holy appointed seasons of the Lord (Passover, Unleavened Bread, First Fruits, Pentecost, Trumpets, Day of Atonement and Feast of Tabernacles) would no longer be celebrated. And their Temple would become a pile of rubble.

Even Zion's virgins were afflicted. Another Hebrew idiom, it indicates these virgins had been raped. They had fallen prey to the common practice of armies raping their captive women.

Moses predicted Zion's destruction in Deuteronomy 32:15-17, 24. *"But Jeshurun* (a name for Israel meaning beloved one) *waxed fat, and kicked: thou are waxen fat, thou art grown thick, thou art covered with fatness; then he* (Israel) *forsook God which made him, and lightly esteemed the Rock of his salvation. They provoked him to jealousy with strange gods, with abominations provoked they him to anger. They sacrificed unto devils, not to God; to gods whom they knew not, to new gods that came newly up, whom your fathers feared not. . .. They shall be burnt with hunger, and devoured with burning heat, and with bitter destruction: I will also send the teeth of beasts upon them, with the poison of serpents of the dust."*

Judah's sins had finally forced God to respond. Jeremiah 25:4-9 says, *"And the LORD hath sent unto you all his servants the prophets, rising early and sending them; but ye have not hearkened, nor inclined your ear to hear. They said, Turn ye again now every one from his evil way, and from the evil of your doings, and dwell in the land that the LORD hath given unto you and to your fathers for ever and ever: And go not after other gods to serve them, and to worship them, and* ***provoke*** *me not to anger with the works of your hands; and I will do you no hurt. Yet ye have not hearkened unto me, saith the LORD; that ye might provoke me to anger with the works of your hands to your own hurt. Therefore thus saith the LORD of hosts; Because ye have not heard my words, Behold, I will send and take all the families of the north, saith the LORD, and Nebuchadnezzar the king of Babylon, my servant, and will bring them against this land, and against the inhabitants thereof, and against all these nations round about, and will utterly destroy them, and make them an astonishment, and an hissing, and perpetual desolations."*

It is God who makes us strong and victorious in life. And when we refuse to acknowledge Him, believing we are fine on our own, disaster can strike. Turning from God produces a downward spiral, proving the expression that sin will take you further than you wanted to go, keep you there longer than you wanted to stay, and cost you more than you wanted to pay.

I am reminded of an interview I saw years ago on a popular Christian program. The woman interviewed was an ex-witch.

Here's a brief synopsis of her story:

While engaged in prostitution, she became interested in white witchcraft. Thinking it was harmless, she immersed herself in it until she was seduced into black witchcraft. She ended up becoming the most powerful witch in England. Among other things, her powers enabled her to kill a bird in midflight. She also had personal encounters with Satan. But instead of bringing her joy, she felt continually tormented. Her lowest point was allowing a warlock to impregnate her so she could offer her baby to Satan as a human sacrifice. Shortly after, Jesus entered her life and rescued her. She is now a forgiven born-again Christian. Her desire is to warn others about the dangers of dabbling in the occult (both white and black witchcraft, tarot cards, etcetera). These things are not innocent or harmless, but very very dangerous.

Her story is not uncommon. Those who have been rescued from this lifestyle by Jesus say much the same thing. We need to understand how seductive and dangerous the occult is, and how seriously God takes it when we traffic in it. Scripture is full of admonitions to avoid any interaction with the occult. Failure to do so carries a heavy penalty.

Continuing with the text:

"Her adversaries are the chief, her enemies prosper; for the LORD hath afflicted her for the multitude of her transgressions: her children are gone into captivity before the enemy. And from the daughter of Zion all her beauty is departed: her princes are become like harts that

find no pasture, and they are gone without strength before the pursuer." Lamentations 1: 5-6

Jeremiah lamented how Judah's enemies prospered while controling and abusing her. He acknowledged it's Judah's fault due to her many offenses against God. Through His prophets, God had pleaded with her to repent. Because Judah refused, now she and her children would suffer captivity and bondage.

While *"daughter of Zion"* refers to Israel, "daughter" figuratively refers to "apple of the eye." This is in keeping with Moses's reference to how God cared for Israel in Deuteronomy 32:10 and that she is *"the apple of his eye."* Again, we see this reference in Zechariah 2:8. *"For thus saith the LORD of hosts; After the glory hath he sent me unto the nations which spoiled you: for he that toucheth you toucheth* ***the apple of his eye."***

This was God's way of saying that He watches over Israel. He never takes His eyes off her. In fact, she is the very center of His attention and care. That's why David, when surrounded and harassed by enemies, prayed in Psalm 17:8, *"Keep me as* ***the apple of the eye****, hide me under the shadow of thy wings."* He understood that God loved him and was his protector.

David's son, Solomon, also understood this, but knew it was a two-way street. If one wanted God to keep focused on him, meaning providing, protecting, and blessing him, then he had to keep focused on God. That's why in Proverbs 7:2, Solomon instructed his son to, *"Keep my commandments* (he was talking about God's commandments which he claimed were also his) *and live; and my law* (God's laws, which he also claimed were his) *as the* ***apple of thine eye."*** This was to be the main thing, the main focus in life.

In Lamentations 2:18, Jeremiah will again refer to Israel as the apple of God's eye by saying, *"let not the **apple of thine eye** cease* (perish)." He was asking God not to utterly destroy Judah. Even so, her beauty had departed. That word "beauty" (*hadar)* means "magnificent, ornament, glorious, goodly, majesty." Israel was meant to be God's ornament. She was to shine with Yahweh's glory and majesty in the midst of a pagan world in order to draw them to the one true God.

Solomon, in Proverbs 1:9, told his son that the fear of the Lord and godly wisdom were *"**ornaments** of grace unto thy head, and chains about thy neck."* In Proverbs 4:9, he said, *"She* (godly wisdom) *shall give to thine head an **ornament** of grace: a crown of glory shall she deliver to thee."*

Ezekiel described God's love for Israel and how He delivered her from the slave pits of Egypt and lifted her up above the nations. *"I have caused thee to multiply as the bud of the field, and thou hast increased and waxen great, and thou are come to excellent **ornaments**: thy breasts are fashioned, and thine hair is grown, whereas thou was naked and bare,"* (Ezekiel 16:7). And in Ezekiel 16:11, God said, *"I decked thee also with **ornaments**, and I put bracelets upon thy hands, and a chain on thy neck."* Both words for ornaments are *adiy* and mean "trappings, finery, excellent." God not only prospered Israel physically but made her spiritually excellent.

Now, Israel had lost her beauty. She had forsaken godly wisdom in favor of worldly wisdom, making herself ugly in God's eyes. Ezekiel 7:20 mentioned what happened. *"As for the beauty of his* (God's) ***ornament*** (Israel), *he set it in majesty: but they made the images of their abominations and of the detestable things* (their idol's) *therein: therefore have I set it far from them."*

Israel was warned about this in Jeremiah 4:30. *"And when thou are spoiled, what will thou do? Though thou clothest thyself with crimson, though thou deckest thee with* ***ornaments*** *of gold, though thou rentest thy face with painting,* ***in vain shall thou make thyself fair****, thy lovers will despise thee, they will seek thy life."* Since everything that made Israel beautiful and great came from God, it couldn't be accomplished by lesser things now. Worldly solutions would never be able to restore her beauty.

It's interesting to note that while Israel was to be God's ornament, the Church was to be Jesus.' Isaiah 49:18 alluded to this when speaking of Gentiles. *"Lift up thine eyes round about, and behold: all these* (the Gentiles) *gather themselves together, and come to thee. As I live, saith the LORD, thou shalt surely clothe thee with them all, as with an* ***ornament*** (adiy), *and bind them on thee, as a bride doeth."* And again in Isaiah 61:10, *"I will greatly rejoice in the LORD, my soul shall be joyful in my God; for he had clothed me with the* ***garments of salvation****, he hath covered me with the* ***robe of righteousness****, as a bridegroom decketh himself with* ***ornaments*** (peer), *and as a bride adorneth herself with her jewels."* We see that the ornaments of Jesus' bride are the garments of salvation and robe of righteousness. But "ornaments" in Isaiah 61:10 is different from the one in Isaiah 49:11. It is *peer* in Hebrew and means "an embellishment, a fancy headdress, beauty, bonnet." Jesus, as head of the Church, is that "fancy headdress." He is our bonnet, our covering, our head.

But we are also His ornament. 1 Peter 3:4 explains. *"But let it be the hidden man of the heart, in that which is not corruptible, even the* ***ornament*** *of a meek and quiet spirit, which is in the sight of God of great price."* We become His ornament when we develop a *"meek and quiet spirit."* How wonderful to know that while God is our everything, He also takes delight in us.

Then Jeremiah said Judah's *"princes are become like harts that find no pasture, and they are gone without strength before the pursuer."* After Assyria conquered the ten northern tribes in 722 B.C., Judah began spiraling downward. In 605 B.C., she became Nebuchadnezzar's vassal and the Babylonian king took many of her nobles into captivity as a symbol of her forced subservience. Then the remainder of the nobles were either killed or captured in 587 B.C. after Jerusalem fell.

And Judah's princes were truly like harts and without strength. During the fall of Jerusalem, Judah's final king, Zedekiah, fled the city, leaving the populace behind to face the calamity which he himself brought upon them. It was a cowardly act and unsuccessful. He and his entourage got as far as Jericho before the Babylonians caught them and brought them to the Syrian town of Riblah. There, at Nebuchadnezzar's command, Zedekiah's sons were killed in front of him and Zedekiah himself was blinded. Disgraced and humiliated, Zedekiah was dragged in chains to Babylon along with most of Judah's population.

Jeremiah said these captives would *"find no pasture."* For seventy years that would be the case. Because they had spurned the very One Who desired to shepherd and pasture them, they would be unprotected and made to cope in an alien land.

God had always desired to be their Shepherd. Ezekiel 34:31 makes that clear. *"And ye are my flock, the flock of my* ***pasture****, are men, and I am your God, saith the Lord GOD."* And Psalms 74:1, 79:13, 95:7, 100:3 all claim that Israel was the sheep of God's pasture.

How far from David's 23rd Psalm they had come! David, the man after God's own heart, understood God's love and power when he penned it. *"The LORD is my shepherd; I shall not want. He maketh me to lie down in green* ***pastures****: he leadeth me beside the still waters. He restoreth my soul: he leadeth me in the paths of righteousness for his name's sake. Yea, though I walk through the valley of the shadow of death, I will fear no evil: for thou art with me; thy rod and thy staff they comfort me. Thou preparest a table before me in the presence of mine enemies: thou anointest my head with oil; my cup runneth over. Surely goodness and mercy shall follow me all the days of my life: and I will dwell in the house of the LORD for ever."*

David knew God would shepherd His people as long as they remained faithful and obedient. When they weren't and their gross sins became very great, God finally engraved those sins on the horns of the altars of their false gods. These engravings were made by *"a pen of iron"* and *"the point of a diamond"* as an indelible testimony against them until God's wrath and judgment were satisfied, (Jeremiah 17:1).

Even so, God's mercy will triumph. In Ezekiel 34:12-14, He promised that sometime in the future He will once again be Israel's Shepherd. *"As a shepherd seeketh out his flock in the day that he is among his sheep that are scattered; so will I seek out my sheep, and will deliver them out of all places where they have been scattered in the cloudy and dark day. And I will bring them out from the people, and gather them from the countries, and will bring them to their own land, and feed them upon the mountains of Israel by the rivers, and in all the inhabited places of the country. I will feed them in a good* ***pasture****, and upon the high mountains of Israel shall their fold be: there shall they lie in a good fold, and in a fat pasture shall they feed upon the mountains of Israel."* That promise was partially fulfilled on May 14, 1948.

But God's mercy doesn't end there. There is a Shepherd who cares for and protects all who come to Him. His name is Jesus. In John 10:9, 11 Jesus said, *"I am the door: by me if any man enter in, he shall be saved, and shall go in and out, and find* ***pasture****. . . ..I am the good shepherd: the good shepherd giveth his life for the sheep."*

Continuing with the text:

"Jerusalem remembered in the days of her affliction and of her miseries all her pleasant things that she had in the days of old, when her people fell into the hand of the enemy, and none did help her: the adversaries saw her, and did mock at her sabbaths. Jerusalem hath grievously sinned; therefore she is removed: all that honoured her despise her, because they have seen her nakedness: yea, she sigheth, and turneth backward. Her filthiness is in her skirts; she remembereth not her last end; therefore she came down wonderfully: she had no comforter. O LORD, behold my affliction: for the enemy hath magnified himself. The adversary hath spread out his hand upon all her pleasant things: for she hath seen that the heathen entered into her sanctuary, whom thou didst command that they should not enter into thy congregation. All her people sigh, they seek bread; they have given their pleasant things for meat to relieve the soul: see, O LORD, and consider, for I am become vile. Is it nothing to you, all ye that pass by? behold, and see if there be any sorrow like unto my sorrow, which is done unto me, wherewith the LORD hath afflicted me in the day of his fierce anger." Lamentations 1:7-12

I don't know who said we don't really appreciate something until we lose it, but it's true. And that's where the inhabitants of Jerusalem found themselves. They had lost everything. Their beautiful city was in ruins. The glorious Temple that Solomon built was now a heap of rubble. Jerusalem, once greatly admired, was now a byword, a curse, and a laughing-stock. *"Her enemies mocked at her sabbaths."* That word "sabbaths" is *mishbath* and means "annihilation, cessation." These enemies taunted the Jewish captives over the utter destruction of their city.

After Israel's liberation from Egyptian bondage and before they even entered the Promised Land, God warned them in Deuteronomy 11:26-28 of this very thing. *"Behold, I set before you this day a blessing and a* ***curse****; A blessing, if ye obey the commandments of the LORD your God, which I command you this day: And a* ***curse****, if ye will not obey the commandments of the LORD your God, but turn aside out of the way which I command you this day, to go after other gods, which ye have not known."*

Proverbs 3:33 is another reminder: *"The* ***curse*** *of the LORD is in the house of the wicked: but he blesseth the habitation of the just."*

Unfortunately, these admonitions went unheeded. As mentioned, by the time Jeremiah came on the scene, the northern kingdom of Israel had already experienced the penalty of their disobedience, and Judah was on the precipice. At God's command, Jeremiah spoke these words over Judah: *"And I* (God) *will deliver them* (the kingdom of Judah) *to be removed into all the kingdoms of the earth for their hurt, to be a reproach and a proverb, a taunt and a* ***curse****, in all places whither I shall drive them,"* (Jeremiah 24:9).

Jeremiah went on to say that Jerusalem and Judah would become a *"desolation, an astonishment, an hissing, and a* ***curse****,"* (Jeremiah 25:18).

But, as usual, God is merciful. He promised there would be a future restoration of both the northern and southern kingdoms. *"And it shall come to pass, that as ye were a* ***curse*** *among the heathen, O house of* ***Judah****, and house of* ***Israel****; so will I save you,* *and ye shall be a blessing: fear not, but let your hands be strong,"* (Zechariah 8:13).

We must understand that Proverbs 3:33 applies even today. The wicked will be cursed and feel the full force of God's wrath. Yet, God's mercy also applies. Always preferring blessing to cursing, God has made a way for everyone to experience His benevolence. Galatians 3:13 tells us that *"Christ hath redeemed us from the* ***curse*** *of the law, being made a* ***curse*** *for us: for it is written,* ***Cursed*** *is every one that hangeth on a tree."* Though we are all sinners and deserved to be cursed by God, He provided the solution. By being made a "curse" for us, Jesus restored us back to Father God. The saddest part is that not everyone will accept His sacrifice and so, remain cursed.

It's interesting to note that Revelation 22:3, when describing New Jerusalem, tells us *"There shall be no more* ***curse****: but the throne of God and of the Lamb shall be in it; and his servants shall serve him."* What a wonderful future awaits God's *"servants."*

Returning to the text: We see Jeremiah is quick to state the reason for this utter destruction. *"Jerusalem hath grievously sinned; therefore she is removed."* The word "grievously" (*chet*) indicates a crime and its penalty. Sinned (*chata*) means "miss the way, sin." Though all sin is serious, this is not talking about some misdeed. Rather, it indicates something treasonous against God. And we see what that is in the following sentence: *"because they have seen her nakedness: yea, she sigheth, and turneth backward. Her filthiness is in her skirts; she remembereth not her last end; therefore she come down wonderfully; she had no comforter."*

The reference to Jerusalem's nakedness and the filthiness in her skirts is an explicit reference to sexual immorality and symbolized Judah's spiritual immorality. Her years of playing the harlot with other gods had finally reaped its just end. Not only did God enact judgment, but for a season He would turn His back on her. During this time, no one will come to her aid. She will be mocked and despised. This fact tears Jeremiah's heart. You can almost hear the agony in his voice when he cried, *"O LORD, behold my affliction: for the enemy hath magnified himself. The adversary hath spread out his hand upon all her pleasant things: for she hath seen that the heathen entered into her sanctuary, whom thou didst command that they should not enter into thy congregation."*

Seeing the desecration of Judah and her people wrecked Jeremiah. But seeing the destruction of the Temple had to be a blow not even Jeremiah anticipated. This was *God's* sanctuary, *God's* meeting place with His people. Its destruction was almost too much to bear.

In addition, those who were not taken captive but were left in Jerusalem were destitute. Food (bread *lechem,* meat *okel*) was scarce and purchased by what little treasures the people had left. Those who had nothing to barter, starved. The land and its people had *"become vile."* That word "vile" is *zalal* and means "to shake, quake, to be loose morally, worthless, prodigal." Because they had become prodigal sons, they were shaken to the core and left as orphans to fend for themselves.

On a deeper level, we must understand that Adam and Eve became prodigals when they disobeyed God by eating the forbidden fruit. Their sin nature was then passed down to their offspring. Psalm 14:3 says, *"They* (mankind) *are all gone aside, they are all together become filthy: there is none that doeth good, no, not one."* And Romans 3:10, 23 says, *"There is none righteous, no, not one . . .. For all have sinned, and come short of the glory of God."*

Thus, as prodigals, we need to be restored back to God through the redemption that Jesus purchased with His blood. Those who do will come under the umbrella of God's love, protection, provision and even receive promotions as kings and priests. But those who don't will be destroyed, first by the pigsty of the world, like the prodigal in Luke 15:11-32, then by a horrifying eternity in hell. Just as Judah was destroyed due to her sins, so those who refuse God's mercy and grace will also be destroyed.

Continuing with the text:

*"From **above** hath he sent fire into my bones, and it prevaileth against them: he hath spread a net for my feet, he hath turned me back: he hath made me desolate and faint all the day. The yoke of my transgressions is bound by his hand: they are wreathed, and come up upon my neck: he hath made my strength to fall, the Lord hath delivered me into their hands, from whom I am not able to rise up. The Lord hath trodden under foot all my mighty men in the midst of me: he had called an assembly against me to crush my young men: the Lord hath trodden the virgin, the daughter of Judah, as in a winepress. For these things I weep; mine eye, mine eye runneth down with water, because the comforter that should relieve my soul is far from me: my children are desolate, because the enemy prevailed. Zion spreadeth forth her hands, and there is none to comfort her: the LORD hath commanded concerning Jacob, that his adversaries should be round about him: Jerusalem is as a menstruous woman among them."* Lamentations 1:13-17

Jerusalem's demise did not come by chance. Jeremiah clearly noted that this calamity was brought about by God and no one else. Notice, he said that it came from "*above*." That word is *marowm*, meaning "altitude, an elevated place." This fire, this burning fury, came down from heaven. But unlike God's fire that fell on Sodom, utterly consuming it and never to rise again, this fire will not completely destroy. Both Judah and Israel will rise again. But for now, Judah was desolate and "faint," meaning sick. It especially referred to a woman during her menstrual period. So, Judah, and by extension Jerusalem, was not only deserted and isolated, but as sick and weak as a menstruating woman. It's a graphic and unpleasant contrast to its former status as princess and jewel among the nations. A menstruating woman was also considered unclean, pointing to Judah being designated "unclean" by God.

Jeremiah also mentioned that "*The yoke of my* (Judah's) *transgressions is bound by his* (God's) *hand,*" again acknowledging that it was God's doing. That word "transgressions" (*pesha*) means "revolt, rebellion." It conveys the seriousness of their sins. They were traitors, rebels against God. And now they must wear their transgressions like a yoke.

According to *Webster's New World Dictionary*, yoke means "to bind together, a wooden frame or bar with loops or bows at either end, used for harnessing together a pair of oxen, etc." Judah's transgressions were now bound around her neck, and she must pay the consequences. God warned of this in Jeremiah 2:19-20: "*Thine own wickedness shall correct thee, and thy backsliding shall reprove thee: know therefore and see that it is an evil thing and bitter, that thou hast forsaken the LORD thy God, and that* ***my fear is not in thee, saith the Lord GOD of hosts****. For of old time I have broken thy yoke, and burst thy bands* (He delivered them from Egyptian bondage)*; and thou saidst, I will not transgress; when upon every high hill and under every green tree thou wanderest, playing the harlot.*" They had lost the fear and reverence of the Lord. A tragic mistake when one realizes that the "*fear of the Lord is the beginning of wisdom,*" (Proverbs 9:10).

Instead, they had become fools, following after other gods. And their foolishness has shackled them to the Babylonians.

It's interesting to note that in Matthew 11:29-30 Jesus said, *"Take my **yoke** upon you, and learn of me; for I am meek and lowly in heart: and ye shall find rest unto your souls. For my **yoke** is easy, and my burden is light."* Either we are bound or yoked to Jesus, or we are bound or yoked to our transgressions.

But what about the Gentile nations? Like Judah, can they be yoked to transgressions? Yes. More than a hundred years before Jeremiah's warning to Judah, Isaiah issued his own warning. He cited the following reasons for God's coming judgment: self-indulgence, lasciviousness, narcissism, pride, injustice, calling evil good and good evil, rewarding the wicked, forgetting God, despising God's Word (Isaiah 5:1-30).

Without any effort, this can describe America. Once a Christian nation that prospered under God's blessings, it has become a nation of self-indulgent narcissists. Our justice system is often two-tiered. Our leaders and officials are corrupt. Good is called evil. The rich are unjustly rewarded. We have forgotten God. Even many churches despise the pure Word of God, preferring instead to pump out shallow feel-good messages that never mention sin. And many of those sitting in churches prefer this to hard, transforming messages. They want their ears tickled (2 Timothy 4:3). Some churches have even bought into the belief that we are in the midst of a "Golden Age," and that by taking over the seven mountains of society (education, family, media, government, business, religion, arts and entertainment) we will usher in the millennial reign of Jesus.

Though these leaders may have good intentions, they will never usher in the Golden Age no matter how hard they try or how many inroads they make into these mountains. Only Jesus can do that. But before it happens, God's judgment will fall on all the nations of the world. Because God punished Judah for her sins, we know He will punish every other nation for theirs. Eventually, nations will be yoked to their transgressions and forced to pay the price.

Returning to Lamentations: Jeremiah continued to bemoan the sad state of Judah's fate: they are not able to rise, they were trodden underfoot, their mighty and strong men were crushed. The very strength and vigor of Judah, as well as its future as symbolized by its promising young men, had been devastated. They had all been trodden in the winepress of God's wrath. This Scripture will see its completion during the Tribulation when evil doers are thrust into God's winepress (Revelation 14:19).

Jeremiah concluded by again comparing Jerusalem to *"a menstruous woman."* I've already cited the obvious implications. But menstruating women were also considered unclean for seven days. We know that seventy years of captivity were designated by God because Judah failed to allow her land its sabbath rests. By comparing Judah to a *"menstruous woman,"* does this indicate that the seventy-year captivity was the time necessary for her uncleanness to be over? Perhaps.

Continuing with the text:

"The LORD is ***righteous****; for I have rebelled against his commandment: hear, I pray you, all people, and behold my sorrow: my virgins and my young men are gone into captivity. I called for my lovers, but they deceived me: my priests and mine elders gave up the ghost in the city, while they sought their meat to relieve their souls. Behold, O LORD; for I am in distress: my bowels are troubled;*

mine heart is turned within me; for I have grievously rebelled: abroad the sword bereaveth, at home there is as death. They have heard that I sigh: there is none to comfort me: all mine enemies have heard of my trouble; they are glad that thou hast done it: thou wilt bring the day that thou hast called, and they shall be like unto me. Let all their wickedness come before thee; and do unto them, as thou hast done unto me for all my transgressions: for my sighs are many, and my heart is faint." Lamentations 1:18-22

In previous verses, Jeremiah admitted that Judah had sinned and that it was God who executed judgement. But here, for the first time, he admitted that God was justified in doing it; that His actions were not only deserved but *"righteous."* Judah deserved what she got. That word "rebelled" in the above verse is *marah*, meaning "bitter, to provoke, to rebel, especially against God." And Judah had done all those things. She had debased her exalted relationship with God, making it bitter. She had provoked God for decades through her idolatry, murders, child sacrifices, thievery, licentiousness, and other sins. And God had had it. His long suffering had finally come to an end.

I've already noted that the reference to Judah calling for her lovers is a Hebrew idiom indicating she called on her allies for help. Especially culpable was king Zedekiah. After he was placed on the throne by Nebuchadnezzar, he took a loyalty oath then reneged when the Egyptian Pharaoh Hophra encouraged him to rebel. Because Zedekiah felt secure in Hophra's assurances that he would support Judah should Nebuchadnezzar retaliate, Zedekiah refused to heed God's command to submit to Babylon. Since Egypt symbolizes the world, it is clear where Zedekiah had placed his trust. But that trust would be violated. When Babylon reacted by sending its army, the Egyptian reinforcements never came, ensuring Judah's defeat.

Jeremiah then mentioned the fate of the priests and elders. They were dead. During the Babylonian siege of Jerusalem, famine or want of "meat" caused many to die. Others died at the hands of the conquering Babylonians. In addition, Zondervan's *Pictorial Encyclopedia of the Bible* says, "The chief priest Seraiah and other leaders were taken to Riblah and executed upon the orders of Nebuchadnezzar."

Continuing to grieve over his beloved nation, Jeremiah pointed out that his enemies were rejoicing over Judah's demise. *"They are glad."* That word "glad" (*suws*) means these enemies were taking great delight in Judah's fate. And because they were wallowing, triumphing, and gloating over her misery, Jeremiah asked God to punish them for their wickedness in the same way He punished Judah for hers. God answered that prayer forty-eight years later when, in 539 B.C., Babylon fell to the Persians under the leadership of Cyrus the Great.

In spite of all this, we need to understand that God's heart is not in judgment. He desires to move in love because He is love itself (1 John 4:16). He is long-suffering and patient. But as Creator, He makes the rules and is justified in enforcing them. That means bringing down the hammer of judgment when necessary. He is a just Judge, One Who cannot deny His holiness. Thus, in the end, judgment must come to all nations and individuals. John 5:22 tells us that God has delegated this judgment to Jesus. *"For the Father judgeth no man, but hath committed all judgment unto the Son."*

I have covered Jesus as Judge in several of my other books and will not repeat it now. But rest assured, God is not an easy-going Santa Clause, one who watches over us from afar, gives us things, and has a harmless little "naughty list" for those who mess up. Nothing could be further from the truth. God is holy. In Revelation 4:8, the four angels around the throne cry day and night, *"Holy, holy, holy"* not "Love, love, love." God cannot nor will He wink at sin. There is no "naughty list" from which one can get expunged. There is only heaven or hell, saved or unsaved.

While God indeed loves us, He is also capable of anger and wrath. This is the aspect of God no one wants to talk about; the aspect of God that even the Church rarely covers.

Yet, it is very real.

Chapter 2

"How hath the Lord covered the daughter of Zion with a cloud in his anger, and cast down from heaven unto the earth the beauty of Israel, and remembered not his ***footstool*** *in the day of his anger! The Lord hath swallowed up all the habitations of Jacob, and hath not pitied: he hath thrown down in his wrath the strong holds of the daughter of Judah; he hath brought them down to the ground: he hath* ***polluted*** *the kingdom and the princes thereof. He hath cut off in his fierce anger all the* ***horn*** *of Israel: he hath drawn back his right hand from before the enemy, and he burned against Jacob like a flaming fire, which devoureth round about."* Lamentations 2:1-3

Jeremiah continues expressing his grief and enumerating the ways God has broken His people. They are now under a cloud of fury and wrath. The *Theological Wordbook of the Old Testament* describes "cloud" as "becloud, being placed under a cloud because of the Lord's anger."

Jeremiah again mentions Israel's former "beauty" (*tipharah*), meaning ornament. This was already covered in chapter one. But suffice it to say, that Israel, destined to be God's ornament, destined to reflect His glory and perfection, was now a ruin and the brunt of jokes. Their glorious God-given destiny was replaced by one of captivity, hardship, and disgrace.

But what seems to shock and distress Jeremiah most is that God *"remembered not his footstool,"* the Temple in Jerusalem. At God's command, David, in 1 Chronicles 28:2, 10, commissioned his son, Solomon, to build the Temple and called it God's footstool. Psalm 132:7 confirms this by saying, *"We will go into his tabernacles: we will worship at his* ***footstool***.*"* To Jeremiah, God destroying His own Temple was unthinkable.

Yet, He did. And in so doing showed His contempt for what the Levitical priesthood had become and their desecration of the Temple. In Jeremiah 32:30-36, God laid out His grievances. *"For the children of Israel and the children of Judah have only done evil before me from their youth: for the children of Israel have only provoked me to anger with the work of their hands, saith the LORD. For this city hath been to me as a provocation of mine anger and of my fury from the day that they built it even unto this day; that I should remove it from before my face, Because of all the evil of the children of Israel and of the children of Judah, which they have done to provoke me to anger, they, their kings, their princes,* ***their priests****, and their prophets, and the men of Judah, and the inhabitants of Jerusalem. And they have turned unto me the back, and not the face: though I taught them, rising up early and teaching them, yet they have not hearkened to receive instruction.* ***But they set their abominations in the house****,* (the Temple) *which is called by my name, to defile it. And they built the high places of Baal, which are in the valley of the son of Hinnom, to cause their sons and their daughters to pass through the fire unto Molech; which I commanded them not, neither came it into my mind, that they should do this abomination, to cause Judah to sin. And now therefore thus saith the LORD, the God of Israel, concerning this city, whereof ye say, It shall be delivered into the hand of the king of Babylon by the sword, and by the famine, and by the pestilence."*

The son of a Zadok priest, Ezekiel, a prophet and contemporary of Jeremiah, as well as a captive taken to Babylon with king Jehoiachin in 597 B.C., confirmed Jeremiah's pronouncement. *"And the word of the LORD came unto me* (Ezekiel), *saying, Son of man, say unto her Thou art the land that is not cleansed, nor rained upon in the day of indignation. There is a conspiracy of her prophets in the midst thereof, like a roaring lion ravening the prey: they have devoured souls; they have taken the treasure and precious things; they have made her many widows in the midst thereof.* ***Her priests have violated my law, and have profaned mine holy things: they have put no difference between the holy and profane, neither have they shewed difference between the unclean and the clean, and have hid their eyes from my sabbaths, and I am profaned among them."*** (Ezekiel 22:23-26)

Nothing or no one is too powerful or important to be taken down if God deems it necessary. Even Moses, who spoke face to face with God, was chastised by being denied entrance into the Promised Land. When trying to get water from the rock in the desert of Zin, Moses struck it, thus disobeying God. He was only to speak to it because he had already smitten a rock at Horeb. His disobedience spoiled the prophetic picture of Jesus, the Rock, being struck (His crucifixion and death) only once for our sins as well as providing living water for all.

When David, the apple of God's eye, sinned by having an adulterous affair with Bathsheba, God punished him by taking the first-born child of that relationship as well as by allowing discord and treachery to permeate his family.

Those who know the Lord and continually and willfully sin without any repentance, will experience God's correction. Usually, this comes through the conviction of the Holy Spirit. But if unheeded, the Potter will take out His wheel and begin carefully crushing and remolding His clay, always with restoration in mind.

Jeremiah then said, *"The Lord hath swallowed up **all** the habitations of Jacob."* That word "swallowed" means "to swallow, destroy, eat up." This is a Hebrew idiom referring to complete destruction. God had destroyed *all* the *"habitations of Jacob,"* referring to the twelve tribes, both the kingdom of Israel and the kingdom of Judah. Though this occurred at different times, God essentially wiped out both kingdoms, thus *all* of Jacob.

It's interesting that the word "Jacob" is used here rather than "Israel." As mentioned, Jacob means "heel-catcher, supplanter," which referred to Jacob's nature as a conniver and schemer. After God got hold of him, He changed his name to Israel, meaning prince with God. This symbolized a change in character as well as position. No longer the supplanter, Jacob and his offspring now held a prominent place with God. They would be the carriers of an incredible destiny. But here, in Lamentation, we see they are no longer worthy to be called Israel. Once again, God sees them as "supplanters, connivers."

And they were "polluted" (*chalal*), "wounded, bore through, pierced, profaned, defiled, desecrated." Not only had they rebelled against God, but they offered their children as sacrifices to Molech in the Hinnom Valley. 2 Chronicles 36:14, when referring to the evil deeds of Zedekiah, says, *"Moreover all the chief of the priests, and the people transgressed very much after all the abominations of the heathen; and **polluted** the house of the LORD which he had hallowed in Jerusalem."* Because the Jews polluted God's holy house, He was now polluting theirs. By lifting His hand of protection, God left Judah defenseless, thus cutting off her horn (a symbol of power or government).

Unlike David, who said in 2 Samuel 22:2-3, *"The LORD is my rock, and my fortress, and my deliverer; The God of my rock; in him will I trust: he is my shield, and the **horn** of my salvation, my high tower, and my refuge, my saviour,"* Judah had forgotten Who her true horn was. She had forgotten that God, her King, was her strength and source of power. Psalm 75:10 says, *"All the **horns** of the wicked also will I* (God) *cut off; but the **horns** of the righteous shall be exalted."*

Jeremiah noted that God *"hath drawn back his right hand from before the enemy."* God's right hand is the hand of power. By withdrawing it, He allowed both Israel and Judah to fend for themselves. He was showing them that all their "horns" were useless.

"And he (God) *burned against Jacob."* Notice, the name Jacob is again used rather than Israel, indicating a fall from grace.

For those who don't know the Lord, judgment often comes by way of God lifting His hand of protection and allowing the consequences of their sins and poor choices to manifest in their lives. But just as with believers, God's desire is always to bring them to Himself.

Because of God's covenant with Israel, He was determined to reinstate both Israel and Judah in the future. He made this promise in Micah 4:13: *"Arise and thresh, O daughter of Zion: for I will make thine **horn** iron, and I will make thy hoofs brass: and thou shalt beat in pieces many people: and I will consecrate their gain unto the LORD, and their substance unto the Lord of the whole earth."*

Luke 1:68-69 carries this theme into the New Testament. *"Blessed be the Lord God of Israel; for he hath visited and redeemed his people, And hath raised up an **horn** of salvation for us in the house* *of his servant David."* That horn of salvation is Jesus, the Lion of the tribe of Judah, the Root of David (Revelation 5:5). And His horn is for *"whosoever believeth in him,"* (John 3:16).

Continuing with the text:

"He hath bent his bow like an enemy: he stood with his right hand as an adversary, and slew all that were pleasant to the eye in the tabernacle of the daughter of Zion: he poured out his fury like a fire. The Lord was as an enemy: he hath swallowed up Israel, he hath swallowed up all her palaces: he hath destroyed his strong holds, and hath increased in the daughter of Judah mourning and lamentation. And he hath violently taken away his tabernacle, as if it were of a garden: he hath destroyed his places of the assembly: the LORD hath caused the solemn feasts and sabbaths to be forgotten in Zion, and hath despised in the indignation of his anger the king and the priest. The Lord hath cast off his altar, he hath abhorred his sanctuary, he hath given up into the hand of the enemy the walls of her palaces; they have made a noise in the house of the LORD, as in the day of a solemn feast. The LORD hath purposed to destroy the wall of the daughter of Zion: he hath stretched out a line, he hath not withdrawn his hand from destroying: therefore he made the rampart and the wall to lament; they languished together. Her gates are sunk into the ground: he hath destroyed and broken her bars: her king and her princes are among the Gentiles: the law is no more; her prophets also find no vision from the LORD. The elders of the daughter of Zion sit upon the ground, and keep silence: they have cast up dust upon their heads; they have girded themselves with sackcloth: the virgins of Jerusalem hang down their heads to the ground."
Lamentations 2:4-10

Jeremiah lists the things God had done to Judah. First, He had *"bent his bow like an enemy."* This implies that God was waging war against Judah as an enemy. "Bow" (*qesheth*) denotes God as a hunter. The people of Judah have become His prey. In His fury, God has "killed, smitten and destroyed" them.

Mourning for the Temple and all that it involves (the feasts of the Lord, the daily priestly sacrifices, etcetera) continues, as well as mourning for the slaughter or removal of their leaders and priests. By destroying *"his strong holds,"* God removed His hedge of protection and allowed the enemy to come in. Not only that, but He *"hath stretched out a line."* That word "line" is *qav,* meaning "a cord for measuring, especially a measuring line for judgment." God had determined the length and scope of Judah's punishment. And it would be poured out in full measure. God even made a "rampart" (*cheyl*) which means an entrenchment. Conquering armies build ramparts around a city it wanted to subjugate in order to keep the inhabitants from escaping. Thus, there would be no escape for Judah.

In addition, her gates and walls were broken down which means anyone can enter. Those who remained inside had no protection. Nor do they have leaders. They were either dead or had become Babylonian captives. And God Himself had *"broken her bars."* That word "bars" is *beriyach* meaning "bolt, bar, something thrust through." According to the *Theological Wordbook of the Old Testament,* it also refers "to the bars which hold together the upright boards forming the walls of the Tabernacle." Their precious *towrah* or Pentateuch could no longer be fully followed because the Temple was no more. It had been thrust through, broken down. Neither could the prophets hear from God.

Then notice, *"The* ***elders*** *of the daughter of Zion sit upon the ground, and keep silence."* That word "elders" (*zaqen*) means "old, old age." According to the *Theological Wordbook of the Old Testament,* the aged were to be respected and honored. They also comprised the ruling body of a city and even formed "an advisory body to the kings." Elders sat at the gate to administer justice. The gate was the center of government and commerce, as well as religious activities. In essence, it was the heartbeat of a city. Proverbs 31:23 notes that being allowed to sit with the elders was considered an honor.

Now, Jerusalem's gates were smashed. Her elders, who had led the people astray and refused to repent or listen to God's warning, had lost everything and sat in the dirt. No longer offering wisdom or advice, they were silent, humiliated, disgraced, and covered in sackcloth and ashes.

What an object lesson! Their pride and disobedience had reduced them to the lowest of the low. Proverbs 1:29-31 says, *"For that they hated knowledge, and did not choose the fear of the LORD: They would none of my counsel: they despised all my reproof. Therefore shall they eat of the fruit of their own* ***way****, and be filled with their own devices."* The elders were now eating the fruit of their "way."

This reminds me of Mark 8:36 where Jesus said, *"For what shall it profit a man, if he shall gain the whole world, and lose his own soul?"* The glory the world bestows is temporary and fleeting. A successful life is more than making a name for oneself. It's more than acquiring riches or power or engaging in pleasure. Rather, our life is a test run for eternity. It is here we will either accept or reject Jesus as our Savior and Lord. Because God greatly desires a family, and because He will not force anyone to come to Him, He has laid a choice before us. Those who come to Him freely will be His forever, in His forever family. Those who do not, will remain part of Satan's family, forever separated from God and residing in hell.

Continuing with the text:

"Mine eyes do fail with tears, my bowels are troubled, my liver is poured upon the earth, for the destruction of the daughter of my people; because the children and the sucklings swoon in the streets of the city. They say to their mothers, Where is corn and wine? when they swooned as the wounded in the streets of the city, when their soul was poured out into their mothers' bosom. What thing shall I take to witness for thee? What thing shall I liken to thee, O daughter of Jerusalem? what shall I equal to thee, that I may comfort thee, O virgin daughter of Zion? for thy breach is great like the sea: who can heal thee? Thy prophets have seen vain and foolish things for thee: and they have not discovered thine iniquity, to turn away thy captivity; but have seen for thee false burdens and causes of banishment. All that pass by clap their hands at thee; thy hiss and wag their head at the daughter of Jerusalem, saying, Is this the city that men call The perfection of beauty, The joy of the whole earth? All thine enemies have opened their mouth against thee: thy hiss and gnash the teeth: they say, We have swallowed her up: certainly this is the day that we looked for; we have found, we have seen it. The LORD hath done that which he had devised; he hath fulfilled his word that he had commanded in the days of old: he hath thrown down and hath not pitied: and he hath caused thine enemy to rejoice over thee, he hath set up the horn of thine adversaries." Lamentations 2: 11-17

Jeremiah continued to be overcome with emotion. Not only did he weep bitterly but the very core of his being was in agony. His *"liver is poured upon the earth."* This is another Hebraic idiom meaning he had been greatly humbled. His pride had been brought to the ground. All those things he once delighted in, his beautiful city, the Temple, the position Israel held as the "apple of God's eye," their mandate to display God to the world through the Torah and Commandments, had now come to naught.

Everything was in shambles. Those remaining in the city were weak and starving. Babies died while futilely trying to suck milk from their mothers' empty breasts. Death was all around them. Their *"breach is great like the sea: who can heal thee?"* Judah was so broken and shattered that Jeremiah wondered how they would ever recover.

Jeremiah again pointed to the prophets who had failed to harken to God's word but proclaimed their own, professing prosperity and safety. They had *"seen vain and foolish things."* That word "vain" is *shav* and means "desolating, uselessness, emptiness, falsehood, idolatry." These prophets had pursued the things of this world rather than the things of God. They had despised God's wisdom and instructions and became fools (Proverbs 1:7).

At the very end of his life, Solomon finally got it right. In Ecclesiastes 1:2 he said, *"all is vanity."* And in Ecclesiastes 12:13, he concluded that everything he had learned in life boiled down to this: *"Fear God, and keep his commandments: for this is the whole duty of man."*

But Judah did not heed. They had become like those five vain and foolish virgins in Matthew 25:1-13, who were unable to enter into the marriage supper of the Lamb and who heard Jesus utter these incredibly heartbreaking words, *"Verily I say unto you, I know you not."* By rejecting God and insulting Him through blatant disobedience, both individuals and nations will eventually hear those same words.

God had carried Israel's burdens for decades. He had made them successful in war and prosperous in peace. He even carried their burden of sin by instituting a system of animal sacrifices. But because they turned their back on Him, they now had to carry their own burdens. And instead of acknowledging their guilt, Judah's prophets had *"seen for thee false* ***burdens*** *and causes of banishment."* They proclaimed their troubles were a result of their failure to honor and sacrifice to the idolatrous "queen of heaven." This is a Romans 1:28-32 mindset: *"And even as they did not like to retain God in their knowledge, God gave them over to a reprobate mind, to do those things which are not convenient; Being filled with all unrighteousness, fornication, wickedness, covetousness, maliciousness; full of envy, murder, debate, deceit, malignity; whisperers, Backbiters, haters of God, despiteful, proud, boasters, inventors of evil things, disobedient to parents, Without understanding, covenant breakers, without natural affection, implacable, unmerciful: Who knowing the judgment of God, that they which commit such things are worthy of death, not only do the same, but have pleasure in them that do them."*

Because I believe this Romans mindset accurately describes our nation as well, we must realize that judgment can't be too far behind.

Our decline has been coming for years and is the result of several factors. I've detailed this in my book, *Destination Hell,* and will repeat some of it here.

Some signposts of America's decline:

1) The disbanding of the Legion of Decency and further depravity of the movie industry
2) the sexual revolution of the '60s
3) removal of prayer in school
4) *Roe v. Wade* and the legalization of abortion
5) the legalization of same-sex-marriage

The Legion of Decency:

The Legion was founded by Catholic Archbishop John McNicholas in 1934. Later, they were joined by Protestant groups to help regulate a film industry that seemed incapable of regulating itself. Films flagged as objectionable or indecent by the Legion meant millions would refuse to see them, thus affecting the studio's bottom line.

But by the mid '60s, the Legion of Decency's influence had waned. And in 1965, it was reorganized into the National Catholic Office for Motion Pictures (NCOMP). Later, the NCOMP morphed into other entities, but they never achieved the same clout as the Legion. Its final form, The Office of Film and Broadcasting, terminated operations in 2010,[4] leaving Hollywood to further disintegrate into a cesspool.

The ill effects of Hollywood and the entertainment industry cannot be overemphasized. Neuromarketing is the big thing and has been for years. It is subliminal messaging designed to manipulate people. Hollywood is a master at it and has used both subliminal and overt messaging to peddle their demonic ideology.

Early on, they portrayed Christians as buffoons or mentally unstable, thus trying to promote a disdain for Christianity. They then began portraying parents as incompetent fools, while their children appeared smarter and wiser, thus promoting disrespect for parental authority and mocking the traditional family structure. Then the messages became even more overt, promoting premarital sex followed by adulterous sex, homosexuality, and lesbianism, then the sexualization of children. Currently, we are bombarded by messages and images of violence and the occult.

But Hollywood has always been comfortable with the occult. Many have sold their souls for fifteen minutes of fame. And while Hollywood has always had its share of practicing Satanists, they are now coming out of the closet in droves, thus guaranteeing their movies will continue to be filled with vice and immorality.

A side note: A holly tree is both ornamental and evergreen. Slow growers, they can reach heights of fifty feet and live up to three hundred years. Druids viewed them as symbols of eternal life and fertility. Believed to have magical properties, its wood was used to make sorcerers' wands. That's why the motion picture industry named itself, "Hollywood" in the 1920's.[5] And it has indeed become a "sorcerer's wand."

But Satan also has his hand in the music industry. Hard rock, by their own admission, is dominated by Satanists. And most rap music glorifies sex, violence, and disrespect for both women and police. Television is no better, nor are secular books that promote sin and hopelessness.

Regarding the book industry, not long ago, the ABA, the American Booksellers Association, issued a pathetic and spineless apology for their "serious, violent incident." Just what was this "incident"? It was mailing flyers promoting an anti-trans book entitled, *Irreversible Damage: The Transgender Craze Seducing Our Daughters*. Written by Abigail Shrier, it was originally hailed as "one of the most important books of our time."[6] Its censorship provides an ominous warning for the book industry and free speech.

Through neuromarketing, subliminal messages in movies, books, music, TV, video games, and advertisements have had a devastating effect. It's a 163-billion-dollar industry based on science, and it works. Their studies define how to manipulate people's brains for a desired outcome whether it's behavioral or psychological. It can affect how you spend money and what products draw you, and even evoke certain emotions through smell, sight, and sound.

The sexual revolution:

This 1960's revolution was a turning point for our nation. It was a time of "sex, drugs, and rock 'n' roll." Attitudes toward morality and sex shifted, impacting homes and marriages. It also fueled feminist groups and energized the fledgling gay rights movement.[7] At the same time, Bob Dylan was telling "everyone" to get stoned, and they did. Young people began experimenting with illicit drugs beginning with marijuana and LSD, followed by amphetamines, barbiturates, cocaine, then heroin in the '70s.[8] By the late '60s, hard rock, a subgenre of classic rock, became more and more popular, with many of its singers being practicing Satanists who also promoted drug use and premarital sex.

The removal of school prayer:

Not surprising, the '60s also saw the removal of school prayer after atheist Madalyn Murray O'Hair filed a lawsuit against Baltimore's school board. The 1963 case, *Murray v. Curlett*, was upheld by the U.S. Supreme Court in a vote of 8 to 1. And here's the tragedy. Not one Christian church or Christian organization presented a case to the court in support of school prayer![9] It's worth noting that from 1941-1971, the Supreme Court was controlled by Freemasons. And four Mason judges were able to influence the Court's decision to remove prayer and God from our schools.[10]

The legalization of abortion and same-sex marriage:

In 1973, the U.S. Supreme Court declared abortion was protected under the constitution in the landmark case, *Roe v. Wade.*[11] Since 1973, over 65.5 million precious babies have been murdered in America,[12] making us a nation of blood and one that has made a covenant with death.

And on June 26, 2015, the Supreme Court, in *Obergefell v. Hodges,* declared that according to the Fourteenth Amendment, same-sex couples had a fundamental right to marry, changing the time-honored Biblical definition of marriage.[13]

Alongside this came the rise of socialism and communism. Few connected the dots that Karl Marx, the father of Communism, came out of the Illuminati, a Satanic organization. His *Communist Manifesto* was virtually a replica of *The Illuminati Manifesto*. It also formed the basis of the secular *Humanist Manifesto.*

All of them, the Illuminati, communism, and secular humanism, have similar beliefs and goals. They want to create a global society with a social and economic order that facilitates the redistribution of wealth. Rejecting the need for salvation, they believe Christian salvation is "harmful." Instead, they believe man must create his own religion. They also have seventeen common strategies deemed necessary to achieve their goals:

1. Reject traditional religion
2. Reject concept of sin, salvation, and the need for God
3. Promote idea that morals and ethics are situational
4. Push idea that a better world can be achieved through intelligence and reason

5. Encourage personal freedom without moral restrictions
6. Promote abortion, sexual exploration, and divorce
7. Promote euthanasia and suicide
8. Promote democracy (mob rule) rather than a democratic republic
9. Promote concept of "separation of church and state"
10. Promote economic socialism
11. Promote government control over every area of life by using "anti-discrimination" as a tool
12. Destroy nationalism and promote concept of a "world community"
13. Promote the need for an international court
14. Promote environmentalism and population control
15. Provide birth control to developing nations
16. Remove all barriers to scientific research
17. Promote international cooperation as absolutely essential[14]

It's clear that most of these seventeen strategies have already been achieved. It's also clear that our nation is on the road to perdition.

Jesus said you would know a tree by its fruits (Matthew 7:16-20).

Let's look at the fruits produced.

Children are a gift from God (Psalm 127:3-5). Satan knows this. He also knows they are every nation's future. That's why one of his primary aims is to destroy them. And he starts in the womb. One of his greatest American success stories is *Roe v. Wade.* To ensure its continuing triumph, he keeps abortion a hot button topic, pushing against any opposition.

Satanists have supported abortion for years, even teaming up with Planned Parenthood in 2017 to help them expand their Missouri clinics. And in 2020, the Satanic Temple came out and tied abortion to their official rituals.[15] So, when Texas passed their "heartbeat" law, they were outraged.

That law codifies that abortions after six weeks are illegal. After that specified time, citizens may take legal action against those who perform them or those who aid others in performing them. Portland's city council, along with the mayor at that time, Ted Wheeler, immediately sprang into action by proposing a ban on Texan goods as well as travel to their state.[16]

Right behind them was the Satanic Temple who protested that this violated their "religious freedom" by impeding their right to have official ritual abortions. They claim these "rituals" should be protected under Religious Liberty laws. Their spokesman, Lucien Greaves, believes this is a "battle of competing religious viewpoints."[17]

We must understand that what Satanists are fighting for here is the right to perform **human sacrifices**! They are killing unborn babies in Satanic rituals. And the added shock is how brazenly the Satanic Temple admits this. That should horrify everyone.

But if Satan can't destroy our children in the womb, he will try other means. Since the 19th century, Satan has been infiltrating our schools. Though many dedicated and sincere teachers remain, he has successfully inserted his anti-God, anti-Christian lackeys as staff, teachers, principals, and school board members. He has also successfully incorporated his ideology and philosophies into official school curriculum.

This became evident by the '60s. Colleges and universities began offering liberal courses that questioned morality. Suddenly, topics like "situational ethics" sprang up. So did the push to replace Biblical morality with the faulty science of evolution.[18] The premise was if we are just an accident of nature, the product of something that crawled out of the primordial ooze, why shouldn't we make up our own moral codes?

Colossians 2:8 cautions us against this very thing. *"Beware lest any man spoil you through philosophy and vain deceit, after the tradition of men, after the rudiments of the world, and not after Christ."*

But the church took no notice. As a result, we now have colleges producing students incapable of honest and respectful debate, and who need "safe spaces" where they can retreat with their "blankies and playdough" to keep from hearing ideas they don't like. And some colleges even encourage students to use violent totalitarian tactics to silence differing opinions.

Early indoctrination is key. It's one of the cornerstones of communism. A young tree is easier to bend than an older one. That's why Vladimir Lenin said, "Give me just one generation of youth, and I'll transform the whole world."[19]

Hitler also understood this principle when he said, "Let me control the textbooks and I will control the state. The state will take youth and give to youth its own education and its own upbringing. Your child belongs to us already."[20] The Hitler Youth program and League of German Girls were implementations of this philosophy.

While America's public schools push their evil agenda on younger and younger children, real education is suffering. Although the U.S. outspends almost every other nation on education, the results are far from inspiring. According to *EducationWeek,* in 2023, The Trends in International Mathematics and Science Study (TIMSS) which evaluates 4th and 8th grade students every four years, confirmed that academic achievement in the U.S. continued to decline. The TIMSS also showed "more American students failing to meet even the lowest level of achievement in math."

Author Mike LaChance, who has been following and evaluating U.S. trends in education since 2012, said in his September 10, 2025, article: "New analysis has found" that "reading and test scores for American 12th graders have hit a 20 year low."

And according to EdSurge, an education journalism website, "In 2025, American students, particularly 12th graders, are testing at historic lows in reading, science, and math. The Nation's Report Card, released by the National Center for Education Statistics, reveals that almost half of high school seniors are now testing below reading level. In math, only about 22% of 12th graders perform at or above proficiency standards."

If California is any indication, these scores will not improve anytime soon. They plan to dumb down their math classes. To this end, they have issued guidelines using philosophies found in Critical Race Theory to "apply social justice principles to math lessons." It will suspend the grading of students in favor of simply allowing them to "view their learning as a process." California had also planned to dispense with all accelerated math programs.[21]

The idea of disbanding accelerated math programs did not sit well with 746 mathematicians and scientists who sent an open letter to the California Department of Education claiming their proposed changes and "one size fits all" approach would "place K-12 public school students at a disadvantage compared with their international and private school peers" and ultimately "cause lasting damage to STEM education in the country and exacerbate inequality by diminishing access to the skills needed for social mobility."[22] Since then, California has backpedaled on the issue.

But if ideology is the measuring rod, our public schools have gotten their money's worth. While most Americans are still proud of their country, according to *Issues & Insights*, most young people are not. In fact, only 36% of them claim to be proud of America.[23]

Not surprisingly, college students and young adults were socialist Bernie Sanders' biggest supporters in his bid for the Presidency. During the Clinton/Sanders race, a whopping 59% of them favored Sanders,[24] as did 57% in the Sanders/Biden contest.[25] That means an incredible number of our young don't value the freedoms America offers. Instead, they are enamored by socialism even though this ideology has failed the world over. It has impoverished the nations that tried it and left them with tyrannical overlords. Millions were killed or imprisoned during the iron-fisted reign of Lenin, Stalin, Mao Zedong, Nicolae Ceausescu, and Pol Pot, all communist dictators. And yet, this is what our young people want to bring to America.

Even so, these and other liberal views continue to be crammed down our children's throats. An LA Alexander Hamilton High School history teacher was forced to remove her classroom flags. Featured were a Palestinian flag, Black Lives Matter Flag, a transgender flag, and two flags that said "F...the Police" and "F...Amerikkka."[26] Why were they there in the first place?

In contrast, a teacher at Marysville Middle School was ordered to remove her Thin Blue Line flag conveying support for law enforcement, while other teachers in that same school were allowed to hang Black Lives Matter and LGBTQ flags.[27]

In Florida, a teacher became unglued over her students supporting another student's right to bring a Trump flag to class. She called the flag carrier, "a racist." Then told her class, "Trump brings out racism in trashy people."[28]

This is not the only incident of teachers bullying their students because they embraced a different philosophy from theirs. Nor is it the first story of unsuitable educators occupying positions they shouldn't. Sadly, there are many of them.

But this next one is unbelievable! Theology professor, Curtis Freeman, at Duke University and Director of its Baptist House of Studies said, "Evangelical Christianity is the greatest threat to human existence today. It must be laid waste." He also compared Christian fundamentalists to the Taliban.[29] And this is a **theology** professor teaching young adults about religion? God help us!

Having our children denied quality education or forced to endure political brainwashing is not enough for some educators. They want them corrupted in every way by promoting sexual immorality and gender confusion. All this is grooming and recruiting our children to accept sexual advances and deviant sexual behavior as normal. So, it wasn't that surprising when the San Francisco Gay Men's Chorus came out with a song called, *"We're coming for Your Children,"* that boldly declared they plan to indoctrinate and seduce our children into the LGBTQ lifestyle, though they deleted their video six days later.[30]

Some teachers have actively recruited students into LGBTQ clubs according to a leaked recording of two seventh grade California teachers. During the October 2021 CTA Conference, these teachers shared how they deceived parents by calling these clubs "equity clubs," and how they found recruits by "spying on students' online searches and activity as well as eavesdropping on their conversations to identify and recruit sixth-grade students into these LGBTQ clubs whose membership rolls were kept hidden from parents." The school responded by suspending all these clubs.[31] Praise God!

Not long after, Allyn Walker, assistant professor of criminal justice and sociology at Old Dominion University, came out "openly suggesting pedophilia is natural and should not be considered wrong." She was placed on leave.[32]

The entire list of other inappropriate behavior by educators is too long to include, but here are just six:

- A Florida Broward County School Board member chaperoned the field trip of elementary students to a gay bar.[33]
- Loudoun County School covered up the rape of a fourteen year old girl by a transgender boy using the girls' bathroom. To add insult to injury, they had the girl's father arrested for bringing it up at a school board meeting. The rapist was transferred to a different school where he sexually assaulted another girl.[34]
- Jacob Engels, a Gateway Pundit contributor, attended an Orange County School Board meeting where he used his time to read portions of *Gender Queer*: a memoir by Maia

Kobabe. The book was carried by and featured in the Boone High School library during Pride Month. Engels was able to read only one section of the sexually graphic interactions of homosexuals before the chairman ordered him to stop, then had him escorted out by police when he refused[35]. Apparently, it was appropriate material for high school students but not for adults.

- Recently, parents exposed a Hudson Ohio School Board when they discovered their high school kids were reading, *642 Things to Write About*, then instructed to "write a sex scene you wouldn't show your mom." To his credit, the Hudson Mayor, Craig Shubert, gave the board an ultimatum: resign or be criminally charged for distributing child pornography.[36]
- Parents in Minnesota discovered that the Richfield School Board had approved a sex-ed program that required their children to act out both transgender and gay roles. Among other things, this K-12 sex education program teaches "gay sex, gender ideology, abortion, racial justice, and more, and utilizes visuals and role-playing activities."[37]
- Over 100 obscene and sexually explicit books were discovered by parents in the North Carolina, Wake County, public elementary, middle, and high schools. Criminal charges have been filed by parents against the school board.[38]

New York and California are already trying to decriminalize sex between children and adults. And members of NAMBLA (North American Man/Boy Love Association) a homosexual, pedophile organization, now call themselves "minor-attracted persons" and claim to champion sexual freedom for children.[39]

As a result of all this, our children are anxious and confused. Some no longer know if they are male or female and are getting hormone therapy and surgeries to artificially change their sex. The American College of Pediatricians has tried to warn of the dangers, claiming that artificially altering one's sexuality most often leads to unhappiness and depression. And when these children become adults, their suicide rate is twenty times higher than the national average.[40]

Because these types of things have been going on for years, is it any wonder that according to a study by Arizona Christian University, 30% of millennials identify as LGBTQ?[41] It was a small study of only six hundred people from age eighteen to thirty-seven, but if accurate what does that mean in terms of numbers? According to marketingcharts.com there were 74.2 million U.S. millennials in 2024. Thirty percent of that translates to 22.3 million!

It's obvious that many in industry, government, and institutions of learning have an ominous agenda. We have given our children over to be taught by godless secular establishments and are surprised when we discover they disrespect our values, have lost faith in God, hate this country, themselves, and each other, have seared consciences, and no foundation.

The cumulative effects of society's moral decline are horrifying. Andrew Powell, in his article, *What the devil? U.S. turns to dark side as Americans make Satan mainstream,* encapsulates what's going on in America by citing, in one paragraph, actual events: "(the erecting of) Satanic statues, witches casting spells, drag queens reading to kids, open pedophilia on streaming services such as Netflix, sex dolls with real child's likeness, cannibal restaurants, Satanic rituals at all-American event like the Super Bowl, radical leftist groups outright saying they want to destroy the nuclear family, a daughter of politicians wishing a Happy New Year to the Church of Satan, a chemical named 'Luciferase' in the COVID-19 vaccine."[42]

In the face of all this, how can we, as a nation, possibly hope to escape God's judgment?

Continuing with the text:

"Their heart cried unto the Lord, O wall of the daughter of Zion, let tears run down like a river day and night: give thyself no rest; let not the apple of thine eye cease. Arise, cry out in the night: in the beginning of the watches pour out thine heart like water before the face of the Lord: lift up thy hands toward him for the life of thy young children, that faint for hunger in the top of every street. Behold, O LORD, and consider to whom thou hast done this. Shall the women eat their fruit, and children of a span long? shall the priest and the prophet be slain in the sanctuary of the Lord? The young and the old lie on the ground in the streets: my virgins and my young men are fallen by the sword; thou hast slain them in the day of thine anger; thou hast killed, and not pitied. Thou hast called as in a solemn day my terrors round about, so that in the day of the LORD'S anger none escaped nor remained: those that I have swaddled and brought up hath mine enemy consumed." Lamentations 2:18-22

Although Jeremiah understood this grave calamity was Judah's fault, he exhorted his people to cry out to the Lord for mercy. *"Let tears run down like a river day and night: give thyself no rest."* But here's the sad part. Instead of tears like a river, God wanted to give them peace *"like a river"* (Isaiah 66:12). He also wanted to give them rest.

Psalm 37 talks about trusting, delighting, committing, and resting in the Lord. Notice the progression. Resting in the Lord is preceded first by our trusting, delighting in, and committing ourselves to Him. Conversely, Psalm 38:3 tells us there is no rest for those who sin. Thus, we can understand why God, in Jeremiah 6:16 said, *"Stand ye in the ways* (His ways), *and see, and ask for the old paths, where is the good way, and walk therein, and ye shall find rest for your souls.* ***But they said, We will not walk therein."*** Because they refused to walk in God's ways they had no rest.

In spite of all this, God, ever loving and merciful, gave His people this promise in Jeremiah 46:27: *"But fear not thou, O my servant Jacob, and be not dismayed, O Israel: for, behold, I will save thee from afar off, and thy seed from the land of their captivity; and Jacob shall return, and be in rest and at ease, and none shall make him afraid."* Even in the face of Judah's gross sins, God would not abandon them. He would once again show Himself strong on their behalf by bringing them, as well as Israel, back to their homeland as a cohesive nation.

Then Jeremiah said that God had *"killed, and not pitied."* "Killed" (*tabach*) means to "slaughter, butcher, kill ruthlessly." This shows the great depth of God's anger. It was fierce and hot and could only be extinguished when it was fully satisfied. And none *"escaped"* (*paliyt*). That word means "a refuge." God was Israel's refuge. *"God is our* ***refuge*** *and strength, a very present help in trouble,"* (Psalm 46:1). And Proverbs 18:10 says, *"The name of the LORD is a strong tower: the righteous runneth into it, and is safe."* But there in is the rub. Notice, it's the righteous who run into His safe arms. Rebels against God remain outside and make easy targets for the enemy.

This applies even today. Jesus is our refuge and strength, our high tower. If we accept Him and what He did for us, we become the righteousness of Christ and are entitled to run under His covering for safety. Jesus said in Luke 19:10, *"For the*

Son of man is come to seek and to save that which was lost." 1 Peter 3:18 says, *"For Christ also hath once suffered for sins, the just for the unjust, that he might bring us to God, being put to death in the flesh, but quickened by the Spirit."* Jesus said in John 8:12, *"I am the light of the world: he that followeth me shall not walk in darkness, but shall have the light of life."*

God has done it all, then made it so simple for us to come to Him.

Chapter 3

"I am the man that hath seen affliction by the rod of his wrath. He hath led me, and brought me into darkness, but not into light. Surely against me is he turned; he turneth his hand against me all the day. My flesh and my skin hath he made old; he hath broken my bones. He hath builded against me, and compassed me with gall and travail. He hath set me in dark places, as they that be dead of old. He hath hedged me about, that I cannot get out: he hath made my chain heavy." Lamentations 3:1-7

Here we see that Jeremiah's lamentations were for himself. God's heavy hand of judgment had greatly affected him. He called himself *"the man that hath seen affliction by the rod of his wrath."* That word "man" is *geber* meaning "valiant man, warrior, person, be strong, to prevail." Jeremiah is a survivor. He had prevailed in the midst of great calamity. He had witnessed the "rod" of God's wrath. "Rod" (*shebet*) means a "branch, stick, correction." Job 9:34 speaks of God's rod of correction. Psalm 89:30-32, referring to God's covenant people, gives this warning: *"If his children forsake my law, and walk not in my judgments; If they break my statutes, and keep not my commandments; Then will I visit their transgression with the* ***rod****, and their iniquity with stripes."* Proverbs 10:13 adds, *"In the lips* *of him that hath understanding wisdom is found: but a* ***rod*** *is for the back of him that is void of understanding."*

Judah failed to walk in God's judgments and commandments. They became fools, *"void of understanding."* All this necessitated the application of God's "rod."

As already mentioned, just as God desired to be Israel's Shepherd, so Jesus desires to be ours. For those in his flock, His rod is one of protection, gentle guidance, and comfort (Psalm 23:4). Isaiah 11:1-4 gives this additional insight. *"And there shall come forth a* ***rod*** *out of the stem of Jesse, and a Branch shall grow out of his roots: And the spirit of the LORD shall rest upon him, the spirit of wisdom and understanding, the spirit of counsel and might, the spirit of knowledge and of the fear of the LORD; And shall make him of quick understanding in the fear of the LORD: and he shall not judge after the sight of the eyes, neither reprove after the hearing of his ears: But with righteousness shall he judge the poor, and reprove with equity for the meek of the earth: and he shall smite the earth with the* ***rod*** (power, correction) *of his mouth, and with the breath of his lips shall he slay the wicked."*

This is King Jesus ruling in power and authority over the world. Revelation 12:5 says, *"And she* (Israel) *brought forth a man child, who was to rule all nations with a* ***rod*** *of iron: and her child was caught up unto God, and to his throne."* And Revelation 19:15, describing Jesus' return says, *"And out of his* (Jesus') *mouth goeth a sharp sword, that with it he should smite the nations: and he shall rule them with a* ***rod*** *of iron."*

As an eyewitness to the power of God's rod, Jeremiah saw only destruction and carnage. Though God had promised Judah's sorrow and captivity would only last seventy years, Jeremiah couldn't see past the current landscape. The enormity of it and its resulting pain plunged him into self-pity and darkness. Sin affects everyone, even those not sinning because it pollutes nations, families, relationships, etcetera.

Proverbs 14:34 tells us that righteousness exalts a nation. Therefore, conversely, sin brings it down. And Judah was a prime example. They had left *"the paths of uprightness, to walk in the ways of darkness,"* (Proverbs 2:13). And because they had *"put light for darkness"* (Isaiah 5:20), God gave them darkness.

Jeremiah was a righteous man who feared the Lord; a prophet who had remained faithful and obedient even in the face of staggering persecution. He even admonished his people to *"Give glory to the LORD your God, before he cause darkness, and before your feet stumble upon the dark mountains, and, while ye look for light, he turn it into the shadow of death, and make it gross darkness,"* (Jeremiah 13:16). But now, his overwhelming sorrow caused him to take his eyes off God and focus on the misery around him. He forgot Isaiah 50:10, *"Who is among you that feareth the LORD, that obeyeth the voice of his servant, that walketh in darkness, and hath no light? let him trust in the name of the LORD, and stay upon his God."*

With all the evil in the world, it is easy to become discouraged and question God. It's also easy to become weary of well-doing and see only doom and gloom. But long ago, Isaiah predicted that a promised One would come, the Messiah Who would bring light into this dark world for both Jew and Gentile. *"I the LORD have called thee in righteousness, and will hold thine hand, and will keep thee, and give thee for a covenant of the people, for a* ***light of the Gentiles****; To open the blind eyes, to bring out the prisoners from the prison, and them that sit in darkness out of the prison house. I am the LORD; that is my name: and my glory will I not give to another, neither my praise to graven images… .And I will* *bring the blind by a way that they knew not; I will lead them in paths that they have not known: I will* ***make darkness light before them****, and crooked things straight. These things will I do unto them, and not forsake them."* (Isaiah 42:6-8, 16)

Now, contrast that to Satan. Darkness is his realm. Desiring to keep people there, he'll use everything in his power, blinding their minds, crippling them with fear and pride, and even appearing as an *"angel of light."* 2 Corinthians 11:14 says, *"for Satan himself is transformed into an angel of light."* That word "transformed" in Greek is *metaschematizo* and means, "to disguise." So, Satan, lord of darkness, will even disguise himself as a light bearer, pretending to bring spiritual enlightenment when in reality it is spiritual darkness. All bogus religions were birthed by this false "angel of light."

Jeremiah also said, *"My flesh and my skin hath he* (God) *made old; he hath broken my bones."* Because of all the tragedy he had witnessed, he felt like an old man. His strength (bones) was broken, diminished. He had become weak. He had been smitten with gall, meaning venom or poison, and couldn't overcome it. His chain was too heavy. That word "chain" is *nechosheth* meaning "copper, metal, fetter." It can also mean "lust and harlotry." Judah's lust and harlotry have brought down God's heavy hand. And because Jeremiah was fettered or shackled to Judah, it had greatly affected him, as well. Psalm 73:6, when speaking about foolish and evil men says, *"Therefore pride compasseth them about as a* ***chain****; violence covereth them as a garment."* Judah was chained to the consequences of her pride and violence, and in a sense, so was Jeremiah.

Continuing with the text:

"Also when I cry and shout, he shutteth out my prayer. He hath inclosed my ways with hewn stone, he hath made my paths crooked. He was unto me as a bear lying in wait, and as a lion in secret places. He hath turned aside my ways, and pulled me in pieces: he hath made me desolate. He hath bent his bow, and set me as a mark for the arrow. He hath caused the arrows of his quiver to enter into my reins. I was a derision to all my people; and their song all the day. He hath filled me with bitterness, he hath made me drunken with wormwood. He hath also broken my teeth with gravel stones, he hath covered me with ashes. And thou hast removed my soul far off from the peace: I forgat prosperity. And I said, My strength and my hope is perished from the LORD." Lamentations 3:8-18

Jeremiah took on or experienced Judah's anguish. He identified with her, felt her demise as if it were his own. He believed God was ignoring his prayers. His grief was so great he even claimed God had made his "paths crooked," implying his moral or physical path was now twisted, distorted, just as Judah's course had become distorted. Israel was destined to be God's oracle, His shining ornament. But Judah had forgotten Proverbs 3:5-6, Psalm 16:11, and Psalm 119:105. *"Trust in the LORD with all thine heart; and lean not unto thine own understanding. In all thy ways acknowledge him, and he shall direct thy* ***paths****."* And *"Thou* (God) *wilt shew me the* ***path*** *of life: in thy presence is fulness of joy; at thy right hand there are pleasure for evermore."* And *"Thy* (God's) *word is a lamp unto my feet, and a light unto my* ***path****."* It is God who makes straight our path, Who keeps us safe and on sure footing. And when we stray, we have no light to see the dangerous potholes before us.

It's interesting to note that Jeremiah also claimed that God had enclosed his *"way with hewn stone."* Exodus 20:25 specifically disqualifies hewn stones in the making of God's altar. Hadn't Judah made her worship "hewn stones," polluted stones that now entrapped her by their desecration, thus entrapping Jeremiah as well?

We are to be living sacrifices. Romans 12:1 says, *"Present your bodies a living sacrifice, holy, acceptable unto God, which is your reasonable service."* Thus, the altars of our life are to be made by unhewn stones, fashioned by God, not us. It is God Who has prepared the work we should do. Ephesians 2:10 makes that clear. *"For we are his* (God's) *workmanship, created in Christ Jesus unto good works, which God hath before ordained that we should walk in them."* When we do our own thing, when we chart our own course, we are surrounding ourselves with "hewn stones" that are unacceptable to God.

Jeremiah continued to lament that he, as well as Judah, were now treated like God's enemy. Like fallen Judah, Jeremiah, as the Lord's prophet, had also been the object of derision. People had made mocking songs about him, illustrating the fact that those who obey God will always be mocked and jeered by those who don't.

Jeremiah mentioned God was like a bear. That's a Hebrew idiom meaning a "great destroyer." That could also apply to the lion. It illustrates how Jeremiah viewed God as the instrument of his and Judah's destruction.

Jeremiah was also *"drunken"* with *"wormwood."* Drunken (*ravah*) means "make drunk, have one's fill." Wormwood is *laanah* and means "to curse, poisonous, hemlock." According to Zondervan's *Pictorial Encyclopedia of the Bible,* wormwood is the "herbaceous perennial *Artemesia absinthium*" and makes a bitter alcoholic drink. Wormwood also symbolizes tragedy, grief, and at times, brutality. Jeremiah was feeling all three. He was experiencing God's curse to the full.

When God gave Israel His commandments at the beginning of their forty years of wilderness wanderings, Moses warned them not to be seduced and serve other gods when they entered the Promised Land. *"Beware lest there should be among you a man or woman, or family or tribe, whose mind and heart turns away this day from the Lord our God to go and serve the gods of these nations; lest there should be among you a* ***poisonous root that bears gall and wormwood****. And lest, when he hears the words of this curse and oath, he flatters and congratulates himself in his mind and heart, saying, I shall have peace and safety, though I walk in the stubborness of my mind and heart bringing down a hurricane of destruction and sweep away the watered land with the dry."* Deuteronomy 29:18-19 (Amplified)

That *"poisonous root that bears gall and wormwood"* had become a massive growth which God could no longer ignore. Years ago, He warned them that their idolatry would bring a curse. Twice, Jeremiah also warned of the same thing, (Jeremiah 9:15 and 23:15). Yet they disobeyed. And they, along with Jeremiah, were now suffering. But one must understand how merciful God was. Though He continually warned His people, His long-suffering and patience kept prolonging the necessary judgment. He loved, and still loves His people. And though more judgment is coming during the seven-year Tribulation, in the end, God will preserve and elevate Israel.

Jeremiah also claimed that God *"hath also broken my teeth with gravel stones, he hath covered me with ashes."* The *Theological Wordbook of the Old Testament* concludes that to break someone's teeth "is to rob him of power." Both Judah and Jeremiah were broken and powerless. And ashes indicate mourning.

Jeremiah also said that God had *"removed"* him, his life, his being from all that was happy and good. That word "removed" (*zanach*) means "to push aside, reject, spurn, cast off." Since *"every good gift and every perfect gift is from above,"* (James 1:17) and because perfect peace belongs to those who are focused on God (Isaiah 26:3), being cast off by God means the loss of both His peace and blessings.

Continuing with the text:

"Remembering mine affliction and my misery, the wormwood and the gall. My soul hath them still in remembrance, and is humbled in me. This I recall to my mind, therefore have I hope. It is of the LORD'S mercies that we are not consumed, because his compassions fail not. They are new every morning: great is thy faithfulness. The LORD is my portion, saith my soul; therefore will I hope in him. Lamentations 3:19-24

In the midst of Jeremiah's grief, he finally turned his eyes from the devastation back to God. He remembered that God was merciful, compassionate, and faithful. Judah's punishment would not last forever.

During dark times, it's important to remember who God is and what He has done in the past and that He is a big God, capable of big things.

Continuing with the text:

*"The LORD is **good** unto them that wait for him, to the soul that seeketh him. It is **good** that a man should both hope and quietly wait for the salvation of the LORD. It is **good** for a man that he bear the yoke in his youth."* Lamentations 3:25-27

Note, the word "good" is used three times. First, Jeremiah, like others before him, extolled God's goodness. 1 Chronicles 16:34 says, *"O give thanks unto the LORD; for he is **good**; for his mercy endureth for ever."* And Psalm 34:8 says, *"O taste and see that the LORD is **good**: blessed is the man that trusteth in him."*

Then Jeremiah made a distinction. God's goodness was directed toward those who *"wait for him"* and *"seeketh"* Him. Jeremiah was beginning to separate the goodness of God from God's holiness which required the dispensing of justice when needed.

Finally, Jeremiah detailed what was good for man to do. He was to *"hope and quietly wait"* for God's deliverance. Until then, Jeremiah had been a noisy gong, crying, wailing, moaning over both his and Judah's fate. Though Judah's judgment was years in the making, and God had given ample warning, Jeremiah had not remained silent in the face of that judgment. Having already been told by God that this punishment would not last, Jeremiah had been impatient, not content to wait upon the Lord. If he had, God would have renewed his strength (Isaiah 40:31).

Jeremiah also claimed that it was good for a man to *"bear the yoke in his youth."* This refers to submitting to God's controlling hand and discipline when young. It's easier for a child to accept the ways of the Lord than an adult. Proverbs 22:6 says, *"Train up a child in the way he should go: and when he is old, he will not depart from it."* And Genesis 8:21 tells us this instruction is necessary because *"the imagination of man's heart is evil from his youth."*

Years of sin by Judah's leaders, priests, and prophets resulted in generations lacking godly examples and training. *"We lie down in our shame, and our confusion covereth us: for we have sinned against the LORD our God, we and our fathers, from our* ***youth*** *even unto this day, and have not obeyed the voice of the LORD our God,"* (Jeremiah 3:25). God confirmed this. *"For the children of Israel and the children of Judah have only done evil before me from their* ***youth****: for the children of Israel have only provoked me to anger with the work of their hands, saith the LORD,"* (Jeremiah 32:30). The tree had become rotten and needed to be felled. Despite his grief, Jeremiah finally acknowledged this.

His people had failed to "*seeketh*" God. That word is *darash* in Hebrew and means "to seek with care, inquire, require, follow." Psalm 32:8 says, *"I will instruct thee and teach thee in the way which thou shalt go: I will guide thee with mine eye."*

God's requirement is still the same. Jesus said in Mark 8:34, *"Whosoever will come after me let him deny himself, and take up his cross, and* ***follow*** *me."* Jesus also said, *"My sheep hear my voice, and I know them, and they* ***follow*** *me,"* (John 10:27). Both Scriptures indicate that true believers in Jesus *follow* Him. And what a promise Jesus made in John 12:26, *"If any man serve me, let him* ***follow*** *me; and where I am, there shall also my servant be: if any man serve me, him will my father honour."* A servant must obey his master. The problem with Judah is that they had become their own master.

Continuing with the text:

"He setteth alone and keepeth silence, because he hath borne it upon him. He putteth his mouth in the dust; if so be there may be hope. He giveth his cheek to him that smiteth him: he is filled full with reproach. For the Lord will not cast off for ever: But though he cause grief, yet will he have compassion according to the multitude of his mercies. For he doth not afflict willingly nor grieve the children of

men. To crush under his feet all the prisoners of the earth, To turn aside the right of a man before the face of the most High, To subvert a man in his cause, the Lord approveth not. Who is he that saith, and it cometh to pass, when the Lord commandeth it not? Out of the mouth of the most High proceedeth not evil and good? Wherefore doth a living man complain, a man for the punishment of his sins? Let us search and try our ways, and turn again to the LORD. Let us lift up our heart with our hands unto God in the heavens." Lamentations 3:28-41

Jeremiah had run the gamut of lamenting, pleading with God, blaming Him, then blaming Judah, and finally admitting this judgment was deserved. He had acknowledged that God's ways were higher (Isaiah 55:9); that He did all things well (Mark 7:37); that His judgments were righteous (Psalm 9:8), and that He was perfect and just (Deuteronomy 32:4).

Jeremiah then described how one should respond to God's judgment. First, he should bear it in silence, without complaining. He should humble himself before the Lord. Putting *"his mouth to the dust"* is a Hebraic idiom meaning to be greatly humbled. He should willingly accept God's judgment (*he giveth his cheek to him that smiteth him*). He should feel shame for what he had done (*he is filled full with reproach)* and repent.

In addition, he should not lose hope because he knew God did not delight in his sufferings and that God would not "cast" him off forever. He also knew that in the midst of his sorrow, he would once again experience God's mercy. In fact, it would be a *"multitude of his mercies."* Jeremiah understood that only those things allowed by God could befall him or His people. And God would never *"turn aside the right of a man before the face of the most High, To subvert a man in his cause, the Lord approveth not,"* meaning He would never deprive a man of his rights or make crooked a man's way. Man does that to himself. Thus, Judah's destruction was deserved, allowed by God, and must be borne with patience and humility. Therefore, neither Judah nor Jeremiah had a right to complain, and should, instead, reflect on their failures and sins, then repent and return to the Lord.

Continuing with the text:

"We have transgressed and have rebelled: thou hast not pardoned. Thou hast covered with anger, and persecuted us: thou hast slain, thou hast not pitied. Thou hast covered thyself with a cloud, that our prayer should not pass through. Thou hast made us as the offscouring and refuse in the midst of the people. All our enemies have opened their mouths against us. Fear and a snare is come upon us, desolation and destruction." Lamentations 3:42-47

Jeremiah again admitted that Judah had sinned against God. They were transgressors, rebels, traitors. Then he recounted their heavy punishment. God was far from them. In fact, He was hidden as though covered by a cloud. And He didn't answer their prayers. They had been slain without pity. They were outcasts (*the offscouring*). They were refuse. That word is *maowe* in Hebrew and means "reject, despise." But it's also a play on words because refuse also means "garbage, that which is thrown out as useless." Judah had become the refuse or garbage of the world, the butt of jokes among their enemies. And those still living, lived in fear, poverty, and misery.

Continuing with the text:

"Mine eye runneth down with rivers of water for the destruction of the daughter of my people. Mine eye trickleth down, and ceaseth not, without any intermission, Till the LORD look down, and behold from

heaven. Mine eye affecteth mine heart because of all the daughters of my city. Mine enemies chased me sore, like a bird, without cause. They have cut off my life in the dungeon, and cast a stone upon me. Waters flowed over mine head; then I said, I am cut off. I called upon thy name, O LORD, out of the low dungeon. Thou hast heard my voice: hide not thine ear at my breathing, at my cry. Thou drewest near in the day that I called up thee: thou saidst, Fear not." Lamentations 3:48-57

Jeremiah recalled how he had been heartbroken over God's prophecy of Judah's impending doom, and wept for them. And despite their abuse of him, Jeremiah had even interceded on their behalf. Then he recalled how during that time *"Waters flowed over mine head."* This is an idiom meaning he was surrounded by trouble and hardship, all brought on him by his own people. He remembered his persecution, the times he was arrested, beaten, and imprisoned. More emphatically, he remembered when he was placed in a muddy cistern and thought he was going to die. As he was sinking into the mire, God heard his cry and comforted him by reassuring him he had nothing to fear. Shortly after, Jeremiah was rescued by the Ethiopian eunuch, Ebed-melech, and brought to the court of the guard.

Continuing with the text:

"O Lord, thou hast pleaded the causes of my soul; thou hast redeemed my life. O LORD, thou hast seen ***my wrong****: judge thou* ***my cause****. Thou hast seen all their vengeance and all their imaginations* ***against me****. Thou hast heard their reproach, O LORD, and all their imaginations* ***against me****; The lips of those that rose up* ***against me****, and their device* ***against me*** *all the day. Behold their sitting down, and their rising up; I am their musick. Render unto them a recompence, O LORD, according to the work of their hands. Give*

*them sorrow of heart, thy **curse** unto them. Persecute and destroy them in anger from under the heavens of the LORD."*
Lamentations 3:58-66

The mood has suddenly changed. Instead of weeping for Judah, Jeremiah reminded God of how horribly his people had treated him. Note the references to "my wrong," "my cause," and the numerous mentions of people being "against" him. Jerusalem's inhabitants rewarded Jeremiah's diligence and faithfulness in proclaiming God's warnings by persecuting him and making him a laughingstock. He was their "musick." That word "musick" is *mangiynah* in Hebrew, meaning "a satire, mocking song." It is also a Hebraic idiom meaning gossip. In other words, they not only made-up songs to mock him, they gossiped about him. He was the joke that circulated around the public square and gates. He was the constant subject of their idle conversations.

Now, instead of Jeremiah asking for mercy for Judah, he was asking God to right the wrongs they had done him. David did this in Psalm 28 when he asked God to bring divine judgment against his enemies. In Psalm 58, he also asked God to *"break the teeth"* of the wicked. In the same way, Jeremiah was asking God to exercise His judgment, to actually "curse" those who persecuted him.

The truth is they were already cursed. Deuteronomy 11:26-28, says those who don't follow God are cursed. *"Behold, I set before you this day a blessing and a **curse**; A blessing, if ye obey the commandments of the LORD your God, which I command you this day: And a **curse**, if ye will not obey the commandments of the LORD your God, but turn aside out of the way which I command you this day, to go after other gods, which ye have not known."*

Every sentence in Deuteronomy 27:15-26, begins with the word "cursed." In these verses God lays out those things that bring curses: idolatry, dishonoring parents, stealing, misleading the blind (both physically and spiritually), perverting justice, sexual relations with your father's wife, bestiality, incest, having sex with your mother-in-law, murder, bribery, blaspheming, or dishonoring God's Word.

Thus, we see we are all cursed because every one of us has sinned. Every one of us has failed to follow God's commandments. The only way the curse can be lifted is if God lifts it Himself, which He did. Galatians 3:13 tells us that *"Christ hath redeemed us from the* ***curse*** *of the law, being made a* ***curse*** *for us: for it is written,* ***Cursed*** *is every one that hangeth on a tree."*

How wonderful to know that even if we have become as wayward as Judah, there is a remedy for the resulting curse if we're willing to take it!

Chapter 4

"How is the gold become dim! how is the most fine gold changed! the stones of the sanctuary are poured out in the top of every street. The precious sons of Zion, comparable to fine gold, how are they esteemed as earthen pitchers, the work of the hands of the potter!" Lamentations 4:1-2

Jeremiah zeroed in on the Temple. Located on Mount Moriah where Abraham was prepared to sacrifice his son, Isaac, it occupied the original threshing floor of Ornan (2 Chronicles 3:1). According to Zondervan's *Pictorial Encyclopedia of the Bible,* the interior of Solomon's Temple (referring to the Holy Place and Holy of Holies) measured sixty by twenty by thirty cubits (one cubit equals eighteen inches), and was made of precut, polished stones. (These chambers were expanded by Herod almost 1000 years later.) The roof was cedar, overlaid with packed clay, followed by a mix of crushed limestone and soil or clay creating a canopy as hard as cement.

1 Kings 7:48-49 says that gold covered many of the Temple furnishings and accessories: the altar of incense, table of show-bread, the lampstand, tongs, cups, snuffers, basins, spoons, firepans, door hinges, and doors. 1 Kings 6:28-35 goes further and tells us that Solomon also covered the carved cherubim

with gold as well as the walls and floors of both the Holy Place and Holy of Holies. It was truly a house of gold. Now, with its gold removed and it being reduced to a pile of rocks, the Temple was *"dim."*

But this dimness can also refer to the fact that the Shekinah glory, God's luminous presence, was no longer there. Ezekiel also prophesied of Judah's coming destruction and the departure of God's glory, (Ezekiel 10:18-19).

I believe both Ezekiel and Jeremiah's warnings prophetically refer not only to the destruction of Judah but to the destruction of Herod's Temple in 70 A.D. by Rome. That Temple was also one of gold. According to the historian, Josephus, the entrance to the Holy Place was covered with "vines of gold-work with gold grape clusters as tall as a man." The face of its porch entrance was also covered with gold plates, creating a brilliant facade when struck by the sun. The parapet and bird spikes surrounding the roof were gold covered. Inside, the walls were decorated with gold covered carvings of angels, palm trees, and flowers.

All this made the Temple shine both inside and out. And when the Temple caught fire during the siege of Jerusalem, Roman soldiers razed it in order to scrape the melted gold from between the stones.

How it must have hurt Jeremiah to witness the "consecrated" stones of Solomon's Temple *"poured out in the top of every street,"* turned into rubble and profaned by being dumped onto these common streets.

In the same way, the *"sons of Zion"* were also dim castoffs. I like the way the Amplified describes it. *"The noble and precious sons of Zion, once worth their weight in fine gold—now they are esteemed merely as earthen pots."* The people of Judah, instead of illuminating God's presence as gold forged by His hand, had become as common as clay pots made by man.

Continuing with the text:

"Even the sea monsters draw out the breast, they give suck to their young ones: the daughter of my people is become cruel, like the ostriches in the wilderness. The tongue of the sucking child cleaveth to the roof of his mouth for thirst: the young children ask bread, and no man breaketh it unto them. They that did feed delicately are desolate in the streets: they that were brought up in scarlet embrace dunghills. For the punishment of the iniquity of the daughter of my people is greater than the punishment of the sin of Sodom, that was overthrown as in a moment, and no hands stayed on her. Her Nazarites **were** *purer than snow, they were whiter than milk, they were more ruddy in body than rubies, their polishing was of sapphire: Their visage* **is** *blacker than coal; they are not known in the streets: their skin cleaveth to their bones; it is withered, it is become like a stick. They that be slain with the sword are better than they that be slain with hunger: for these pine away, stricken through for want of the fruits of the field. The hands of the pitiful women have sodden their own children: they were their meat in the destruction of the daughter of my people."* Lamentations 4:3-10

Jeremiah described the condition of his people. Graphic and disturbing, it points to their utter debasement. Starvation was rampant and cruelty reigned. Women were like "ostriches" (*yaen*). Some translate *yaen* as "screamer," but most believe it is better translated as "greedy." Job 39:16-17 described a female ostrich as *"hardened against her young ones, as though they were not hers."* He also claimed they lack wisdom and understanding. Ephesians 4:18-19, when describing the spiritual condition of Gentiles, says this about them: *"Having the* ***understanding*** *darkened, being alienated from the life of God through the* **ignorance** (lack of wisdom) *that is in them, because of the blindness of their heart: Who being past feeling have given themselves over unto lasciviousness, to work all uncleanness with* ***greediness.***" That word "greediness" (*Moab*) in Greek is only used this one time in the New Testament. It means "from the mother of her father, incestuous."

During and after the siege by Babylon, these Judean mothers behaved like uncaring, unfeeling ostriches and godless Gentiles. They refused to feed their suckling babies, causing them to die. Jeremiah found this abhorrent and said even "*sea monsters*" fed their young. That word "sea" is *yam*, meaning "large body of water, west, westward, opposite of north." Since God's throne was considered to be in the north, being opposite of north implies being far from God. The *Theological Wordbook of the Old Testament* states that "heathen nations are likened to the roaring sea." And Daniel 7:3 prophesized of four demonic kingdoms as coming out of the sea.

That word "monsters" completes the picture. It is *tannah* in Hebrew, meaning "a jackal, dragon." Both are pictures of evil. Thus, by this reference to "sea monsters," Jeremiah was saying that even the vilest creatures feed their young, while the daughters of Judah did not.

Then in Lamentations 4:10, Jeremiah described what these women were doing. "*The hands of the pitiful women have sodden their own children: they were their meat in the destruction of the daughter of my people.*" Their **greediness**, their selfish desire to satisfy and protect themselves at the expense of their own offspring, revealed their lack of wisdom and understanding, and enabled them to cook and eat (*sodden*) their own babies!

The word "incestuous" applies to these women eating their own children's flesh. Without God's restraining power, man is capable of horrendous deeds. This happened again in 70 A.D., during Rome's siege of Jerusalem, when women ate their own babies.

If that weren't bad enough, Jeremiah said that little children (toddlers or young children) could find no man to give them bread, meaning the surviving males kept what food they had for themselves. Their refusal to share, allowed the little ones to die from starvation, making these men almost as bad as the women.

Next, those who once *"did feed delicately are desolate in the streets: they that were brought up in scarlet embrace dunghills."* Scarlet (*towla*) means crimson or red. This red or crimson dye is expensive and comes from a worm (*coccus ilicis*). It symbolized wealth and power. But their wealth and power meant nothing now. No longer dining on delicacies, these elites scoured the garbage heaps for food.

This is also a play on words. Scarlet can symbolize sin. Isaiah 1:18 says, *"Come now, and let us reason together, saith the LORD: though your sins be as* ***scarlet****, they shall be as white as snow; though they be red like* ***crimson****, they shall be as wool."* These elites, who wore scarlet clothes, were covered in sin and had led many astray. And since they had yet to *"reason together"* with the Lord and repent, they remained scarlet.

Jeremiah then said Judah's punishment was worse than Sodom's. Why? Sodom was quickly destroyed by God while Judah was forced to endure prolonged suffering at the hands of man. Because Jeremiah was watching his people become unrecognizable skeletons, he concluded that a quick death by the sword was preferable to death by starvation. Obviously, his pain made him shortsighted. Sodom was utterly destroyed, never to rise again, while Judah was destined to suffer for only seventy years before being allowed to return to the land.

But why seventy years? Leviticus 25:4, 2 Chronicles 36:21, and Jeremiah 25:1-11 tell us. In Leviticus, God commanded Israel to let their land rest every seven years. That meant no plowing, no planting, no harvesting. Because Israel failed to do so for 490 years, God would now rest their land by bringing Israel into Babylonian captivity, a captivity that would last one year for every seven-year period they disobeyed this command.

Note, in the KJV, Jeremiah made a distinction between Sodom and Judah. *"The punishment of the **iniquity** of the daughter of my people is greater than the punishment of the **sin** of Sodom."* It uses the words "iniquity" and "sin" which have different connotations. Biblehub.com defines sin (*chattaah*) as "missing the mark." God has set down laws governing what is acceptable behavior for man, and when we disobey, either willfully or out of ignorance, we sin. Iniquity (*avon*) means "perversity, evil." Biblehub defines it as "something twisted or bent out of proper shape." Basically, it is the type of continuous unrepentant sin that eventually perverts an individual or nation, causing them to scorn God without fear.

But *The Septuagint* says, *"The **iniquity** of the daughter of my people has been increased **beyond** the **iniquities** of Sodoma."* This clearly implies that Judah's degradation was even worse than that of debauched Sodom's. Is it any wonder that between Jeremiah 2:22 and Jeremiah 51:6, the prophet mentioned "iniquity" twenty-one times?

Then in Lamentations 4:7, Jeremiah bemoaned the fact that Judah's Nazarites once were consecrated to the Lord and symbolically clean. They *"were more ruddy in body than rubies."* "Ruddy," (*adam*) meaning "to show blood, flush, red," indicated these men were healthy (physically and spiritually). They were even better than red rubies (*paniyn*), indicating their superior vigor. That word "rubies" also refers to the gem as well as "corals or as round as a pearl," again indicating health. However, if we look at Job 28:18, which speaks of God's wisdom, we get a better understanding. *"No mention shall be made of* ***coral****, or of* ***pearls****: for the price of wisdom is above* ***rubies****."* These Nazarites were better than rubies because they were full of God's wisdom.

In addition, *"their polishing was of sapphire."* Polishing points to separation. And according to the *Theological Wordbook of the Old Testament*, sapphires were gems "used for scratching other substances, to score with a mark, to inscribe." In other words, these Nazarites were separated and inscribed or marked by God.

This is in direct contrast to their current "so called" Nazarites who were *"blacker than coal."* Jeremiah was referring not only to their wasted physical state due to starvation, but their wasted, blackened spiritual state due to their iniquities.

Continuing with the text:

"The LORD hath accomplished his ***fury;*** *he hath poured out his* ***fierce anger****, and hath kindled a* ***fire*** *in Zion, and it hath* ***devoured*** *the foundations thereof. The kings of the earth, and all the inhabitants of the world, would not have believed that the adversary and the enemy should have entered into the gates of Jerusalem. For the sins of her prophets, and the iniquities of her priests, that have shed the*

blood of the just in the midst of her, They have wandered as blind men in the streets, they have polluted themselves with blood, so that men could not touch their garments. They cried unto them, Depart ye, it is unclean; depart, depart, touch not: when they fled away and wandered, they said among the heathen, They shall no more sojourn there. The ***anger*** *of the LORD hath divided them; he will no more regard them: they respected not the persons of the priests, they favoured not the elders."* Lamentations 4:11-16

Notice the words "fury," "fierce anger," "fire," "devoured," and "anger" all denoting the depth of God's wrath. His full vengeance had been poured out and had accomplished the intended purpose, namely, to destroy Judah's evil foundations. She had become polluted and corrupt to the core. Thus, she needed to be leveled: her cities, her government, her priests, her supposed "holy men," her elites. They all had a hand in persecuting and shedding innocent blood. They had killed prophets like Uriah during King Jehoiakim's reign (Jeremiah 26:20-30). They had persecuted Jeremiah and those who followed him. These sins made the prophets and priests as filthy as lepers. Their garments, once the symbol of separation and holiness which people touched in hopes of obtaining a blessing, were now nothing but dirty rags. They had lost the respect of the people who demanded they now declare their uncleanness just as lepers were required to declare theirs. Their spiritual blindness, their failure to live holy and consecrated lives, their failure to be godly leaders and examples reduced them to the status of outcasts. They had not esteemed their office nor followed the wisdom of the elders who reverenced and obeyed God.

Though this judgment was deserved, it was so complete, so terrible, even the heathen nations couldn't believe its severity. They never believed breaching Jerusalem's walls was possible.

But because they had been breached, it made them believe Judah was finished, that she would never rise again, that the God of Abraham, Isaac, and Jacob had abandoned her, never to *"regard"* her. But they were wrong.

According to the historian Josephus, the reign of king David's line ended with the Babylonian sacking of Jerusalem. It was a reign that included twenty-one kings, although Josephus counted Saul, a Benjaminite, among them. This Davidic reign lasted 514 years. In the millennial kingdom, it will be reestablished and last 1000 years.

Continuing with the text:

"As for us, our eyes as yet failed for our vain help: in our watching we have watched for a nation that could not save us. They hunt our steps, that we cannot go in our streets: our end is near, our days are fulfilled; for our end is come. Our persecutors are swifter than the ***eagles*** *of the heaven: they pursued us upon the mountains, they laid wait for us in the wilderness. The breath of our nostrils, the anointed of the LORD, was taken in their pits, of whom we said, Under his shadow we shall live among the heathen. Rejoice and be glad, O daughter of Edom, that dwellest in the land of Uz; the cup also shall pass through unto thee: thou shalt be drunken, and shalt make thyself naked. The punishment of thine iniquity is accomplished, O daughter of Zion; he will no more carry thee away into captivity: he will visit thine iniquity, O daughter of Edom; he will discover thy sins."* Lamentations 4:17-22

Jeremiah acknowledged that nothing could thwart God's judgment and that no help was coming. Their ally, Egypt, was nowhere to be seen. Judah was on her own and at the mercy of her oppressors. And these oppressors were savage. They were *"swifter than the eagles of the heaven."* That word "eagles" is *nesher,* meaning "to lacerate, large bird of prey." And that is what they did to Judah. They lacerated her. They killed, raped, and burned at will. Those who survived and fled were followed and captured. There were no safe havens. Judah was finished as a nation, at least for now.

The sad reality is that Israel (both north and south) was meant to live *"under the shadow"* of God's protection. Psalm 91:4 says, *"He* (God) *shall cover thee with his feathers, and under his wings shalt thou trust."* They were to trust in God. He was to shelter and cover them with His protecting "feathers." That's why David prayed in Psalm 17:8, *"Keep me as the apple of the eye, hide me* ***under the shadow of thy wings****."*

Instead, their rebellion forced them to live "under the shadow of death." Jeremiah 13:16 warned of this. *"Give glory to the LORD your God, before he cause darkness, and before your feet stumble upon the dark mountains, and, while ye look for light, he turn it into the* ***shadow of death*** *and make it gross darkness."*

Rebellion against God always brings darkness. Those who desire to rule or be king over their own lives will always end up *"under the shadow of death."* That's why it's important to be part of the right kingdom.

First, let's define "kingdom." It's not a democracy. It's a territory governed by an absolute ruler, the king. He makes the laws. He enforces them. Even so, a king has responsibilities to those he governs. Among them are the proper maintenance of structures like roads and bridges. He and his surrogates must also enforce laws to protect his people. And when those laws are violated, he must see that justice is done. And finally, a king must protect his kingdom from invaders, and if required, fend them off in battle, which necessitates having a sufficient army. In this way, he keeps the borders of his kingdom from being breached and overrun by hostiles.

But what about his subjects? Do they have any responsibility? Yes. It can be summed up in one word: obedience.

As mentioned in Hosea chapter thirteen, there are three spiritual kingdoms. I list them in order of power: the Kingdom of God, the Kingdom of Satan, and the Kingdom of Self. Because we have free will, it is up to us to determine under which kingdom we will live. Since God's kingdom was already covered in Hosea, I will only touch upon the Kingdom of Satan and Self.

The kingdom of Satan:

How do we know Satan has a kingdom? Because it was revealed during Jesus' temptation in the wilderness. Matthew 4:8-9 says that Satan showed Jesus, *"all the **kingdoms** of the world…and saith unto him, All these things will I give thee, if thou wilt fall down and worship me."* Jesus didn't dispute Satan's claim. He didn't say, "These kingdoms aren't yours." Rather, He said, *"It is written, thou shalt not tempt the Lord thy God."* Indeed, the Bible calls Satan *"prince of this world"* (John 12:31) and *"god of the world"* (2 Corinthians 4:4)." Make no mistake, Satan's evil and corrupt kingdom is very real. This explains why our world is so wicked and chaotic. Its systems are currently ruled by him.

The kingdom of Self:

The last and weakest kingdom is the Kingdom of Self. We need to understand that God's kingdom is more powerful than Satan's, but Satan's kingdom is more powerful than Self's. We need to understand that if "Self" is king, our kingdom is not under the provision and protection of God's kingdom and becomes easy prey for Satan's takeover. That's why Satan wants us to reign as King Self because that's the only kingdom he can defeat. Why do you think Satan tempted Eve with the promise of *"ye shall be as gods?"* He was telling her, "Eat the fruit. Do it your way. Make yourself king!"

Because of free will, we can choose whether we want God as King, Satan as King, or Self as King. James 4:7 says, *"Submit yourselves therefore to God. Resist the devil, and he will flee from you."* Submission to God indicates He is King. Joshua 24:15 says, *"choose you this day whom ye will serve."* He was telling the Israelites they were free to choose who they would serve (God, Satan, or Self). Though Satan is powerful and should not be discounted, the biggest obstacle to the Kingdom of God is the Kingdom of Self. We've already seen that Saul, Israel's first king, was an illustration of this. We also saw how miserable his life became.

Returning to Lamentations: Jeremiah, in verse 21-22, warned those heathen nations that brought Judah down, specifically Edom and Uz.

Edom, meaning red, refers to Jacob's twin brother, Esau, or to Esau's descendants. Because Esau's birthright as first born fell to Jacob, Esau hated him, thus fueling the "ancient hatred" already operating because of Ishmael's animus towards Isaac.

Esau and his descendants lived in mountainous Seir, a territory covering over a hundred miles. It was a land that enabled them to prosper due to its iron and copper mines, as well as its important intersecting trade routes. Its capital, Sela (Petra), was situated on the plateau of *Umm el-Biyara*. Esau and his clan intermarried with the indigenous Canaanites and Horites, which opened them up to gross idolatry.

Edom was eventually subdued by king David. By the time of Solomon's reign, Edom's lucrative trade routes, as well as their copper and iron mines, were under Israel's control. This increased Edom's resentment. They ultimately rebelled and regained their freedom. But in 732 B.C., Edom became a tributary of Assyria. In due time, the heavy burden levied against them stripped their wealth and resulted in their decline. In 604 B.C., they were conquered by Babylon. To their shame, they were part of Nebuchadnezzar's forces during the capture of Jerusalem in 587 B.C. Thus, Judah's own blood relatives were among those who perpetuated that slaughter and destruction.

Jeremiah singled out those Edomites dwelling in the land of Uz. Believed to be situated east of Israel bordering Arabia, specifically the *Wadi Sirhan*, Uz was once Job's home (Job 1:1). A flat plain with pastureland, it was conducive for raising livestock and could support thousands of animals due to its plenteous water supply. Their reservoirs were in the form of both wells and natural rain basins, making it a popular trade route during Biblical times.

Jeremiah went on to say that "*the cup also shall pass through unto thee* (Edom)*: thou shalt be drunken, and shalt make thyself naked.*" In modern language, he's saying "what goes around comes around." Edom will have their day in court. Although God lifted His hand of protection from Judah, enabling her enemies to oppress and destroy her, that didn't mean those enemies would escape judgement for their own sins or for their treatment of Israel. Jeremiah 49:7-22 prophesied Edom's coming judgment in incredibly harsh terms. He used words such as "calamity," "destroy," "made bare," "desolation," "reproach." Verse 12 says, *"For thus saith the LORD; Behold, they whose judgment was not to drink of the cup have assuredly drunken; and art thou he* (Edom) *that shall altogether go unpunished? thou shalt not go unpunished, but thou shalt surely drink of it."*

Ezekiel 35:5-6 confirms this. Regarding Edom's ancient hatred of Israel, it says, *"Because thou* (Seir/Edom) *hast had a* ***perpetual hatred****, and hast shed the blood of the children of Israel by the force of the sword in the time of their calamity, in the time that their iniquity had an end: Therefore, as I live, saith the Lord GOD, I will prepare thee unto blood, and blood shall pursue thee: sith thou hast not hated blood, even blood shall pursue thee."* While Judah's punishment was complete, the Edomites still had to face theirs. God would eventually punish them for their intense hatred of Israel and for shedding innocent blood by allowing others to shed theirs.

We must understand that God is holy. Our sins, as well as the sins of our nation, can provoke His anger and judgment. Both are very real. And when God is provoked, there is no remedy. Though judgment may not be immediate, it will come. Then nothing will be able to stay His wrath. Hebrews 10:31 says, *"It is a fearful thing to fall into the hands of the living God."*

Chapter 5

"Remember, O LORD, what is come upon us: consider, and behold our reproach. Our inheritance is turned to strangers, our houses to aliens. We are orphans and fatherless, our mothers are widows. We have drunken our water for money; our wood is sold unto us. Our necks are under persecution: we labour, and have no rest. We have given the hand to the Egyptians, and to the Assyrians, to be satisfied with bread." Lamentations 5:1-6

Jeremiah asked the Lord not to forget Judah. The siege was over. The results were in. The people had been shamed and lived in disgrace. Survivors had buried family and friends. Still, their oppressors showed no mercy, placing heavy yokes upon Judah's neck. Prior to this, Judah gave her "hand" to the Egyptians and Assyrians by making alliances with them against Babylon. A Hebraic idiom meaning power, it indicates that Judah had surrendered hers. Now, Judah submitted herself to Babylon's authority and pledged her loyalty just so her people wouldn't starve. Even so, her overlords forced them to purchase the water on their own land and the wood from their own trees. This taxation was probably part of the tribute Judah was forced to pay. And Judah was helpless to do anything about it. Friendless and with nowhere to turn, they were now ruled by strangers.

Continuing with the text:

"Our fathers have sinned, and are not; and we have borne their iniquities. Servants have ruled over us: there is none that doth deliver us out of their hand. We gat our bread with the peril of our lives because of the sword of the wilderness. Our skin was black like an oven because of the terrible famine." Lamentations 5:7-10

The sins of their forefathers had brought this on Judah. And yes, the sons had to bear these iniquities. But they were not guiltless. Rather, they had also filled that iniquitous cup to the level where God had to finally act. Now, instead of God ruling over them or an anointed kinsman, "servants" ruled, those installed by king Nebuchadnezzar.

Even so, the terror continued. According to Josephus, Nebuchadnezzar appointed Gedaliah governor of Judah. As the son of a moderate political family that supported and tried to protect Jeremiah, Gedaliah was seen as a minimal threat by the Babylonian king. But Gedaliah served only two months before he and other Jewish leaders, along with the Babylonian garrison, were murdered by Ishmael, a member of Judah's royal family who sought control.

Fearing a Babylonian reprisal, most of the Jews in Jerusalem migrated to Egypt for safety, forcing Jeremiah to come along. He eventually died there. Those who remained in Israel continually faced danger. When tending their crops outside the city, they were often molested or killed by Arab marauders. This, coupled with the already scarcity of food produced by Babylon's nearly thirty months of on-again-off-again siege, made the inhabitants malnourished, sickly, and gaunt.

Continuing with the text:

"They ravished the women in Zion, and the maids in the cities of Judah. Princes are hanged up by their hand: the faces of elders were not honoured. They took the young men to grind, and the children fell under the wood. The elders have ceased from the gate, the young men from their musick. The joy of our heart is ceased; our dance is turned into mourning. The crown is fallen from our head: woe unto us, that we have sinned! For this our heart is faint; for these things our eyes are dim. Because of the mountain of Zion, which is desolate, the foxes walk upon it." Lamentations 5:11-18

Jeremiah lamented the horrific atrocities committed against his people. Women were raped. Princes (*sar,* leaders, chieftains) were impaled (hanged by their hand), meaning their bodies were driven through with a spike anchored to the ground. Impalement, the instrument of a repulsive but quick death, was the forerunner of crucifixion. According to the *World History Encyclopedia,* ancient Egyptian hieroglyphics indicate it was practiced by pharaohs from Sobekhotep II to Merneptah (son of Ramesses II), a period covering 1800 B.C. to 1203 B.C. It was also described in the Babylonian Code of Hammurabi (1755-1750 B.C.) indicating that this practice carried over into the Assyrian, Babylonian, and later Persian Empires. Inscriptions show that Sennacherib, the Assyrian king, used impalement in 701 B.C. as a means of terrifying any would-be rebel after his conquest of Jewish Lachish. Now, Babylon used it to punish Judah's chiefs as a warning against further rebellion.

Even the elderly, once sought for their advice or approval, were not respected. They no longer sit at the gate dispensing wisdom. The young men, the pride and future of Judah, were humiliated by being forced to grind meal, traditionally a woman's job. In this same way, the Philistines humiliated

Samson almost 460 years earlier. Children crumbled under the hard labor they were forced to endure. No one sang. No one danced. All was sadness and despair. From being God's intended "head of nations," Judah was now powerless and disparaged; her people, defeated, weak, and hopeless.

It's interesting to note that while there was plenty of mourning and an acknowledgement that their calamity was the result of sin, no mention was made that Judah, either her remaining elites or common people, repented on a national level. Thus, foxes now walked in their holy city. While fox in Hebrew (*shuwal)* means "fox," it more often means "jackal." According to *Webster*, jackals are animals that hunt in packs. But that word can also negatively refer to a person, indicating he is cruel and underhanded. Therefore, a double meaning emerges. Judah had become like a pack of jackals, unrighteous in their cruelty and deceit. Now, they were oppressed by jackals, conquerors who were even crueler and more underhanded.

David, when praying about the wicked, said in Psalm 63:10, *"They shall fall by the sword: they shall be a* ***portion*** *for* ***foxes****."* Portion (*menath*) means "allotment. *The Theological Wordbook of the Old Testament* goes further and says it can mean "a portion of the sacrifice; to be prey for jackals." The *Wordbook* further states that David, in his prayer, was not only requesting a "violent death" for the wicked, but that they would be "a sacrifice (portion) for the wild beasts." And that's just what happened. Jackal-like Judah had become a portion, a sacrifice for jackal-like Babylon.

Continuing with the text:

"Thou, O LORD, remainest for ever, thy throne from generation to generation. Wherefore dost thou forget us for ever, and forsake us so

long time? Turn thou us unto thee, O LORD, and we shall be turned; renew our days as of old. But thou hast utterly rejected us; thou art very wroth against us." Lamentations 5:19-22

Jeremiah ended his lamentation by exalting God. Though Judah's kingdom had come to an end, God's kingdom never would. His throne is everlasting. Then Jeremiah asked God why He had forgotten them and left them for so long. It's a rhetorical question. He knew God was still their God, that He still loved His people based on His promise to restore them. But Jeremiah also knew his people were stiff necked and needed God's wooing if they are to return (*"turn thou us unto thee)."* He also knew that his people must turn back to God before He would turn back to them. They needed to repent and live according to God's laws as they once had.

Jeremiah ended by acknowledging the reality of God's anger, knowing that it, too, will have an end.

Conclusion:

What a saga! It's a picture of the just and inescapable ending of those who spurn God. Being in the presence of God brings fullness of joy (Psalm 16:11). His absence brings dimness and sorrow. Jeremiah described the misery of Judah's destruction following years of sin and willful disregard of God's warnings to repent. While God's love is amazing and deep, His anger and wrath are just as amazing and deep. And His holiness requires satisfaction in the face of unrepentant sin.

Though Jeremiah understood the reason and even the necessity for God to level Judah, his tender heart caused him to deeply lament the outcome. He mourned Judah's fall from her exalted position to become the contempt of the world. His firsthand witness of the carnage made him deeply depressed and, at times, seem to forget God's promise of restoration. But in the end, he acknowledged that God's actions were both just and deserved, and prayed for His forgiveness.

God's first choice is always mercy. And He extends it freely to those who come to Him with a repentant heart. No matter how low we sink, He is always willing to forgive.

Joel

Chapter 1

The name "Joel" means "Yahweh is God." A common name in Israel, it included the name of the prophet Samuel's eldest son, as well as a prince in Simeon's tribe, some chiefs in the tribes of Gad, Issachar, Manasseh, Levi, and one of king David's mighty men.

Due to the mention of Jerusalem's Temple and the priesthood, most scholars believe Joel was a prophet to the southern kingdom at a time when apostasy was rampant. Some put this around 830 B.C. Others put it somewhere between the 9th to 5th century B.C. Because so little is known about Joel and because no specific historical references are mentioned in the text, scholars are unable to accurately establish a timeline. Even so, Joel's ministry applies as much today as it did prior to the advent of Christ, therefore I've saved it for last.

Now going to the text:

"The word of the LORD that came to Joel the son of Pethuel. Hear this ye old men, and give ear, all ye inhabitants of the land. Hath this been in your days, or even in the days of your fathers? Tell ye your children of it, and let your children tell their children, and their children another generation. That which the palmerworm hath left

hath the locust eaten; and that which the locust hath left hath the cankerworm eaten; and that which the cankerworm hath left hath the caterpiller eaten." Joel 1:1-4

We are told right from the start that this is a word from God, not from man. The fact that Joel's father, Pethuel, was mentioned establishes a family connection that was undoubtedly known at that time. Pethuel means "vision of God" or "enlarged of God." *The Septuagint* claims his name was Bathuel, meaning "house of God" or "man of God," further indicating Pethuel was a godly man, someone who received divine revelations. Thus, a spiritual connection is indicated, pointing to an anointed family who loved and followed Yahweh.

It's addressed to the elders or rulers (*ye old men*) and general population (*all ye inhabitants of the land)*. Judgment had come! And it was so harsh the people are admonished to emblaze it into their collective memory by reminding their children and children's children about it.

The disaster was in the form of an incredibly destructive insect plague, one never seen before. The above verses list this catastrophe in order. First came the palmerworm or cutting locust. Then the swarming locust. Next, the cankerworm or destroying locust. And finally, the caterpillar. Each one devouring what the other left.

This is a picture of the utter devastation of their nation's fields and crops. Such plagues were always believed to come from the hand of God. Exodus chapter ten is an example when God unleashes the eighth plague of devouring locusts on Egypt. It's interesting that Moses was also instructed to tell the people and their progeny of this calamity. *"And that thou* (Moses)

mayest tell in the ears of thy son, and of thy son's son*, what things I have wrought in Egypt, and my signs which I have done among them; that ye may know how that I am the LORD,"* (Exodus 10:2).

There's no reason to believe Joel's account was not the description of an actual plague occurring sometime in Judah's history. However, I believe it also has prophetic significance and points to the time of Jacob's Trouble or seven-year Tribulation, which will also be a time never seen before.

Continuing with the text:

"Awake, ye drunkards, and weep; and howl, all ye drinkers of wine, because of the new wine; for it is cut off from your mouth. For a nation is come up upon my land, strong, and without number, whose teeth are the teeth of a lion, and he hath the cheek teeth (molars) *of a great lion. He hath laid my vine waste, and barked my fig tree: he hath made it clean bare, and cast it away; the branches thereof are made white. Lament like a virgin girded with sackcloth for the husband of her youth. The meat offering and the drink offering is cut off from the house of the LORD; the priests, the LORD'S ministers, mourn. The field is wasted, the land mourneth; for the corn is wasted: the new wine is dried up, the oil languisheth. Be ye ashamed, O ye* ***husbandmen****; howl, O ye* ***vinedressers****, for the wheat and for the barley; because the harvest of the field is perished. The vine is dried up, and the fig tree languisheth; the pomegranate tree, the palm tree also, and the apple tree, even all the trees of the field, are withered: because joy is withered away from the sons of men. Gird yourselves, and lament, ye priests: howl, ye ministers of the altar: come, lie all night in sackcloth, ye ministers of my* (Joel's) *God: for the meat offering and the drink offering is withholden from the house of your God."* Joel 1:5-13

There is so much here. God was telling His people to "wake up." They had become self-indulgent (drunkards), corrupt, and foolish. Wine was forbidden a priest before he was scheduled to minister in the Temple (Leviticus 10:9). Some scholars believe Joel was referring to the conduct of the priests who became drunk before performing their duties.

I see no reason to doubt this, but I also believe it refers to the southern kingdom of Judah as a whole, to their moral and spiritual decay. Proverbs 26:9 says, *"As a thorn goeth up into the hand of a* ***drunkard****, so is a parable in the mouth of fools."* As a nation, they had become oblivious (drunken) to the dangers around them. Symbolically, they couldn't even feel a thorn when jammed into their hands. They had become so inebriated with their own importance, success, and prosperity that they didn't see the danger of losing God's favor and His coming judgment. Or that one day, the lion, Babylon, would rip them with his teeth. That their land would be decimated. And as a sign of their desolation, there would be no new wine for the people to enjoy.

"He hath laid ***my vine*** *waste, and barked* ***my fig tree****; the branches thereof are made white."* Israel is God's fig tree. And Israel was His vine. Psalm 80:8-9 refers to this: *"Thou* (God) *hast brought a* ***vine*** *out of Egypt: thou hast cast out the heathen* (from the Promised Land), *and planted it* (His vine, Israel). *Thou preparedst room before it, and didst cause it to take deep root, and it filled the land."*

Psalm 80:12-16 prophetically described what would happen after Israel turns from God. *"Why hast thou then broken down her* (Israel's) *hedges, so that all they which pass by the way do pluck her? The boar out of the wood doth waste it, and the wild beast of the field doth devour it. Return, we beseech thee, O God of hosts: look down from heaven, and behold, and visit this* ***vine****; And the vineyard which thy right hand hath planted, and the branch that thou madest strong for thyself. It is burned with fire, it is cut down: they perish at the rebuke of thy countenance."*

Jeremiah, the weeping prophet, endlessly prophesied against Judah and foretold the coming Babylonian conquest. In Jeremiah 2:21, he broadcasted God's indictment against them. *"Yet I had planted thee a* ***noble vine****, wholly a right seed: how then art thou turned into the* ***degenerate plant*** *of a strange vine unto me."* Drunken Judah had become a *"degenerate plant,"* one God would rip out of the soil before He could replant. And that meant He would keep Judah in Babylonian captivity for seventy years.

Even so, Malachi 3:11 gave this future promise: *"And I will rebuke the devourer for your sakes, and he shall not destroy the fruits of your ground; neither shall your vine cast her fruit before the time in the field, saith the LORD of hosts."* Instead of a locust-ravaged land, stripped of everything good, God would once again restore and prosper Israel.

But the prophetic message is clear and mirrors Matthew 24:37-38 where Jesus described the last days and the signs of His second coming. *"But as the days of Noe* (Noah) *were, so shall also the coming of the Son of man be. For as in the days that were before the flood they were eating and drinking, marrying and giving in marriage, until the day that Noe entered into the ark."*

Like foolish drunkards, the people of Judah were oblivious to the judgment that would come upon them. They went about their lives as if nothing was wrong. And just as those unprepared people in Noah's day were swept away by the flood, so were the people of Judah. And so will those who fail to heed the Lord's warning in the last days. They, too, will be swept into the seven-year Tribulation. In all three, the pattern is the same: godless obtuse rebels will be swept away and destroyed.

And just as Israel was Yahweh's vine, a vine which was to display His love, statutes, and goodness to the pagan nations, so Jesus, our vine, displays God the Father's love, statutes, and goodness to a dying world. And we, as His branches, are to reflect Him as His ambassadors. Jesus, in John 15:1, 5-6, said, *"I am the true **vine,** and my Father is the husbandman.... I am the **vine,** ye are the branches. He that abideth in me, and I in him, the same bringeth forth much fruit: for without me ye can do nothing. If a man abide not in me, he is cast forth as a branch, and is withered; and men gather them, and cast them into the fire, and they are burned."*

And just as Israel failed to become that *"noble vine"* in Jeremiah 2:21, and was destroyed, if we do not attach ourselves to the Vine of heaven instead of the "vine of the earth," we will also be destroyed. *"And another angel came out from the altar, which had power over fire; and cried with a loud cry to him that had the sharp sickle, saying, Thrust in thy sharp sickle, and gather the clusters of the **vine of the earth**; for her grapes are fully ripe. And the angel thrust in his sickle into the earth, and gathered the **vine of the earth**, and cast it into the great winepress of the wrath of God,"* (Revelation 14: 18-19).

There is one more symbol I'd like to discuss. It's Babylon's great teeth and how he comes as a devouring locust. As mentioned, this happened in 587 B.C. But it is also prophetic and points to the seven-year Tribulation. During that time, another devouring "locust" will be allowed to plague those who have refused to attach themselves to the Vine and have taken the mark of the beast. Revelation 9:3, 7-8 gives a horrifying description of these demonic entities. *"And there came out of the smoke* ***locusts*** *upon the earth: and unto them was given power, as the scorpions of the earth have power. . .. And the shapes of the* ***locusts*** *were like unto horses prepared unto battle; and on their heads were as it were crowns like gold, and their faces were as the faces of men, And they had hair as the hair of women, and* ***their teeth were as the teeth of lions.****"*

In Joel, God called His people to *"Lament like a virgin girded with sackcloth for the* ***husband*** *of her youth."* God had been Israel's Husband in her youth. *"For thy Maker is thine* ***husband****; the LORD of hosts is his name; and thy Redeemer the Holy One of Israel; The God of the whole earth shall he be called,"* (Isaiah 54:5. But they abandoned Him and turned to Baal, making him their "husband."

Even so, had Israel repented, God would have forgiven her, and she wouldn't have been afflicted by Babylon. But during the seven-year Tribulation this will change when a remnant of Jews return to God and accept Jesus as their Messiah. At that time, Hosea 2:19 tells us what will happen. *"And I* (God) *will betroth thee* (Israel) *unto me for ever; yea, I will betroth thee unto me in righteousness, and in judgment, and in lovingkindness, and in mercies."*

Joel described the lack of sacrifices in the Temple. The famine had made that impossible. The land had been ravaged; the corn, new wine, and oil *"languisheth."* That word is *"amal"* meaning to droop, be exhausted."

But notice what Joel said about the wheat and barley. They had "perished." It's *abad* in Hebrew and means "destroyed," meaning there was none to be had. In addition to this being historical, it again has prophetic applications. A famine occurred after the Babylonian siege of Jerusalem in 587 B.C. And it will occur again during the time of Jacob's Trouble. That famine will be so severe it will cost a day's pay to purchase a *"measure of wheat"* or *"three measures of barley,"* (Revelation 6:6). A measure is about what it takes to make one loaf of bread.

Then Joel mentioned that *"the vine is dried up, and the fig tree languisheth."* Isreal, the *"degenerate vine,"* the *"fig tree,"* had been cut off. Any plant severed from its roots will always dry up and die.

Also affected were the pomegranate, palm, and apple trees, and *"all the trees of the field."* They were withered. That word 'withered" is *yabesh* and means "become dry, wither, to be ashamed, confused." What does that imply?

Let's look at each.

Pomegranate: It was known for its upright growth as well as its fragrance and delicious fruit. Judah had become bent in her ways. No longer following God, she ceased to be upright and was steeped in immorality and idolatry. Thus, she produced unacceptable fruit. And instead of a pleasing fragrance, she became a stench in God's nostrils. Jeremiah 6:20 alluded to this. *"To what purpose cometh there to me incense from Sheba, and the sweet cane from a far country? your burnt offerings are not acceptable, nor your sacrifices sweet unto me."*

Palm tree: According to the *Theological Wordbook of the Old Testament,* palm trees were "among the tallest and most graceful of all trees found in the Middle East. . .. They were used as landmarks, for shade and food. Some considered them as 'trees of life." Psalm 92:12-14, *"The righteous shall flourish like the palm* ***tree:*** *he shall grow like a cedar in Lebanon. Those that be planted in the house of the LORD shall flourish in the courts of our*

God. They shall still bring forth ***fruit*** *in old age; they shall be fat and flourishing."* No longer tall and graceful, unrighteous Judah had withered. She had ceased to be a landmark that pointed to God or His goodness, becoming instead as filthy and evil as the pagan nations that surrounded her.

Apple tree: This tree was known for its fragrance as well as its nourishing fruit. Just as believers are to be a *"sweet savor of Christ"* (2 Corinthians 2:15) so Israel was to be a sweet savor of Yahweh. Now, she was neither sweet nor nourishing.

All the trees in the field: Scripture talks about how trees produce either good or bad fruit. This refers to produce and the fruit of our body (Deuteronomy 28:4) as well as the fruit produced by our actions as seen in the following Scriptures:

- Proverbs 11:30 comes right out and says, *"The* ***fruit*** *of the righteous is a* ***tree*** *of life."*
- And Proverbs 8:19 says, regarding spiritual fruit, *"My* ***fruit*** *is better than gold, yea, than fine gold; and my revenue than choice silver."*
- Proverbs 10:16b says that while the labor/fruit of the righteous tends to life, *"the* ***fruit*** *of the wicked* (tends) *to sin."*

Because Judah produced "bad fruit," she was no longer acceptable to God or useful as an example to the world.

Notice, Joel 1:11 singled out the husbandmen and vinedressers and said they should be ashamed (*Be ye ashamed*). These were the tenders of the fields, in charge of production and harvest. But they hadn't done their job. I liken them to the spiritual watchmen on the wall who were supposed to watch over the people and alert them at the first sign of danger.

Today, these husbandmen and vinedressers are those in ministry, especially our pastors. I have talked about their failures in several of my books and won't do it now. But suffice it to say, many who are supposed to minister to the flock, watch over them, and fight against heresy, etcetera, have failed miserably. Today, too few churches preach the full council of God, preferring instead not to offend anyone in order to keep their attendance high and their offering plates full. One day, they will have to answer to God.

But that doesn't mean individual believers are exempt. We, too, will have to answer to God if we stay in dead or worldly churches instead of seeking one faithful to Scripture and one not afraid of addressing current moral issues.

Joel ended this section by telling priests and ministers to lament and mourn because the daily Temple sacrifices had ceased. While historically accurate, it is again prophetic. Sometime in the future, a third Temple will be built in Jerusalem only to be desecrated during the midpoint of the seven-year Tribulation. That's when the antichrist will cause all sacrifices to cease. Daniel 9:27 describes this event. *"And he* (the anti-Christ) *shall confirm the covenant with many for one week* (a *shabuwa* or period of seven, especially a week of years or seven years): *and* ***in the midst of the week he shall cause the sacrifice and oblation to cease****, and for the overspreading of abominations he shall make it desolate, even until the consummation, and that determined shall be poured upon the desolate."*

Continuing with the text:

"Sanctify ye a fast, call a solemn assembly, gather the elders and all the inhabitants of the land into the house of the LORD your God, and cry unto the LORD. Alas, for the day! for the day of the LORD is at

hand, and as a destruction from the Almighty shall it come. Is not the meat cut off before our eyes, yea, joy and gladness from the house of our God? The seed is rotten under their clods, the garners are laid desolate, the barns are broken down; for the corn is withered. How do the beasts groan! the herds of cattle are perplexed, because they have no pasture; yea, the flocks of sheep are made desolate. O LORD, to thee will I cry: for the fire hath devoured the pastures of the wilderness, and the flame hath burned all the trees of the field. The beasts of the field cry also unto thee: for the rivers of waters are dried up, and the fire hath devoured the pastures of the wilderness."
Joel 1:14-20

Conditions were so dire there was a call to fast. Drought and famine had devastated the land. People, as well as livestock, were starving. Garners (*owtsar*) (storehouses) were empty. Is that because they had failed to bring their tithes and offerings into God's storehouse? Perhaps. It's notable that almost 190 years later, Malachi will criticize Isreal for this very failure. *"Will a man rob God. Yet ye have robbed me. But ye say, Wherein have we robbed thee? In tithes and offerings. Ye are cursed with a curse: for ye have robbed me, even this whole nation. Bring ye all the tithes into the* ***storehouse****, that there may be meat in mine house, and prove me now herewith, saith the LORD of hosts, if I will not open you the windows of heaven, and pour you out a blessing, that there shall not be room enough to receive it,"* (Malachi 3:8-10).

Judah was certainly cursed, perhaps partly due to the fact that for decades they had been more concerned with their own storehouses rather than God's. They were also like the man in Jesus' parable. *"The ground of a certain rich man brought forth plentifully: And he thought within himself, saying, What shall I do, because I have no room where to bestow my fruits? And he said, This will I do: I will pull down my barns, and build greater; and there will I bestow all my fruits and my goods. And I will say to my soul, Soul, thou hast much goods laid up for many years; take thine ease, eat, drink, and be merry. But God said unto him, Thou fool, this night thy soul shall be required of thee: then whose shall those things be, which thou has provided?"* (Luke 12:16-20)

Like this rich man, Judah's wealth and prosperity went to her head. She thought she had secured her future by making deals with pagan nations and serving fertility gods to ensure bountiful harvests. Now, her soul was required. Instead of full barns, her people would have to scour the land for scraps.

And note, *"the fire hath devoured the pastures of the wilderness, and the flame hath burned all the trees of the field."* Fire is *esh* in Hebrew. According to the *Theological Wordbook of the Old Testament,* it's used "in context to either God's revelation of himself to man or man's approach to God through worship and sacrifice." This revelation of God can come like the fire on top of Mt. Sinai when Moses went up to receive the commandments or it can reveal God as fiery judgment on Sodom and Gomorrah. Here, in Joel, it was revealed as fire devouring pastures and trees. And everyone knew that it was all *"as a **destruction from the Almighty**."* Isaiah prophesied this very thing. *"Howl ye; for **the day of the LORD** is at hand; it shall come as a **destruction from the Almighty**,"* (Isaiah 13:6).

Though Joel spoke of the terrible times he witnessed, like Isaiah, he was also speaking of a time even more terrible. Both were specifically talking about the day of the Lord, the seven-year Tribulation. Because God is merciful, He never administers judgment without first notifying His prophets. Amos 3:7 makes that clear. *"Surely the Lord GOD will do nothing, but he revealeth his secret unto his servants the prophets."*

It's interesting to note that when Jesus opened the scroll of Isaiah and began reading chapter 61 in order to announce His ministry, He stopped after proclaiming that this was the acceptable year of the Lord, meaning the Age of Grace. Omitted was the rest of that sentence: *"and the day of vengeance of our God."* Why? Because that applies to the day of the Lord and His second coming.

There are numerous Scriptures foretelling the day of the Lord. Other references alluding to that time include the phrases "that day," "those times," "latter days," "time of the end," "last days," or "the day of wrath." I list some below. They are, by no means, the only ones.

- Isaiah 13:9, *"Behold,* ***the day of the LORD cometh****, cruel both with wrath and fierce anger, to lay the land desolate: and he shall destroy the sinners thereof out of it."*
- Jeremiah 30:7, *"Alas! for* ***that day*** (the day of the Lord) *is great, so that none is like it: it is even the time of Jacob's trouble; but he shall be saved out of it."*
- Zephaniah 1:7, *"Hold thy peace at the presence of the Lord GOD: for* ***the day of the LORD is at hand****: for the LORD hath prepared a sacrifice, he hath bid his guests. And it shall come to pass in the day of the LORD'S sacrifice, that I will punish the princes, and the king's children, and all such as are clothed with strange apparel."*
- Amos 5:18, *"Woe unto you that desire* ***the day of the LORD****! to what end is it for you? the day of the LORD is darkness, and not light."*
- Malachi 4:5, *"Behold, I will send you Elijah the prophet before the coming of the great and dreadful* ***day of the LORD****."*
- Matthew 24, Jesus describes this day. In verse 21, He says, *"For then shall be great tribulation, such as was not since the beginning of the world to this time, no, nor ever shall be."*

- 2 Corinthians 1:14: Peter says he will be proud of the Corinthian church in the **day of the Lord Jesus**, which includes the Rapture and the Bema Seat judgment when rewards are given to believers.
- 1 Thessalonians 5:2, *"For yourselves know perfectly that* ***the day of the Lord*** *so cometh as a thief in the night."*
- 2 Peter 3:10, *"But* ***the day of the Lord*** *will come as a thief in the night; in the which the heavens shall pass away with a great noise, and the elements shall melt with fervent heat, the earth also and the works that are therein shall be burned up."* This includes the creation of the new heaven and earth.
- Revelation 6:17, *"For* ***the great day of his wrath*** *is come; and who shall be able to stand?"*
- Isaiah 2:2, *"And it shall come to pass in* ***the last days****, that the mountain of the LORD'S house shall be established in the top of the mountains, and shall be exalted above the hills; and all nations shall flow unto it."*

We can see from the above Scriptures that the day of the Lord will be both terrible and wonderful. For Jews, it heralds the coming of the Messiah, and these are the birth pains preceding it. For a Christian, I believe the day of the Lord refers to a series of events, beginning with the end of the Church Age or Rapture and culminating in the creation of the new heaven and earth. In between are the Tribulation, Jesus' millennial reign, and the white throne judgment. The Tribulation will be covered at the end of this book.

Chapter 2

"Blow ye the trumpet in Zion, and sound an alarm in my holy mountain: let all the inhabitants of the land tremble: for ***the day of the LORD*** *cometh, for it is nigh at hand; A day of darkness and of gloominess, a day of clouds and of thick darkness, as the morning spread upon the mountains:* ***a great people*** *and a strong; there hath not been ever the like, neither shall be any more after it, even to the years of many generations. A fire devoureth before them; and behind them a flame burneth: the land is as the garden of Eden before them, and behind them a desolate wilderness; yea, and nothing shall escape them. The appearance of them is as the appearance of horses; and as horsemen, so shall they run. Like the noise of chariots on the tops of mountains shall they leap, like the noise of a flame of fire that devoureth the* ***stubble****, as a strong people set in battle array. Before their face the people shall be much pained: all faces shall gather blackness."* Joel 2:1-6

Blowing the trumpet, whether the silver long horned trumpet or the ram's horn, could both be sounded in war. But here, Joel specifically referred to a ram's horn which was sounded at the first sign of danger. He was warning his people. In chapter one, he described a horrendous plague of locusts and their ensuing destruction. Then he inlayed a prophetic warning that something even worse would come, namely the day of the Lord.

Joel continued the theme by describing this future time as one of darkness and gloom. Instead of insects, the locust are now described as an army of *"great people."* Aside from the connection to the Babylonian army as already mentioned, this points to the Tribulation and the armies found in Revelation 9:1-12, 16. Verse 7 says, *"And the shapes of the locusts were like unto horses prepared unto battle."* While verse 16, speaking of a second army, numbers the horsemen: *"And the number of the army of the horsemen were two hundred thousand thousand: and I heard the number of them."* They will be like a devouring fire, destroying everything in their path, even the stubble or what's left after everything else has been destroyed.

Isaiah 5:24 also warned about this. *"Therefore as the fire devoureth the* ***stubble****, and the flame consumeth the chaff, so their root* (of the wicked) *shall be as rottenness, and their blossom shall go up as dust: because they have cast away the law of the LORD of hosts, and despised the word of the Holy One of Israel."*

The devastation, horror, and terror will be beyond imagination. *"Before their face the people shall be much pained: all faces shall gather blackness."* People will become pale from fright (*gather blackness*). Blackness is also associated with starvation, sickness, and disease. Additionally, it's a Hebrew idiom meaning "all faces shall be ashamed, confused." Thus, shame and confusion are added to the mix. I believe these things will be perpetrated by demonic armies. Nothing like them has ever been seen before nor will be again.

Continuing with the text:

"They shall run like mighty men; they shall climb the wall like men of war; and they shall march everyone on his ways, and they shall not break their ranks: Neither shall one thrust another; they shall walk

every one in his path: and when they fall upon the sword, they shall not be wounded. They shall run to and fro in the city; they shall run upon the wall, they shall climb up upon the houses; they shall enter in at the windows like a thief. The earth shall quake before them; the heavens shall tremble: the sun and the moon shall be dark, and the stars shall withdraw their shining: And the LORD shall utter his voice before ***his army****: for his camp is very great: for he is strong that executeth his word: for* ***the day of the LORD*** *is great and very terrible; and who can abide it?"* Joel 2:7-11

Joel continued to describe this demonic army. They *"run like mighty men."* That word "mighty" is *gibbowr,* meaning "powerful, warrior, tyrant, valiant man." It's the same word used in Genesis 6:4 when describing the Nephilim, those human-angelic hybrids who terrorized the world before the flood.

They are a disciplined force and will *"not break their ranks."* That's an interesting phrase indicating this army will not leave their assigned path. Ranks (*orach*) means a "well-trodden road, caravan, path." But "break" (*abat*) has added meaning, including "to pawn, borrow, break, lend, take or give a pledge for a debt." This army, though it is demonic, is under the command of God. *"And the LORD shall utter his voice before* ***his army****."* Perhaps in order to escape the abyss for a while, this demonic army has pledged to do God's bidding. At any rate, they will terrorize the world while under God's control.

Notice, there is no place they are unable to enter: up walls, over houses, through windows. No one is safe. And there is nowhere to hide. They are unstoppable (*they shall not be wounded*).

Revelation 9:2-4 describes the unleashing of this army. *"And he* (an angel) *opened the bottomless pit; and there arose a smoke out of the pit, as the smoke of a great furnace; and the sun and the air were darkened by reason of the smoke of the pit. And there came out of the smoke locusts upon the earth: and unto them was given power, as the scorpions of the earth have power.* ***And it was commanded them*** *that they should not hurt the grass of the earth, neither any green thing, neither any tree; but only those men which have not the seal of God in their foreheads."* Notice, this army can't do just anything they want, again indicating they are controlled by God.

This is just one of the horrors of the day of the Lord. Isaiah 26:20-21 also refers to this day. ***"Come, my people, enter thou into thy chambers, and shut thy doors about thee: hide thyself as it were for a little moment, until the indignation be overpast.*** *For, behold, the LORD cometh out of his place to punish the inhabitants of the earth for their iniquity: the earth also shall disclose her blood, and shall no more cover her slain."* Here, reference is made to the Rapture of God's people prior to the Tribulation. It also reveals a purpose for this terrible seven-year period, that of punishing the wicked on earth.

Isaiah 34:1-4, 8 gives added details. *"Come near, ye nations, to hear; and harken, ye people: let the earth hear, and all that is therein; the world, and all things that come forth of it. For the indignation of the LORD is upon all nations, and his fury upon all their armies: he hath utterly destroyed them, he hath delivered them to the slaughter. Their slain also shall be cast out, and their stink shall come up out of their carcases, and the mountains shall be melted with their blood. And all the host of heaven shall be dissolved, and the heavens shall be rolled together as a scroll: and all their host shall fall down, as the leaf falleth off from the* ***vine****, and as a falling fig from the* ***fig tree****. ... For it is the day of the LORD'S vengeance, and the year of recompences for the controversy of Zion."*

Note, this will be a time when God deals with all the nations as well as Israel, His vine and fig tree.

Continuing with the text:

"Therefore also now, saith the LORD, Turn ye even to me with all your heart, and with fasting, and with weeping, and with mourning: And ***rend your heart, and not your garments****, and turn unto the LORD your God: for he is gracious and merciful, slow to anger, and of great kindness, and repenteth him of the evil. Who knoweth if he will return and repent, and leave a blessing behind him; even a meat offering and a drink offering unto the LORD your God? Blow the trumpet in Zion, sanctify a fast, call a solemn assembly: Gather the people, sanctify the congregation, assemble the elders, gather the children, and those that suck the breasts: let the bridegroom go forth of his chamber, and the bride out of her closet. Let the priest, the ministers of the LORD, weep between the porch and the altar, and let them say, Spare thy people, O LORD, and give not thine heritage to reproach, that the heathen should rule over them: wherefore should they say among the people, Where is their God?"* Joel 2:12-17

Joel's message was clearly one of repentance. Because God is merciful and loving, it wasn't too late. If Judah repented, they would be spared. It was common practice during mourning to show one's grief by tearing his garments. But that wasn't good enough. God wanted a rending or circumcision of the heart, (*"rend your heart, and not your garments"*).

We've already seen that Isaiah 26:20 referred to both the Rapture and Tribulation. Joel pointed to the time when the Tribulation was over, a time when a remnant of Israel will repent, accept Jesus as their Messiah, and be restored as head of nations. Zechariah 8:23 points to this: *"Thus saith the LORD of hosts; In those days* (after the Tribulation and during the millennial reign of Christ*) it shall come to pass, that ten men shall take hold out of all languages of the nations, even shall take hold of* *the skirt of him that is a Jew, saying, We will go with you: for we have heard that God is with you."*

Continuing with the text:

"Then will the LORD be jealous for his land, and pity his people. Yea, the LORD will answer and say unto his people, Behold, I will send you corn, and wine, and oil, and ye shall be satisfied therewith: and I will no more make you a reproach among the heathen: But I will remove far off from you the northern army, and will drive him into a land barren and desolate, with his face toward the east sea, and his hinder part toward the utmost sea, and his stink shall come up, and his ill savour shall come up, because ***he had done great things****. Fear not, O land; be glad and rejoice: for the* ***LORD will do great things****."* Joel 2:18-21

Both Assyria and Babylon came from the north. Assyria conquered Israel, the northern kingdom. Babylon conquered Judah, the southern kingdom. Ezekiel 38 talks about a future northern invasion when Iran, Russia, Turkey, and an assortment of other nations will again come against Israel. But they will be utterly defeated by God, Himself. Then, toward the end of the Tribulation, nations again come against Israel. And again, they will be destroyed by God/Jesus when He appears on a white horse. A great stench will arise from this destruction. Revelation says the blood from this slaughter will come up to the horses' bridles (Revelation 14:20). After this, no nation will ever bother Israel again.

Notice, although the world's kingdoms have tried to wipe Israel out *("he had done great things")* God does even greater things (*the Lord will do great things*) because in the end, these nations will not survive, yet Israel does.

Daniel 2:35 tells us what will become of these nations. *"Then was the iron, the clay, the brass, the silver, and the gold, broken to pieces together, and became like the chaff of the summer threshing floors; and the wind carried them away, that no place was found for them: and the* ***stone*** *that smote the image became a great mountain, and filled the whole earth."* This refers to Nebuchadnezzar's dream statue which represented those nations that would be Israel's overlords. It begins with the last kingdom, the revived Roman Empire, which is yet to come, and ends with gold or Nebuchadnezzar's empire. In between are the iron or Roman Empire, the brass or Greek Empire, the silver or Medo-Persian Empire.

But who is the stone? Isaiah 8:14, speaking of Jesus, says, *"And he shall be for a sanctuary; but for a* ***stone*** *of stumbling and for a rock of offence to both the houses of Israel, for a gin and for a snare to the inhabitants of Jerusalem."* And Isaiah 28:16 says, *"Therefore thus saith the Lord GOD, Behold, I lay in Zion for a foundation a* ***stone****, a tried* ***stone****, a precious corner* ***stone****, a sure foundation: he that believeth shall not make haste."* Yes, Jesus is that tried and precious stone!

Continuing with the text:

"Be not afraid, ye beasts of the field: for the pastures of the wilderness do spring, for the tree beareth her fruit, the ***fig tree*** *and the* ***vine*** *do yield their strength. Be glad then, ye children of Zion, and rejoice in the LORD your God: for he hath given you the former rain moderately, and he will cause to come down for you the rain, the former rain, and the latter rain in the first month. And the floors shall be full of wheat, and the fats shall overflow with wine and oil. And I will restore to you the years that the locust hath eaten, the cankerworm, and the caterpillar, and the palmerworm,* ***my great army*** *which I sent among you. And ye shall eat in plenty, and be*

satisfied, and praise the name of the LORD your God, that hath dealt wondrously with you: and my people shall never be ashamed. And ye shall know that I am in the midst of Israel, and that I am the LORD your God, and none else: and my people shall never be ashamed." Joel 2:22-27

Although in 1948 we saw Israel restored in part, God will restore her completely in the future, returning everything she lost. (*I will restore to you the years that the locust hath eaten*). Notice, Joel mentioned the locust, cankerworm, caterpillar, and palmerworm, the very plagues God sent in chapter 1:4. God called them *"my great army,"* again indicating He was in control. And that word "restore" is *shalam*, meaning not only to be "safe in mind, body or estate," but "to make complete, friendly." Israel will be complete as a nation and enjoy God's friendship.

He also said that after this restoration, His people *"shall never be ashamed."* And He said this twice, driving home the point that this is in total contrast to the fact that during most of their history Israel ***was*** "ashamed."

Whereas Joel chapter one began in gloom, heralding the terrible day of the Lord, chapter two focuses on the wonderful end of that terrible day. It also mentioned Israel's former and latter rains which are needed to ensure bountiful crops. Thus, God was assuring them of an abundant and prosperous future. But these rains also symbolically point to the promised outpouring of the Holy Spirit.

Continuing with the text:

"And it shall come to pass afterward, that ***I will pour out my spirit upon all flesh****, and your sons and your daughters shall prophesy,*

your old men shall dream dreams, your young men shall see visions. And also upon the servant and upon the handmaids in those days will I pour out my spirit." Joel 2:28-29

God has been pouring out His Spirit for almost 2000 years. It's called the Church Age. After the baptism of the Holy Spirit at Pentecost, when the people thought the disciples were drunk, Peter told them, *"But this is that which was spoken by the prophet Joel; And it shall come to pass in the last days saith God, I will pour out of my Spirit upon all flesh: and your sons and your daughters shall prophesy, and your young men shall see visions, and your old men shall dream dreams. And on my servants and on my handmaidens I will pour out in those days of my Spirit; and they shall prophesy,"* (Acts 2:16-18).

But this outpouring will continue even after the Church Age ends. It will be poured out in double measure during the Tribulation when millions upon millions will come to the Lord. And according to Zechariah 12:10, there will be a special outpouring over God's people, Israel.

Continuing with the text:

"And I will shew wonders in the heavens and in the earth, blood, and fire, and pillars of smoke. The sun shall be turned into darkness, and the moon into blood, before the great and the terrible day of the LORD come. And it shall come to pass, that whosoever shall call on the name of the LORD shall be delivered: for in mount Zion and in Jerusalem shall be deliverance, as the LORD hath said, and in the remnant whom the LORD shall call." Joel 2:30-32

Acts 2:19-21 repeats this: *"And I will shew wonders in heaven above, and signs in the earth beneath; blood and fire, and vapour of smoke: The sun shall be turned into darkness, and the moon into blood, before that great and notable day of the Lord come: And it shall come to pass that whosoever shall call on the name of the Lord shall be saved."*

This references the Tribulation which heralds the Messianic Age. It will be a time of great signs and wonders, as well as horrendous upheaval and distress, all paving the way for the glorious 1000-year reign of the Jewish Messiah, Jesus.

Chapter 3

"For, behold, ***in those days, and in that time****, when I shall bring again the captivity of Judah and Jerusalem, I will also gather all nations, and will bring them down into the valley of Jehoshaphat, and will plead with them there for my people and for my heritage Israel, whom they* ***have scattered among the nations, and parted my land.*** *And they have cast lots for my people; and have given a boy for a harlot, and sold a girl for wine, that they might drink."* Joel 3:1-3

Again, regarding the end times and the day of the Lord, Joel describes how God will gather all nations in the valley of Jehoshaphat. *"That time"* will mark global anti-Semitism. That's when God will judge the nations for scattering His people, selling them into slavery, and parting their land. The ancient kingdoms did this. Hitler carried it to new heights by killing six million Jews. Following that, many heads of state, including U.S. presidents, have forced Israel to give up land for "peace," a peace that never materialized.

It's not surprising that Jehoshaphat (Armageddon), the last valley mentioned in the Bible, is similar to the first two valleys in Genesis—the valley of rebellion (Shinar) and the valley of war and strife (Siddim). Like bookends, they tell us that man is incapable of governing himself or living in peace with others without God.

Revelation talks about this valley and what will happen there. Armageddon (Har-Megiddon) is the hill overlooking the Valley of Megiddo or Megiddone and means "to gather or rendezvous." So, Megiddo is a place where, in the future, a gathering or rendezvous of nations will take place. There they hope to completely annihilate Israel. But unbeknown to them, God has gathered them for judgment.

As mentioned, this valley is also known as the Valley of Jehoshaphat (meaning "God will judge"), and the Valley of Decision. Megiddo is vast, a natural battleground and the site of dozens of wars over the centuries. It's the perfect gathering place for God to judge the nations (Revelation 16:16) for the reason given in Joel 3:2.

Revelation 19:11-16 tells what will happen. *"And I* (the apostle John who was taken to heaven in Revelation 4:1 and given an eyewitness view of the seven-year Tribulation) *saw heaven opened, and behold a white horse; and he that sat upon him was called Faithful and True, and in righteousness he doth judge and make war. His eyes were as a flame of fire, and on his head were many crowns; and he had a name written, that no man knew, but he himself. And he was clothed with a vesture dipped in blood: and his name is called The Word of God. And the armies which were in heaven followed him upon white horses, clothed in fine linen, white and clean. And out of his mouth goeth a sharp sword, that with it he should smite the nations: and he shall rule them with a rod of iron: and he treadeth the winepress of the fierceness and wrath of Almighty God. And he hath on his vesture and on his thigh a name written, KING OF KINGS, AND LORD OF LORDS."*

Because the world will not only be against Israel but be in rebellion against God by following the demonic antichrist, God will judge them. This battle will mark the end of the Tribulation.

Continuing with the text:

"Yea, and what have ye to do with me, O Tyre, and Zidon, and all the coasts of Palestine? will ye render me a recompence? and if ye recompense me, swiftly and speedily will I return your recompence upon your own head; Because ye have taken my silver and my gold, and have carried into your temples my goodly pleasant things: The children also of Judah and the children of Jerusalem have ye sold unto the Grecians, that ye might remove them far from their border. Behold, I will raise them out of the place whither ye have sold them, and will return your recompence upon your own head: And I will sell your sons and your daughters into the hand of the children of Judah, and they shall sell them to the Sabeans, to a people far off: for the LORD hath spoken it." Joel 3:4-8

God now turned to the nations that subjugated and wounded Israel, namely Tyre, Zidon (Sidon), and Palestine (Philistia). Tyre and Zidon were important Phoenician cities. They sold Israelites as slaves while Palestine continuously looted Israel. What these nations had sown, God tells them they would now reap. This happened, in part, when the Babylonians laid siege to Tyre in 586 B.C. Then in 332 B.C., Alexander the Great completely destroyed Tyre, then dominated Zidon, forcing it to pay tribute. But it's complete destruction won't come until the Tribulation.

The land of Sheba (Sabeans) now Yemen, is located in the southern Arabian Peninsula, a good distance from Israel. Since I found no record of Isreal ever selling the sons and daughters of Tyre, Zidon, or Palestine as slaves, I believe this is an unfulfilled prophecy stating that those who trafficked in Jewish slaves would themselves become slaves.

Continuing with the text:

"Proclaim ye this among the Gentiles; Prepare war, wake up the mighty men, let all the men of war draw near; let them come up: Beat your plowshares into swords, and your pruninghooks into spears: let the weak say, I am strong. Assemble yourselves, and come, all ye heathen, and gather yourselves together round about: thither cause thy mighty ones to come down, O LORD. Let the heathen be wakened, and come up to the valley of Jehoshaphat: for there will I sit to judge all the heathen round about." Joel 3:9-12

Again, this speaks of God judging the heathen nations during the Tribulation. At that time, He will render a heavenly decree upon earth and its inhabitants. Notice, He said, ***"Beat your plowshares into swords, and your pruninghooks into spears."*** This is in stark contrast to what will happen during the 1000-year Messianic Kingdom. Isaiah 2:4, speaking of this time, says, *"And he* (Jesus) *shall judge among the nations, and shall rebuke many people: and* ***they shall beat their swords into plowshares, and their spears into pruninghooks****: nation shall not lift up sword against nation, neither shall they learn war anymore."* Though the earth will go through the horrendous Tribulation, a wonderful future awaits it!

Continuing with the text:

"Put ye in the sickle, for the harvest is ripe: *come, get you down; for the press is full, the fats overflow; for their* ***wickedness is great****. Multitudes, multitudes in the valley of decision: for the day of the LORD is near in the valley of decision."* Joel 3:13-14

Joel again referred to the Tribulation. Revelation 14:18-20 clarifies the event. *"And another angel came out from the altar, which had power over fire; and cried with a loud cry to him that had the sharp sickle, saying,* ***Thrust in thy sharp sickle, and gather the cluster of the vine of the earth; for her grapes are fully ripe*** (man's cup of iniquity is full). *And the angel thrust in his sickle into the earth, and gathered the vine of the earth, and cast it into the great winepress of the wrath of God. And the winepress was trodden without the city, and blood came out of the winepress, even unto the horse bridles, by the space of a thousand and six hundred furlongs."*

Note, the world's wickedness is great. Thus, God's judgment will also be great. From His winepress of wrath, blood will flow for a *"space of a thousand and six hundred furlongs."* That's 200 miles!

Continuing with the text:

"The sun and the moon shall be darkened, and the stars shall withdraw their shining. The LORD also shall roar out of Zion, and utter his voice from Jerusalem; and the heavens and the earth shall shake: but the LORD will be the hope of his people, and the strength of the children of Israel. So shall ye know that I am the LORD your God dwelling in Zion, my holy mountain: then shall Jerusalem be holy, and there shall no strangers pass through her any more."
Joel 3:15:17

During the Tribulation, the earth and its inhabitants will experience many horrors. At its end, dramatic signs in the heavens will appear. Jesus spoke about this in Matthew 24:29-30. *"Immediately* ***after*** *the tribulation of those days shall the sun be darkened, and the moon shall not give her light, and the stars shall fall from heaven, and the powers of the heavens shall be shaken: And* ***then*** *shall appear the sign of the Son of man in heaven: and* ***then*** *shall all the tribes of the earth mourn, and they shall see the Son of man coming in the clouds of heaven with power and great glory."*

Notice, right after these heavenly signs, Jesus, the Son of man, comes in power (*The LORD also shall roar out of Zion*). All those left on earth will see Him. Zechariah 14:3-4 describes this event. *"Then shall the LORD* (Jesus) *go forth, and fight against those nations, as when he fought in the day of battle. And his feet shall stand in that day upon the mount of Olives, which is before Jerusalem on the east, and the mount of Olives shall cleave in the midst thereof toward the east and toward the west, and there shall be a very great valley; and half of the mountain shall remove toward the north, and half of it toward the south."*

And while Scripture tells us two-thirds of the Jews on earth will die during the Tribulation, God will protect a remnant. *"And to the woman* (Israel) *were given two wings of a great eagle, that she might fly into the wilderness, into her place, where she is nourished for a time, and times, and half a time, from the face of the serpent,"* (Revelation 12:14). God's provision and protection will cover a span of three and a half years (*a time, and times, and half a time*). Without His mercy, the Jews would not survive.

Continuing with the text:

"And it shall come to pass in that day, that ***the mountains shall drop down new wine****, and* ***the hills shall flow with milk****, and all the rivers of Judah shall flow with waters, and a* ***fountain shall come forth of the house of the LORD, and shall water the valley of Shittim****. Egypt shall be a desolation, and Edom shall be a desolate wilderness, for the violence against the children of Judah, because they have shed innocent blood in their land. But Judah shall dwell for ever, and Jerusalem from generation to generation. For I*

will cleanse their blood that I have not cleansed: for the LORD dwelleth in Zion." Joel 3:18-21

According to George M. Lamsa's *Idioms in the Bible Explained,* the above verses contain three Hebrew idioms.

1. *"The mountains shall drop down new wine,"* refers to "new teaching and new joy."
2. *"The hills shall flow with milk,"* indicate "a period of peace and prosperity."
3. *"A fountain shall come forth of the house of the LORD,"* means that from the Lord's house will come the "light of truth; reformed Judaism."

Joel was telling us that God's people and land will once again prosper and bloom. Amos 9:13 also refers to this: *"Behold, the days come, saith the LORD, that the plowman shall overtake the reaper, and the treader of grapes him that soweth seed; and the mountains shall drop sweet wine, and all the hills shall melt."*

Even the valley of Shittim, a dry wilderness, will be watered, symbolizing how lush and beautiful everything will become. In contrast, Egypt and Edom, symbols of Israel's enemies, will be desolate. Then God will cleanse His land and make it His holy habitation.

Conclusion:

Though it was a warning to ancient backsliding Judah, Joel is primarily prophetic. It points to a future Jacob's Trouble or seven-year Tribulation, a time so terrible it will devastate the planet and make mankind as scarce as the gold in Ophir (Isaiah 13:13). Even so, God's mercy and love is more than evident throughout.

Since this entire series is about God's judgment, I have included, as the last chapter, the Tribulation, the culmination of that judgment. This was covered in my book, *Destination Hell.* Those who have read it may want to skip it now.

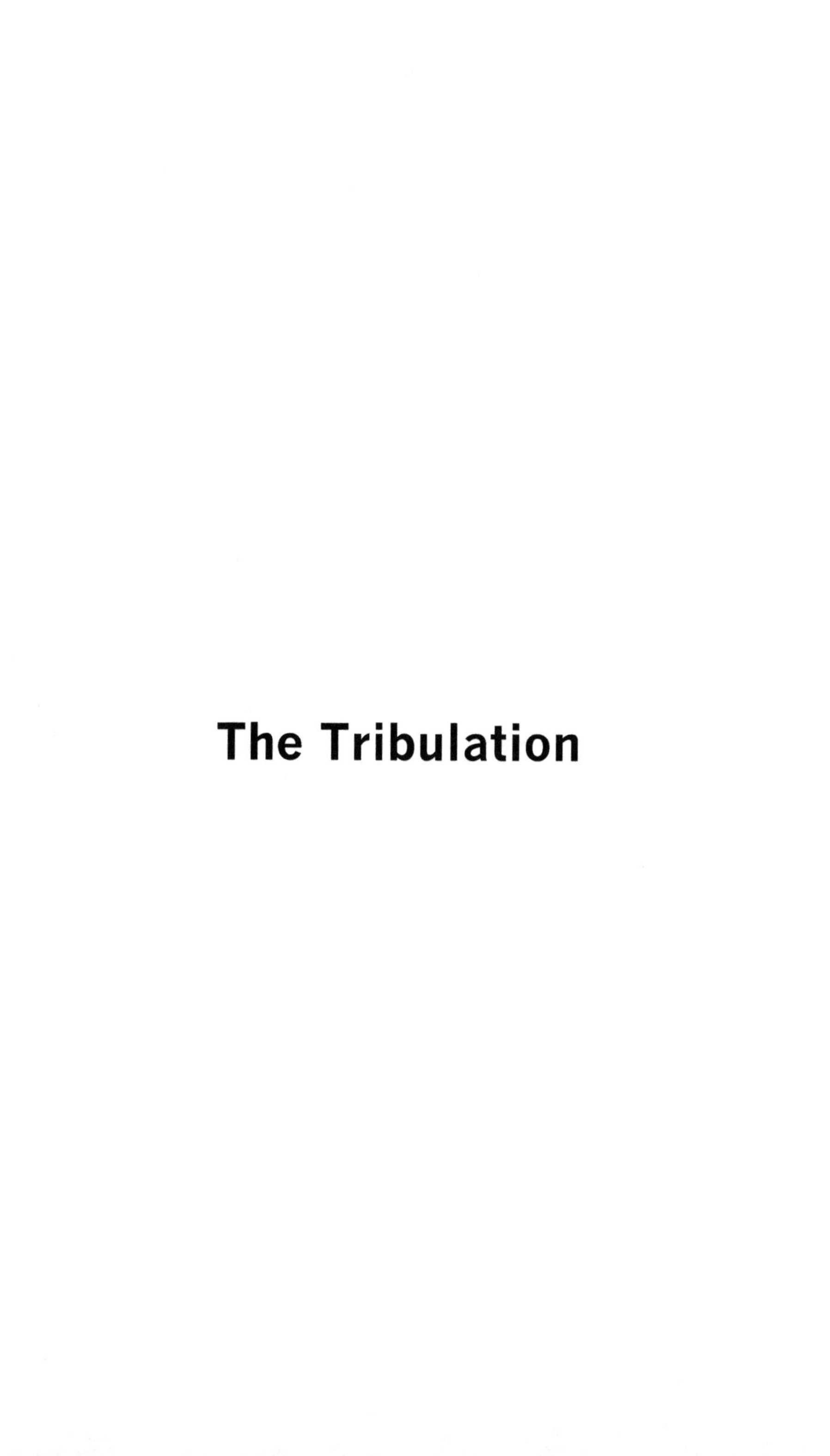

The Tribulation

The Tribulation

Below are the main reasons for the Tribulation:

The Tribulation will reveal God's amazing character, His goodness, patience, and omnipotence. He is in total control. And even though it will be horrendous, He continuously shows mercy by giving people opportunities to repent and turn to Him. He does this by sending two witnesses from heaven, by the 144,000 Jewish evangelists, and by the flying angel who proclaims the gospel throughout the world. In addition, Satan's character will also be revealed through the demonically possessed devious and murderous antichrist.

This will also be a time of transition. God will turn His attention from the church to both Israel and the sinful world. Through various judgements, He will purge the earth in preparation for His 1000-year reign.

Paul wrote in Acts 17:31 that, *"He* (God) *hath appointed a day, in which he will judge the world in righteousness."* That "day" is the seven-year Tribulation.

Daniel 9:24 also gives the following reasons for the Tribulation or 70th week:

- To finish transgression
- To make an end of sins
- To make reconciliation for iniquity
- To bring in everlasting righteousness
- To anoint the most Holy One

John's Rapture:

Revelation 4:1 (*"Come up hither"*) is the Rapture, signaling the end of the Church Age. After this, John found himself in the presence of God. Revelation 4:2-3 describes what he saw. *"And immediately I was in the spirit: and behold, a throne was set in heaven, and one sat on the throne. And he that sat was to look upon like a jasper and a sardine stone: and there was a rainbow round about the throne, in sight like unto an emerald."*

I love evangelist, teacher, and author, Perry Stone's commentary. He mentions that the sardine (sardius) and jasper stone were the first and last stones on the breastplate of Israel's high priest. In addition, Reuben (Jacob's firstborn) is represented by the sardius, and his name means, "behold a son." Benjamin, (Jacob's last son, is represented by the jasper and means, "son of the right hand" Both names symbolically point to Jesus as the "Son" Who sits at the "right hand of God." What a wonderful picture!

Perry Stone goes on to say that the emerald rainbow is not only the sign of God's covenant with Noah, but that an emerald was the fourth gem on the breastplate and represented the tribe of Judah, the very tribe from which Jesus came. Also, in ancient Jewish weddings, emeralds were the common wedding stones of the wealthy. It's a beautiful picture of Jesus as Bridegroom and John representing His bride, the church.

Also notice that while the jasper stone was the last stone on the high priest's breastplate, it was the first gem John mentioned, indicating he first saw Jesus sitting at the right hand of God. In addition, John doesn't call the jasper and sardius a gem, but a stone. That word stone is *lithos* and means, "a stone, a stumbling stone."

So, John not only saw Jesus as the Son, sitting at the right hand of God, he saw Him as a stumbling stone. 1 Corinthians 10:4, and other Scriptures, tell us that Jesus is our Rock (stone). While Romans 9:33 specifically calls Jesus a *"**a stumbling stone and rock of offence.**"* But those who believe in Him have nothing to worry about. To them, He will be their Rock, a firm foundation, reliable and strong. And so He was to John.

On the other hand, those who reject the Son of God have much to worry about. Isaiah 8:13-14 says, *"Sanctify the LORD of hosts himself; and let him be your fear, and let him be your dread. And he shall be for a **sanctuary;** but for a **stone of stumbling and rock of offence,** to both the houses of Israel, for a gin and for a snare to the inhabitants of Jerusalem."* This refers to how God will be a comfort to those who fear Him but great sorrow to those who don't.

Peter quoted Isaiah when talking about Jesus and unbelievers. *"And **a stone of stumbling, and a rock of offence,** even to them which stumble at the word* (of God), *being **disobedient:** whereunto also they were appointed,"* (1 Peter 2:8).

So, when John saw the "Stone" it pointed to the fact that to believers, Jesus is not only their Husband but their solid Rock. To unbelievers, He is the Judge, the stumbling stone, the very stone that will crush them.

Then John noticed twenty-four elders sitting on thrones all dressed in white and wearing gold crowns. These elders fell on their faces and tossed their crowns at Jesus' feet saying: *"Thou are worthy, O Lord, to receive glory and honour and power: for thou hast created all things, and for thy pleasure they are and were created,"* (Revelation 4:10-11). What a sight! John was standing in the very presence of the Creator of the Universe! His majesty and power had to be overwhelming.

After that, John saw the scroll in God's hand and heard an angel ask, *"Who is worthy to open the book, and to loose the seals thereof?"* The angel was really asking, "Who is the rightful heir?" Revelation 5:3 says, *"no **man** in heaven, nor in earth, neither under the earth was able to open the book, neither to look thereon."* That's when John began to cry.

The heir had to be a man. And we are told He is none other than the Lion of the tribe of Judah, the Root of David. It's Jesus, the Son of man, our Kinsman Redeemer. But when John looked, he saw a Lamb who had been slain, indicating why He was worthy to open the scroll. He had paid for it with His blood. And the Lamb was in the midst of the throne, surrounded by four beasts who worshipped Him, indicating He is God.

Revelation 5:7 says, *"And he* (the Lamb) *came and took the book out of the right hand of him that sat upon the throne."* And when He did, all heaven burst into praise and worship, *"Worthy is the Lamb that was slain to receive power, and riches, and wisdom, and strength, and honour, and glory and blessing."*
(Revelation 5:12).

Because this scroll was sealed, it implies it is a legal document. In ancient Israel, property contracts were often sealed this way. Copies were stored in the Jewish Temple until the debtor proved that any debt made against his property was satisfied. Wills of affluent Romans were also sealed with seven seals. Thus, we can deduce that the scroll Jesus holds is a legal will involving property, the very title deed to earth. Before his rebellion, Satan, as "covering cherub" held this deed. Then it was given to Adam and Eve. But after the fall, Satan obtained it again by default.

Now, Jesus is ready to appropriate His rightful inheritance. Because He left the glory of heaven and became a man, and died for the sins of the world, He paid the debt in full on this property (the world) and can legally claim it.

And He, the Lamb, was the one who *"prevailed to open the book and to loose the seven seals thereof,"* (Revelation 5:5), meaning Jesus breaks all seven seals. The entire Tribulation wrath is contained in this scroll.

Seven is the number of completion, perfection, and fullness. Thus, the seven seals, seven trumpets and seven bowls or vials complete God's perfect judgment and usher in the millennial reign. Jesus is about to break the back of sinful, unrepentant man, and pound the planet in judgment.

The enormity of the Book of Revelation:

Revelation talks about things that had already happened, was happening in John's day, and would happen in the future. Chapter one is about Jesus, who He is, His death, burial, and resurrection. Chapters two to three are about seven churches, as well as the entire Church Age. Chapter four is the Rapture. In chapter five, Jesus takes the scroll in preparation for the seven-year Tribulation. Chapters six to eighteen refer to that Tribulation. Chapters nineteen to twenty-two cover the disposal of both the antichrist and false prophet, the chaining of Satan, the millennial reign, the great White Throne Judgment, and the creation of a new heaven and earth.

The clock is set, the covenant signed.

Daniel 9:27 tells us the exact moment the Tribulation begins. It is when the antichrist *"shall **confirm** the covenant with many for one week."* It's interesting to note that the word "confirm" is *gabar* and means, "to be strong, to prevail, act insolently, to rise up in arrogance against God." It is the same root word used when describing Nimrod, the "mighty hunter" in Genesis 10:9. That word in Genesis is *gibbor* and comes from *gabar*, and means, "arrogant, tyrant, powerful." It's no coincidence that Nimrod is a type of antichrist or that secret societies are looking for his return/resurrection so he can finish the work he began at the Tower of Babel. Here, Daniel 9:27 hints that the antichrist also acts in arrogance.

This covenant is with the nation of Israel. Many Bible scholars believe it's a peace treaty that allows Israel to build her third Temple. Isaiah 28:15-18 talked about this last-days covenant and called it a *"covenant with death and hell."* Israel enters this agreement knowing it is evil but do so because they believe that *"when the overflowing scourge shall pass through, it shall not come unto us."* A lot is happening. There is an *"overflowing scourge"* covering planet earth, and apparently Israel's leaders see this covenant as a way of escape.

What is this *"scourge"*? Bill Salus talks about the end times in his many books. Using Scripture, he lays out the various conflicts he believes will happen prior to the Rapture, immediately after it, and during the Tribulation. They include:

- Iran's nuclear Bushehr facility becoming a Chernobyl like catastrophe, forcing people to relocate.
- The Psalm 83 war involving the ten nations or people groups sharing common borders with Israel. Their purpose is to take land. *"They have said, come let us cut them off from being a nation; that the name of Israel may be no more in remembrance."* But Israel will subdue them. As of 2026, I believe this has happened, at least in part, with the decimation of Iran's proxies, those populating Israel's surrounding nations. As a result, the Israeli army has become feared and known as the "exceeding great army," (Ezekiel 37:10). And finally, Israel will expand her territory.
- Somewhere along the line, Damascus becomes a ruinous heap (Isaiah 17:1). *"Behold, Damascus is taken away* (will cease) *from being a city, and it will be a ruinous heap."* This has never happened. Damascus has been continuously inhabited for nearly 5000 years. But it's interesting to note that many terror groups have their headquarters in Damascus.
- The Ezekiel 38-39 war. Along with more territory, Israel will also acquire great spoils, making her wealthier. This sets her up for the second Arab-Israeli conflict, the War of Gog and Magog. This war is for "spoils." Regarding Russia, Ezekiel 38:10-12 says, *"Thou shalt think an evil thought And thou shalt say, I* (Russia) *will go up to the land of unwalled villages; I will go to them that are at rest, that dwell safely, all of them dwelling without walls, and having neither bars nor gates,* ***To take a spoil, and to take a prey.****"*
    - It is a Russian-Iranian led coalition against Israel with nine different nations or people groups involved. They are what Salus calls the "outer ring," those nations not bordering

> Israel. This time, God Himself will supernaturally destroy the invaders in order to make His holy name known (Ezekiel 39:7).

Anti-Semitism is always demonically inspired. Satan hates the Jews. Remember, it was the Seed from their bloodline that sealed his doom. And it will be to their capital, Jerusalem, where that Seed, Jesus, will oust Satan's men, the antichrist and false prophet, and chain Satan himself for a thousand years while Jesus goes on to rule and reign.

Does worldwide hatred of Jews and the threat of constant war prior to the Tribulation make Israel ripe for the antichrist and create their willingness to enter into a *"covenant of death and hell"*? If so, they must believe it is the only way to protect themselves and ensure peace for their nation. Whatever the reason, Israel will enter this evil covenant which is "confirmed" by the antichrist, thus starting the Tribulation clock.

The first half of the seven-year Tribulation:

The stage is set. The restrainer, via the church, has been removed. Scripture tells us that the Spirit of God will not strive with man forever (Genesis 6:3). There comes a time when God will leave man to his own evil devices and their consequences. That time comes when Jesus takes the scroll. In the first half of the Tribulation, seven seals and seven trumpet judgments will be poured out on earth.

The first seal:

Revelation 6:1-2 says, *"and I saw when the Lamb opened one of the seals, and I heard as it were the noise of thunder, one of the four beasts saying, Come and see. And I saw, and behold a white horse: and he that sat on him had a bow; and a crown was given unto him: and he went forth conquering and to conquer."* Here we see a rider galloping out on a white horse. But notice, the rider comes out only after Jesus opens the seal, indicating that Jesus is in total control.

The rider is the antichrist.

God's first judgment on the world is to give it a false leader who promises a false peace and a false Utopia. A world that has rejected Jesus is now ready to embrace an imposter. The Rapture has occurred, and the world is in chaos. Referring to the end times, Jesus spoke of this in Luke 21:8. The first thing He mentioned was deception. *"Take heed that ye be not* ***deceived:*** *for many shall come in my name, saying I am Christ."* Now, the granddaddy of all deceivers has come upon earth's stage!

As many as two billion people have disappeared. Confusion and lawlessness abound. Government agencies are strained and unable to meet all the demands for help. Police departments aren't big enough to quell the chaos, looting, or violence. Fear and terror permeate the world. And because the restrainer is no longer restraining, evil is out of control.

If children killed other children for their sneakers while the restraining influence of the church was still here, and if people shot and killed others for cutting them off in their car, imagine what is going to happen after the church is removed!

Next, notice the horse. It's white. Biblically speaking, white is symbolic of purity and righteousness. In Revelation 19, Jesus returns on a white horse, confirming the first rider is a usurper, one who is not only against Christ, but who puts himself in place of Christ, and even audaciously tries to mimic Him.

Then note that the rider carries a bow but no arrows indicating he has not obtained his position through war. Perhaps a deal was made in some backroom or by a committee of elites. It also suggests dishonesty and subterfuge. He comes under the false colors of peace while planning conquest. Revelation 6:2 clearly tells us his motives, *"conquering and to conquer."* He will eventually conquer three kings or leaders to secure power. He will also bring about a world war. Jesus, on the other hand, carries a sword and His intentions are perfectly clear.

1 Thessalonians 5:3, referring to the end times, says, *"For when they shall say, Peace and safety; then sudden destruction cometh upon them, as travail upon a woman with child; and they shall not escape."* This is a sobering warning. Instead of peace, destruction is coming. And once the first seal is opened, there will be no stopping what follows.

The rider is given a crown (singular). It is a ***stephanos***, a wreath. Perhaps it's his reward for confirming that *"covenant with many"* spoken about in Daniel. In contrast, when Jesus returns, He wears many crowns or ***diadema,*** which are kingly crowns, not a wilting crown of leaves handed to him by man, but crowns of gold given to Him by God the Father for laying down His life for the world.

Also, a *stephanos* was the kind of wreath presented to a Roman general in honor of his military achievements. During his triumphant procession, the general rode in a chariot. Beside him stood a slave holding a *stephanos* over the general's head and gently reminding him that though he was a god that day, it would not last. It's interesting to note the rider in the first seal will also try to make himself a "god" and demand to be worshipped, but that won't last, either.

Next, the antichrist rides alone while Jesus will be followed by the armies of heaven.

The antichrist on the white horse in Revelation 6 and Jesus on the white horse in Revelation 19 are spiritual opposites. The first rider (antichrist) will usher in a time of terror so brutal that, by comparison, Hitler will look like a kindergarten teacher. On the other hand, Jesus Christ will usher in 1000 years of peace and blessing.

Sometime at the beginning of the Tribulation, God sends His two witnesses from heaven to Jerusalem. For three and a half years, they testify and prophesy, preparing Israel for Christ's return. They have the power to send plagues and kill those who try to stop or harm them. Most scholars believe they will either be Elijah and Moses, or Elijah and Enoch.

No doubt Elijah will be one of the witnesses. For centuries, Jews have anticipated his arrival and even set a place for him at every Passover meal. And Malachi 4:5 speaks about the coming of Elijah *"before the great and dreadful day of the LORD."*

These witnesses are allotted three and a half years to preach. Revelation 11: 3 says, *"I* (God) *will give power unto my two witnesses, and they shall prophesy a thousand two hundred and threescore days in sackcloth."* Then they are killed by the antichrist during the middle of the Tribulation. *"And when they shall have finished their testimony the beast that ascendeth out of the bottomless pit shall make war against them, and shall overcome them, and kill them,"* (Revelation 11:7).

In addition, there are 144,000 Jewish evangelists who faithfully share God's Word and will bring many to Christ. We learn more about them in Revelation 7.

Also, early in the first half of the Tribulation, the Jews will begin building their Temple. It is interesting to note that many Jews believe this will usher in the coming of their Messiah. The Temple must be finished by the middle of the Tribulation since that is when the antichrist desecrates it and proclaims himself god. Much to their dismay, the Jews will realize this is not the Messiah they have longed for.

The second seal:

Revelation 6:3-4, *"When He* (the Lamb) *had opened the second seal, I* (John) *heard the second beast say, Come and see. And there went out another horse that was red: and* ***power*** *was given to him that sat thereon to take peace from the earth, and that they should* ***kill*** *one another: and there was given unto him* ***a great sword.****"*

This time the horse is red, signifying blood, sorrow, death, and destruction. The rider is given two things: power to take peace from the earth, and a great sword. Notice these are **given** to him, again indicating Jesus is in control.

The results are terrifying. You are talking about global warfare and violence. People are killing and being killed. To add to this picture, the rider's **great sword** is a *megas machaira.* This implies butchery and slaughter. While the world has seen many wars and conflicts, they are nothing compared to what's going to happen during this second seal judgment.

The third seal:

Revelation 6:5-6, *"And when he had opened the third seal, I heard the third beast say, Come and see. And I beheld, and lo a black horse; and he that sat on him had a pair of balances in his hand. And I heard a voice in the midst of the four beasts say,* ***A measure of wheat for***

a penny; and three measures of barley for a penny *and see thou hurt not the oil and wine."* Here we see a black horse. Black in Scripture is ominous, symbolizing judgment, darkness, and terror. It's a foreboding that something awful is coming.

This rider carries scales to measure the wheat and barley, the amount that can be purchased with a day's pay. In ancient times, normally twenty-four measures of barley could be had for a day's wages. The people in the Tribulation will only get three measures. Likewise, fifteen measures of wheat were the norm, not one. You're talking hyper-inflation and global shortages, especially of basic food supplies. These will not only be rationed but expensive, costing a day's wage to feed one adult with wheat and three adults with barley. These shortages could be the result of the global war because shortages often follow war since people are displaced and cannot plant crops. Again, this is going to be **worldwide famine.** This is **starvation** on a massive scale.

When famines produce mass starvation, it devastates entire populations. To understand how horrible they can be, we just need to look at what's happened in the past. During World War II and immediately after, the world experienced famines. From the Warsaw Ghetto to Kiev to the Netherlands, millions died due to starvation. And although not all the horrendous things mentioned below occurred in each locale, this composite shows that as things become progressively more desperate, people become more willing to do the unthinkable.

In past famines, streets were littered with dead bodies that looked like skeletons. Some began eating their pets. Others turned to cannibalism and began eating the bodies of the dead or even killing and eating their own babies. Some murdered others for food. Still others roved in small bands, breaking into the homes of those they believed were hiding provisions, then torturing them to reveal the hiding places. Those who couldn't bring themselves to do these things began eating toothpaste, glue, leather, sawdust, the bark of trees, grass, or anything else they could find. Others shuttered themselves in their homes waiting for death. It's an ugly picture of the depth of human degradation such tragedies produce.

During the Tribulation, it will become necessary to move about in groups for it won't be safe to walk the streets alone due to marauding thugs. If caught alone, there will be no one to help. Even if others see your struggle, they won't care. Self-preservation will be the rule.

Even now, we see the beginning of this. Years ago, if someone witnessed an assault or robbery, he called the police or tried to help. No longer. Americans have become hardened toward crime and its victims. Not long ago, a woman riding a suburban Philadelphia train at night was raped while onlookers neither tried to stop it nor bothered to call the police. It's believed that some even recorded the incident on their phones.

What a sad commentary on where we are as a nation. But imagine how much worse it will be when pure evil is unleashed. The world will be filled with violence and cruelty. It will be every man for himself. No one will care what happens to his neighbor.

Going back to Revelation 6:5, it's interesting to note that the oil and wine are left unharmed, indicating this famine will be hard on the poor and those with limited incomes, while the rich can still obtain the things they want.

The fourth seal:

Revelation 6:7-8, *"And when he had opened the fourth seal, I heard the voice of the fourth beast say, Come and see. And I looked, and behold a pale horse: and his name that sat on him was Death, and Hell followed with him. And power was given unto them over the fourth part of the earth, to kill with sword, and with hunger, and with death, and with the beasts of the earth."*

When the Lamb opens this seal, Death, riding a pale horse, comes galloping out with Hell following closely behind. That word "pale" indicates a "yellowish green" color. Picture the color of a rotting corpse and you'll get the idea. Again, it is Jesus Who gives this rider power.

But notice, Jesus sets boundaries. Death and Hell can only take one-fourth of the world's population. How many people is that? According to StatisticsTimes.com, the world's population in early 2026 was 8.3 billion. And according to Princeton Theological Seminary, in 2026 there were 2.6 billion Christians across all denominations worldwide.

Assuming two billion are raptured that leaves a population of 6.3 billion. One-fourth of that means nearly 1.6 billion people are going to die as a result of the culmination of what these four horsemen unleash. That's seven times more deaths than those which occurred in all the wars of the last century!

The earth will be covered with pale, decaying corpses. So many people will die that Hell is at Death's heels scooping them up. The fact that Hell is doing the collecting indicates those dying are unsaved.

How is all this death accomplished? We are told in Revelation 6:8 that it will be with *"sword, and with hunger, and with death, and with the beasts of the earth."* We've already seen that sword and famine have killed people. Now "death," which the Amplified Bible calls "plague" instead, and "beasts" are added to the list. I don't think it unreasonable to assume that all the dead bodies lying around, along with the mass starvation, trigger plagues and problems with animals.

Plagues are common during and after a war. They can decimate a population with incredible speed. Perhaps biological weapons have also been used. If so, it's going to be something never seen before and incredibly horrible because, in the past, even ordinary plagues have wiped out huge sections of the population.

And then there are the wild beasts. If there is a food shortage and animals can't find anything to eat, it's not unrealistic to believe they will soon start hunting man. But these plagues can also involve rats, snakes, killer bees, etcetera, that carry diseases or torment man. Amos 5:18-20 hints at this: *"Woe unto you that desire* ***the day of the LORD*** (the Tribulation)! *to what end is it for you? The day of the LORD is darkness and not light. As if a man did flee from a lion, and a bear met him; or went into the house and leaned his hand on the wall, and a serpent bit him."*

In the face of such death, destruction, and tragedy, no government agency in the world will be able to cope. There won't be enough hospital beds, medicine, or first responders. The world will be dark, dangerous, and spiraling out of control. The globe will look like one giant third-world nation. Along with food shortage, if there is limited electricity, no garbage collection, sewers backing up, it will no longer resemble the world we know.

The fifth seal:

Revelation 6:9-11 says, *"And when he* (the Lamb) *had opened the fifth seal, I saw under the altar the souls of them that were slain for the word of God, and for the testimony which they held: And they cried out with a loud voice, saying, How long, O Lord, holy and true, does thou not judge and avenge our blood on them that dwell on the earth. And white robes were given unto every one of them; and it was said unto them, that they should rest yet for a little season, until their fellow servants also and their brethren, that should be killed as they were, should be fulfilled."*

This is global martyrdom, the mass murder of believers. The two witnesses and 144,000 have been busy. A great world-wide revival has taken place, showing God's tremendous mercy and love for all mankind. But this mass murder also implies it's government orchestrated. Those heading the New World Order and One World Religion are not only condoning these actions but implementing them. Depraved men are now butchering those who have turned to God.

These martyrs cry out, asking God to avenge them. They say, *"How long, O Lord, holy and true, does thou not judge and* ***avenge our blood*** *on them that dwell on the earth."* I've already covered the role of a blood avenger in Hosea chapter four. As a reminder, innocent blood had to be avenged. Jesus, our Kinsman Redeemer, will now become the blood avenger. The evil world has seen nothing yet!

Though God does indeed plan to avenge these martyrs, He tells them to *"wait a little longer until the number of their fellow servants and brothers who were to be killed as they had been was completed."* That means there will be more martyrs, more bloodshed. Revelation 17:6 confirms this gross slaughter by saying, *"the woman was drunken with the blood of the saints, and with the blood of the martyrs of Jesus."* The woman is Mystery Babylon which is the harlot One World Religion supported by the One World Government. This bloodbath will be another inquisition but far worse than any before it.

It was Nimrod who successfully instituted Mystery Babylon, the false religious system that encompassed forbidden occult knowledge, the worship of the twelve constellations, as well as the worship of himself and his family (ancestor worship). They then went on to become "gods" in various cultures. And all the above will be part of the One World Religion, which even now is being cobbled together by the U.N. and various secret organizations.

Remember that the apostate church has been left behind. It's from this group that the One World Religion will be formed. Certainly, included among them will be some of the hierarchy of both the Catholic and Protestant churches, as well as leaders of other religions. But I believe it will be the Catholic contingency that heads it all. Apparently, others thought so, too.

Steeped in paganism and tradition, the Catholic Church has played a large role in creating an apostate faith. In 1948, the Vatican opposed the formation of the Jewish state while in 1962 their *Nostra Aetate* declared that the god of Islam and the God of Christianity were one and the same. Vatican II (1962-1965) went on to open its door for a One World Religion with its ecumenicalism. In 1982, Pope John Paul II had a prayer meeting in Assisi, Italy which included pagans and voodoo priests, and where he claimed that voodoo possessed *"truth and good, seeds of the Word."*[43]

Renowned Catholic Bishop Fulton Sheen even predicted that the false prophet of Revelation would come from one of their own (a Catholic cardinal). But this was not a new fear. Martin Luther and Calvin believed it. So did John Knox, John Wesley, Charles Spurgeon, George Whitefield, and Jonathan Edwards. Dr. Henry Edward Cardinal Manning in 1861 also predicted a crisis and apostasy in the Catholic Church.[44]

Since then, many others have come forward and sounded the same alarm, including Father E. Sylvester Berry in his book, *The Apocalypse of Saint John*, Father Herman Bernard Kramer in his, *"The Book of Destiny,"* Father John F. O'Connor, Father Alfred Kunz, and Father Malachi Martin.[45]

Before he died, Father O'Connor preached a sermon in which he claimed that a "Masonic Conspirator" would control the pope and assist the false prophet in "deceiving the world's faithful into worshipping Antichrist."[46]

A March 11, 2010, ABC News article quoted Pope Benedict XVI's exorcist, Reverend Amorth, as saying, "The devil resides in the Vatican" and that "The consequences of the devil's work are evident: Cardinals who don't believe in Jesus, bishops who are linked with the devil."

Some believe it won't be the official pope who fills the role of false prophet but the power behind him. That person is the Black Pope who heads and guides the Jesuit society. He typically wears the black cassock of a Jesuit, hence the name. He is the power behind the power, and promotes the heresy of Liberation Theology which depicts Jesus as a social justice warrior rather than the Savior of the world. Their goal is social justice by any means including assassination, deception, theft, as well as creating world chaos.

Under the Black Popes, Jesuits have affiliated themselves with heretical organizations such as Free Masonry, the Illuminati, Knights of Malta, Club of Rome, and the Bilderbergs. The Black Pope's goals and that of his organization are 1) one world religion 2) one world government and 3) the rebuilding of the Temple in Jerusalem in order to establish the Catholic Church there.

Over the years, several Jesuits have worked hard to conceal their organization's ties to demonic groups. While others, like Jesuit Malachi Martin wrote startling exposés of both the Jesuits and the Vatican hierarchy.[47]

Martin was an eminent Catholic theologian, spoke seventeen languages, was a member of the Vatican Advisory Council and advisor to three popes. In addition, he was the Vatican's researcher on the Dead Sea Scrolls.

His startling claim is this: An Illuminati-Masonic (Freemason) group had infiltrated the upper ranks of the Catholic Church and conspired to bring about a one world government. In his book, *Windswept House,* thinly disguised as fiction in order to protect sources, Martin talks about "prominent clerics who worship Satan" and that "networks . . . had been established between certain clerical homosexual groups and Satanic covens." This lends insight into the worldwide coverup of pedophile clerics by the church.

Martin also talked about a secret ceremony, which he called the "enthronement of Satan" and took place at the Vatican in 1963 in order to ensure two outcomes: 1) Satan's control over Rome and 2) a demonically controlled end-time pope. Paul VI (pope from 1963-1978) called this ceremony, "the smoke of Satan which has entered the Sanctuary."[48]

Monsignor Luigi Marinelli backed this up in his 1999 book, *Gone with the Wind in the Vatican,* in which he details how Catholic priests have made pacts with Satanists and serve communion at Black Sabbath masses. Then Archbishop Milingo, another senior cleric, also claimed that "high ranking Vatican officials were followers of Satan."

In 1999, Father Malachi Martin died under "suspicious" circumstances while working on another book connecting the Catholic Church with the New World Order.[49] Because he was a Jesuit and knew their inner workings, it appears that someone wanted him silenced.

Clearly, Satan has had a foothold in the Vatican for centuries through members of the Freemasons and Illuminati. Pope Pius IX, serving as pope from 1846-1878, called it the "Synagogue of Satan." And in 1884, Pope Leo went so far as to issue an encyclical damning these Masonic efforts.[50]

In November 2021, Archbishop Carlo Maria Vigano, a strong critic of the Vatican, called for "the creation of an anti-globalist alliance to defeat the evil elites who wish to enslave free men and women and promote a 'Religion of Humanity' that cancels Faith in Christ."[51]

Even before this, the Vatican in 2011, under Pope Benedict XVI, had already shown its true colors and made its objectives clear when it published, *Toward Reforming the International Financial and Monetary Systems in the context of a* ***Global Public Authority***. It espoused the same goals as those of the New World Order, declaring the need for individuals and nations to surrender their rights and authority in order to achieve "global civil and economic security." And how was this to be accomplished? Their answer: "At the cost of a gradual balance transfer of a part of each nation's powers to a world authority and to regional authorities."[52]

Remember, Jesus said you will know them by their fruits.

The sixth seal:

Revelation 6:12-17 says, *"And I beheld when he had opened the sixth seal, and lo, there was a* ***great earthquake;*** *and the sun became black as sackcloth of hair, and the moon became as blood; And the stars of heaven fell unto the earth, even as a fig tree casts her untimely figs, when she is shaken of a mighty wind. And the heaven departed as a scroll when it is rolled together, and every mountain and island were moved out of their places. And the kings of the earth, and the great men, and the rich men, and the chief captains, and the mighty men, and every bondman, and every free man, hid themselves in the dens and in the rocks of the mountains, And said to the mountains and rocks, Fall on us, and hide us from the face of him that sitteth on the throne, and from* ***the wrath of the Lamb:*** *For the great day of his wrath is come, and who shall be able to stand?"*

Now, the very elements of heaven and earth turn against man. God uses them in His role of blood avenger to punish man for murdering His people, as well as for their many other sins. And the thing is, the people know it. Notice, they understand that all that happens is due to *"the wrath of the Lamb,"* yet they refuse to repent. Instead, they hide in fear. One must wonder what it will take to bring these people around. So much devastation has occurred, it's hard to believe they aren't falling on their faces before God and begging His forgiveness.

It's probably the **great earthquake** that triggers most of the other calamities in this seal. Those words "great earthquake" are *megas seismos*. This is a block buster. It's off the scale. In addition, earthquakes trigger other disasters like mudslides, tsunamis, and volcanic eruptions. These in turn cause more problems. Tsunamis flood entire towns, while mudslides bury them, and volcanoes burn them down. Volcanoes also fill the air with ash, debris, and toxic gases, which in turn can create a solar winter by darkening the sun. This darkening can, in turn, cause crop failure. Volcanic eruptions can also change the color of the moon and affect the planet's temperature. When this great earthquake hits, millions will die.

What about the falling stars? That word "stars" in Greek is *aster* from which we get our word, asteroid. Many scholars believe this could be a meteor shower. And it's serious because they are going to be dropping like figs from a tree shaken *"by a mighty wind."* As they fall, they can produce shock waves in the air or explosions when they land. They can also create tsunamis, change the temperature of land, air, sea, and wipe out every structure in a wide radius. And if the shower falls on a major city, it could turn it into rubble. All this translates into more death and destruction.

What about the heaven departing as a scroll? That word "departed" literally means, "to rend apart, to separate." Some Bible scholars believe the sky will split open and for a brief moment people on earth will be able to see into another dimension, that of God's throne as He orchestrates this destruction. It could also mean that this earthquake is so powerful it creates a shift in the earth's axis causing the constellations to no longer line up to their former settings.

The sealing of the 144,000:

After the sixth seal, God is ready to further damage the earth via the four winds. But before He does, He pauses. Revelation

7:1-4 says, *"And after these things* (the opening of the first six seals) *I* (John) *saw four angels standing on the four corners of the earth, holding the four winds of the earth, that the wind should not blow on the earth, nor on the sea, nor on any tree. And I saw another angel ascending from the east, having the seal of the living God: and he cried with a loud voice to the four angels, to whom it was given to hurt the earth and the sea, Saying, Hurt not the earth, neither the sea, nor the trees, till we have* ***sealed*** *the servants of our God in their foreheads. And I heard the number of them which were sealed: and there were sealed an hundred and forty and four thousand of all the tribes of the children of Israel."*

I believe these 144,000 were already commissioned at the beginning of the Tribulation along with the two witnesses, but now God seals them. That word "seal" is *sphragizo* and means, "to stamp for security or preservation." Why does He do this? Because what comes next will kill so many people, God needs to keep them safe until their work is completed. This is His great mercy and love on display. He wants as many as possible to hear from these 144,000, repent, and come to Him.

Revelation 7:5-8 gives more information. These 144,000 are 12,000 from every tribe of Israel except Dan's. His tribe is replaced by the tribe of Manasseh (Joseph's son).

Why?

Daniel 9:25-26 says, *"Know therefore and understand, that from the going forth of the commandment to* ***restore*** *and to build Jerusalem unto the* ***Messiah the Prince*** *shall be seven weeks, and threescore and two weeks: the street shall be built again, and the wall, even in troublous times.* ***And after threescore and two weeks shall Messiah be cut off, but not for himself****: and the people of the prince that shall come shall destroy the city and the sanctuary; and* *the end thereof shall be with a flood, and unto the end of the war desolations are determined."*

Daniel was prophesying the coming of Jesus as Messiah. Digging deeper, we see that Daniel wasn't talking about literal weeks. That word "weeks" is *shabuwa* and means, "weeks of years." A week of years is seven years. Therefore, Daniel's scenario would cover seventy weeks of years or 490 years. This is further broken down into two distinct time frames. First comes 7 plus 62 weeks of years for a total of 69 weeks of years or 483 years from the time Jerusalem is restored and rebuilt to the time when Messiah would be cut off **but not for himself**.

Did that happen? Yes! Cyrus decreed that Jerusalem's Temple should be rebuilt in 538/537 B.C. Darius confirmed Cyrus' decree in 520 B.C. But it wasn't until 457 B.C. that Artaxerxes granted autonomy to Judah, then confirmed it by a second decree in 445/444 B.C. It is this date that is significant because that word "restore" in Daniel 9:25 means, "return ownership," not just rebuild. And that didn't happen until 445/444 B.C. when ownership of Jerusalem was fully restored to the Jews. Using this date as a springboard, Julius Africanus, an early church father, calculated the time when Messiah would *"be cut off"* by converting the Jewish calendar, which is based on the phases of the moon, to the Gregorian/Roman calendar, based on the solar year. When he did, he came up with the date, April 6, 32 A.D., the very year many Bible scholars believe Jesus was crucified.

But that leaves one more week of years or seven years before, according to Daniel, the Messiah would reign in His earthly kingdom. It's been almost 2000 years since Jesus left this earth. What happened? The Church Age! For nearly 2000 years we have experienced a pause in Daniel's timetable during this Age of Grace. But that will soon end. Sometime after it does, the final week of Daniel's prophecy will be fulfilled. It's called the seven-year Tribulation, last days, Jacob's Trouble, end times, day of the Lord, etcetera. During this time, the antichrist will appear. Daniel mentions this person when he said, *"the people of the prince that shall come"* and who *"shall destroy the city* (Jerusalem) *and the sanctuary* (Temple)."

Who are the people of the prince, the ones who destroyed Jerusalem and the Temple in 70 A.D.? They were the Romans headed by Titus and Vespasian. Therefore, this prince or antichrist will come from their lineage. Prior to the destruction of the Second Temple, Israel's Jewish ruling class began mingling their bloodline with both Greek and Roman rulers so it's possible that the antichrist could be a Gentile but also have a Jewish bloodline. J.R. Church believed this Jewish bloodline would be connected to the tribe of Dan, and cites as a clue, that Dan is not among the 144,000 Jewish evangelists mentioned in Revelation. For more insight, I recommend his book, *Daniel Reveals the Blood Line of the Antichrist.*

I think this is reasonable because the Jewish nation would never accept a Muslim (as many believe) or a Gentile (as many others believe) as their Messiah. He would at least have to be part Jewish.

In addition, in Genesis 49:16-17, when Jacob blesses his sons, he says this about the tribe of Dan: *"Dan shall **judge** his people as one of the tribes of Israel. Dan shall be a **serpent** by the way, an **adder** in the path, that biteth the horse heels, so that his rider shall fall backward."* This prophecy infers that Dan is treacherous (snake and adder) and that at some point, will act as judge. This was certainly fulfilled when Samson became Israel's 14th judge and served twenty years in a rather malevolent manner.

However, some early church fathers viewed Genesis 49 as prophesying that the antichrist would be a Danite. I think they and J.R. Church make a good point.

Returning to the 144,000. These Jews will bring in a great harvest. Millions will come to Christ. And the fruits of it are revealed in verse 9. *"After this* (after the sealing of the 144,000) *I* (John) *beheld, and lo, a* ***great multitude****, which no man could number, of all nations, and kindreds, and people, and tongues, stood before the throne, and before the Lamb, clothed with white robes, and palms in their hands."*

These people accepted Christ before dying during the Tribulation. Their robes are clean, and they are worshipping in heaven. Just to make sure there is no question of who these people are, verse 14 says, *"These are they which came out of* ***great tribulation****, and have washed their robes, and made them white in the blood of the Lamb."*

We know they have suffered greatly because verse 17 says that Jesus *"shall feed them, and shall lead them unto living fountains of waters: and God shall wipe away all tears from their eyes."* This indicates they experienced great hunger and thirst. But Jesus Himself will care for them now. He will console them, wipe away their tears, and heal their trauma as they cry in His arms.

What a wonderful God we serve! He is so tender, kind, and loving. He rewards those who come to Him and wants no one to perish!

The seventh seal:

Revelation 8:1-2 says, *"And when he had opened the seventh seal, there was silence in heaven about the space of half an hour. And I saw the seven angels which stood before God; and to them were given seven trumpets."*

Again, it is the Lamb Who opens this seal which begins the seven trumpet judgments. Since we are told about the silence in heaven it must be significant. Is this the eye of the storm? Is it a chance for mankind to repent? Is it the prelude for something so terrible it makes those in heaven remain with their mouths open, unable to speak?

Whatever it is, mankind doesn't repent. Perhaps they thought the worst was over and now the One World Government could get on with creating Utopia. But their worst nightmare is just beginning. There are still fourteen judgments left.

But here is an interesting point. In Revelation 8:3, an angel holds a golden censer, and the smoke of it, along with the **prayers of the saints**, ascends before God. This triggers the first of seven angels to sound a trumpet. God is not only unleashing His wrath, He is now answering the prayers of the saints and their request that their blood be avenged.

The first trumpet:

The result of this first trumpet sounding is the falling of hail, fire, and blood upon the earth, burning one-third of all the trees along with all the grass. Picture an out-of-control fire sweeping through acres and acres of land, destroying everything in its path while additional hail, fire, and blood continue raining down on everyone's head. This could be supernatural or the result of nuclear war. Either way, it's devastating.

The second trumpet:

The world hardly has time to draw breath when the second trumpet sounds, sending a *"**great mountain** burning with fire"* into the sea. Many scholars believe this could be an asteroid. Even now, NASA is monitoring hundreds of asteroids and has issued warnings of possible collisions in the future. It could also refer to an erupting volcano spilling burning lava into the sea. Or, again, it could indicate nuclear warfare and the type of destruction that comes with it.

Whatever it is, it results in one-third of the sea turning to blood, the killing of one-third of all sea creatures, and the destruction of one-third of the ships.

The third trumpet:

Following that, the third trumpet causes a burning star, called Wormwood, to fall into earth's rivers making the water bitter, and killing many.

The fourth trumpet:

When the fourth trumpet sounds, one-third of the sun, moon, and stars are smitten, causing daylight to be decreased by one-third. It appears that the first to fourth trumpets sound in rapid fire. People will reel from the devastation as one disaster after the other hits them. And if things couldn't get any worse, this is followed by an angel who flies over the earth shouting, *"Woe, woe, woe, to the inhabiters of the earth by reason of the other voices of the trumpet of the three angels which are yet to sound!"* (Revelation 8:13)

His three woes are dire warnings that something even worse is coming. Daniel 12:1 calls these times *"a time of trouble, such as never was since there was a nation* (Israel)," while Isaiah 13:9 says, *"Behold, the day of the LORD cometh, cruel both with wrath and fierce anger, to lay the land desolate: and he shall destroy the sinners thereof out of it."* Though this is a forewarning of more disaster, it also reflects God's mercy. He is telling people to wake up and repent before it's too late; to come to Him, because in this next round the chances are good they won't survive, and they'll be lost forever.

The fifth trumpet:

Immediately after the angel's warning, the fifth trumpet sounds and *"a star falls from heaven unto the earth: and to* ***him*** *was given the key of the bottomless pit,"* (Revelation 9:1). Although this word for "star" is also *aster,* it cannot mean an asteroid or meteor because of the pronoun "him." This is not an object but a living being. Thus, we can assume it is an angel. That word "fall" is *pipto* and means, "alighting, light on, to fly." So, this is an angel who flies from heaven and lands on earth. This angel opens the bottomless pit. When he does, *"the smoke of a great furnace"* comes pouring out. This is the putrid smoke from the pit of hell itself. It is so dense it darkens the sun and moon.

But that's not the worst of it. The Bible says that a horde of locusts come rushing out. These are not insects, but demonic beings who are given power to torment those not marked by God. In other words, those not sealed like the 144,000 Jews were fair game. The only thing these demonic locusts can't do is kill. The irony is that during this time people will want to die but can't. Revelation 9:6 says, *"And in those days shall men seek death, and shall not find it; and shall desire to die, and death shall flee from them."*

Scripture gives a macabre picture of what these locusts look like: horses with faces of men, having wings and stinging tails. It says their king is Apollyon, which is another name for Satan.

The sixth trumpet:

The six trumpet looses the four angels *"bound in the great river Euphrates"* to slay one-third of those remaining on earth. The sounding of the fourth and fifth trumpets have already caused mass casualties. Now, the sixth trumpet looses a two-million-man army. Some scholars believe this is a demonic army. They ride horses with lion heads. Their breastplates are of fire and brimstone and their mouths spew fire and brimstone. Other scholars believe they are tanks or helicopters or some other modern implements of war. I believe it could be either, though I favor the demonic version.

Whatever they are, the horror they unleash is obvious. But the sad part is that no one repents. Revelation 9:20-21 says, *"And the rest of the men which were not killed by these plagues* (trumpets four to six) *yet repented not of the works of their hands, that they should not worship devils, and idols of gold, and silver, and brass, and stone, and of wood: which neither can see, nor hear, nor walk: Neither repented they of their murders, nor of their sorceries* (that word is *pharmakeia* meaning, 'medication, pharmacy, magic, drug use'), *nor of their fornication, nor of their thefts."*

Notice the five sins emphasized: idolatry, murder, occult activities (including drug use), fornication, and thefts. They are hardly the only sins. But this tells us that evil will be rampant and demonstrates the utter depravity of man. It shows the depths to which man can sink and still justify himself when the restraining power of the Holy Spirit is removed. Every village, town, and city will be affected. There will be no escape. And those who come to the Lord and try to live righteously will be hunted down and killed.

The midpoint between the first and second half of the Tribulation:

Chapters six to nine describe the first half of the Tribulation while chapters sixteen to eighteen describe the second half. At the midpoint, between the two, several important things occur.

In Revelation chapter ten, an angel gives John a book that he is told to eat. Then the angel swears *"that there shall be time no longer,"* indicating no more delays. Soon, the fullness of God's wrath will be complete.

Then John is given a measuring rod to measure the third Jewish Temple, the one built during the first half of the Tribulation. We are also given insight into the two witnesses who have been prophesying for three and a half years, and who the antichrist finally kills. Their bodies lie on a Jerusalem street for three and a half days. Revelation 11:8 says, *"And their dead bodies shall lie in the street of the great city, which spiritually is called Sodom and Egypt, where also our Lord was crucified."*

The world will celebrate their deaths by sending each other gifts. At last, they are rid of their tormentors who spoke of God and pronounced judgments. Now, life can get back to normal, and once again they can live the way they want without consequences. But their joy won't last because suddenly, a loud voice from heaven issues the command to *"Come up hither,"* and the dead witnesses come to life, then are taken to heaven. An earthquake follows, destroying one-tenth of Jerusalem and killing 7000 people, (Revelation 11:13).

Revelation chapter 12 talks about Israel, the birth of Jesus, Satan's rebellion and how he first tried to destroy the Seed (Jesus), then the nation of Israel. There is also a war in heaven between Satan and Michael, the archangel, ending with Satan and his cohorts being cast down to earth. Now, knowing his time is short, Satan becomes really vicious. Revelation 12:13 says, *"And when the dragon* (Satan) *saw that he was cast unto the earth, he persecuted the woman* (Israel) *which brought forth the man child* (Jesus)."

Revelation chapter 13 gives us additional insight into the antichrist and false prophet. It is at this midpoint that the antichrist will violate the covenant with Israel and declare himself god. 2 Thessalonians 2:4 tells us this happens in Jerusalem's Temple. The antichrist, *"Who opposeth and exalteth himself above all that is called God, or that is worshipped: so that he as God, sitteth in the temple of God, shewing himself that he is God."* This desecrates the Temple. In addition, the antichrist stops all Temple sacrifices, (Daniel 9:27).

The Jews are horrified. This is the *"abomination of desolation"* spoken about by both Daniel and Jesus. They offend the antichrist by refusing to accept him as god, causing him to initiate a massive extermination campaign against them. According to Zechariah 13:8, two-thirds of the Jews will die.

But God will protect a remnant by bringing them into a desert city and feeding them for the remainder of the Tribulation or 1,260 days. Many believe this refuge will be Petra, a city carved into the mountains of Jordan. This is the Jewish remnant who realize Jesus is their Messiah and cry out for His return. Recall that Hosea 5:15 spoke about this: *"I* (the Messiah Jesus) *will go and return to my place, till they* (the Jewish people) *acknowledge their offence, and seek my face: in their affliction* (the Tribulation) *they will seek me early."* Zechariah 12:10 adds to this: *"And I* (Jesus*) will pour upon the house of David, and upon the inhabitants of Jerusalem, the spirit of grace and of supplications: and they shall look upon me whom they have pierced, and they shall mourn for him, as one mourneth for his only son, and shall be in bitterness for him, as one that is in bitterness for his firstborn."*

During this time, the false prophet begins performing demonic miracles. In Revelation 13:11, he is described as having *"two horns like a lamb."* Because Jesus is also pictured as a lamb, this suggests the false prophet will be a religious leader. Indeed, he is the one who commands everyone to worship the image of the beast and take his mark or be executed. *"And he* (the false prophet) *had power to give life unto the image of the beast, that the image of the beast should both speak, and cause that as many as would not worship the image of the beast should be killed. And he causeth all, both small and great, rich and poor, free and bond, to receive a mark in their right hand, or in their foreheads: And that no man might buy or sell, save he that had the mark, or the name of the beast, or the number of his name. Here is wisdom. Let him that hath understanding count the number of the beast: for it is the number of a man; and his number is Six hundred threescore and six* (666)*,"* (Revelation 13:15-18). Satan now wants to seal his followers by marking them just as God sealed His 144,000 and born-again believers.

And if a talking image that can kill people sounds farfetched, then consider the technology already here. "The Giant" was created by a company in Dublin, Ireland. It's a ten-story tall statue that talks and sings and can even take on the image of any person.[53] Imagine what a thing like this can do in the hands of the antichrist!

But what about a mark capable of monitoring every purchase a person makes? This means a global digital economy, which the World Economic Forum is already trying to implement. And the technology is here. Bill Gates is funding those working on a vaccine ID containing Luciferase which is an enzyme that makes an "implantable quantum dot microneedle vaccine delivery system work."[54]

You are talking about a vaccine/tattoo that is computer-like and can track not only everyone's movements, but their buying, selling, bank accounts, health history, and even their moods. You are also talking about a mark that can possibly alter human DNA making them "other" or human 2.0, something detestable to God. Current technology can track every human on earth; can enable the world to view the dead bodies of the two witnesses via satellite television; can control people's ability to buy or sell; can enable a statue to move and talk. All the antichrist has to do is flip the switch.

By Revelation 14, we see the results of this evil duo. Their killing spree is swift because the 144,000 are with the Lamb singing a new song. These evangelists brought many to Christ during the first half of the Tribulation, and now are rejoicing in heaven, indicating they have been martyred sometime after the antichrist declared war on the Jews. They are called, *"the first fruits unto God and to the Lamb."* But this isn't the end of God's mercy because He sends another angel to fly over the earth to proclaim, *"the everlasting gospel,"* to *"them that dwell on the earth, and to **every** nation, and kindred, and tongue, and people,"* (Revelation 14:6).

Bear in mind, the antichrist and his henchmen have been killing Jews and every believer in Jesus they can find. Yet, amid this bloodbath, God still desires *"whosoever will"* to come to

Him. He is concerned about the people who are still alive. In spite of all the evil they have done, after all the hatred and contempt they have shown Him, God still desires that none should go to hell. What an amazing God! Who can understand His great love? It defies human logic. Considering how great His love is and considering the many opportunities He has given all the people during this time to come into His waiting and outstretched arms, it's hard to believe there are those who still reject Him. But when it's over and they stand before the Great White Throne they will be without excuse. They will be unable to say they weren't warned or given every opportunity.

The One World Religion doesn't fare well, either. For three and a half years the antichrist has put up with this apostate religion, allowing its leaders to persecute and kill true believers. Now, its usefulness is over. What need has he of any other religion when ***he*** is god? It's time to get rid of all those other gods and have the world just worship him.

So, Revelation 14: 8-11 tells us that this harlot Babylonian religion has fallen. But it also includes a warning for those who take the mark of the beast. *"Babylon is fallen, is fallen, that great city, because she made all nations drink of the wine of the wrath of her* (spiritual) *fornication. And the third angel followed them, saying with a loud voice, If any man worship the beast and his image, and receive his mark in his forehead, or in his hand, The same shall drink of the wine of the wrath of God, which is poured out without mixture* (not diluted, it's full strength!) *into the cup of his indignation; and he shall be tormented with fire and brimstone in the presence of the holy angels, and in the presence of the Lamb: And the smoke of their torment ascendeth up* ***for ever and ever****: and they have no rest day nor night, who worship the beast and his image, and whosoever receiveth the mark of his name."*

Praise God, there will be many who refuse this mark because Revelation 14:13 says, *"blessed are the dead which die in the Lord from henceforth."* And Revelation 15:2 mentions them in heaven. *"And I saw as it were a sea of glass mingled with fire: and them that had gotten the victory over the beast, and over his image, and over his mark, and over the number of his name, stand on the sea of glass, having the harps of God."* What a glorious day that will be! All their pain and suffering will be forgotten as they worship the Lord.

But for those who take the mark, God's sickle is about to cast them in the *"great winepress of the wrath of God."* It's a winepress so full that *"blood came out of the winepress even unto the horse bridles, by the space of a* ***thousand and six hundred furlongs,"*** (Revelation 14:20). A furlong is 220 yards or one-eighth of a mile. As mentioned, that's 200 miles. Imagine blood splashed on the bridle of warhorses (or modern counterparts) scattered over a two-hundred-mile battlefield!

The stage is set. The final seven plagues or vials are about to be poured upon earth. And according to Revelation 15:8, *"no man was able to enter into the temple, till the seven plagues of the seven angels were fulfilled."* Why was man kept out? The Bible doesn't say. But as I thought about it, I came up with the following. (Please note this is simply my opinion.) I think God refuses entrance into His temple because first, He is unwilling to hear any petitions to stay His wrath since He is determined to end it. And secondly, I believe this is breaking His heart. He loves those who are dying on earth. He desires that they come to Him. He also loves the world He created. Now, because His justice must be satisfied, He is destroying both, and this grieves Him.

I even imagine He is weeping. I say this because Ezekiel reveals God's heart. *"**Have I any pleasure** at all that the wicked should die? Saith the Lord GOD: and not that he should return from his ways, and live?"* (Ezekiel 18:23). And Ezekiel 33:11 says, *"As I live, saith the Lord GOD, I have **no pleasure** in the death of the wicked: but that the wicked turn from his way and live: turn ye, turn ye from your evil ways; for why will ye die, O house of Israel?"*

It is evident that God **wants** to forgive everyone's sins. But there are only two ways He can deal with sin: through grace—forgiveness obtained through the shed blood of Jesus, or wrath—judgment and eternal damnation.

The last three and a half years of the Tribulation:

Now it's really going to get rough! As we've seen, Satan has been kicked out of heaven and knows his time is short. And he's furious. Through the antichrist, who he indwells, he will ruthlessly pursue his dream of being worshipped and will destroy anyone who refuses to do so.

The antichrist has already shown his true colors. Revelation chapter 13 describes him as a "beast." Other Scriptures call him: the insolent and willful king, a vile person, the son of destruction, and the man of lawlessness. Empowered by Satan, he will be vile, vicious, treacherous, and the embodiment of evil. A hater of God, he will speak great blasphemies. And with an iron fist, he will establish his ruthless, anti-God kingdom.

The first through fifth vials:

These vials seem to come in rapid order, much like the first through fourth trumpets. The first vial is poured out in Revelation 16:2, causing all those who have taken the mark of the beast to develop *"a grievous sore."* That word "grievous" means "pain, hurtful, anguish," while "sore" means "ulcer." This is a painful ulceration of some kind. Perhaps it covers their whole body or just where they have the mark. In any case, it is no ordinary sore.

The second vial turns the sea into blood, killing every living creature in it. No more fishing, crabbing, or using lobster traps. Nothing in the sea is edible anymore. This will add to the food shortages. Not only will grain products be a day's wage, but now, people living near coastlines can't even supplement their rations by catching food themselves. Life continues to become increasingly difficult.

The third vial turns the rivers and *"fountains of waters"* into blood, meaning much of the water in rivers, aquifers, and underground streams become polluted and undrinkable. People can go weeks without food, but only three to seven days without water. And certainly, there will be no water for bathing or brushing teeth. This lack of personal hygiene will only add to everyone's poor health.

The fourth vial affects the sun, causing a heatwave and men to be "scorched."

The fifth vial produces darkness. During this blackness, Revelation 16:10-11 says, *"and they gnawed their tongues for pain, and blasphemed the God of heaven because of their pains and their sores, and repented not of their deeds."*

Imagine there is little food or water. People are covered with painful ulcers. The rivers and streams stink because everything in them is dead and decaying. You can't go outside because of the violent roving gangs. You can't call the police or

EMT for help. There are no assistance programs left. They have all gone bankrupt. Many of the people you know are dead. And now it's pitch-black outside. It's also sweltering. Temperatures are off the charts. But because of the rolling blackouts you have no electricity, which means no air conditioning. You are hot, hungry, thirsty, and frightened, and probably alone, and all you can do is sit in the dark and hope no one breaks into your house looking for food or valuables.

But if you have not taken the mark of the beast your fate will be even worse. Remember, you can't buy or sell so where do you get food? Maybe from the black market if you have anything left to barter. Or perhaps you find some rotten, moldy scraps in a trashcan.

Your bank account has been frozen. You've lost your job because you're not marked. You can't go home because the antichrist's Gestapo-like police have staked out your house and will arrest you, then take you to the extermination camp for non-compliance. So now, you're alone and on the street, homeless and subject to the elements as well as easy prey for the roving thugs who seem to be everywhere. And even though you have nothing worth stealing, they could, just for sport, rough you up, or rape you, or even kill you. And if they don't get you, chances are the police patrols, who have an APB out for your arrest, will. There is no rest day or night because you must stay one step ahead of them all. It's just a matter of time before you die of starvation or are murdered.

There will be so much death that by the end of the Tribulation a man will be as scarce and rare as gold. Isaiah 13:9-13 sums it up this way: *"Behold, the day of the LORD cometh, cruel both with wrath and fierce anger, to lay the land desolate: and he shall destroy the sinners thereof out of it. For the stars of heaven and the constellations thereof shall not give their light: the sun shall be darkened in his going forth, and the moon shall not cause her light to shine. And I will punish the world for their evil, and the wicked for their iniquity; and I will cause the arrogancy of the proud to cease, and will lay low the haughtiness of the terrible.* ***I will make a man more precious*** (rare) ***than fine gold, even a man*** (scarcer) ***than the golden wedge of Ophir.*** *Therefore, I will shake the heavens, and the earth shall remove out of her place, in the wrath of the LORD of hosts, and in the day of his fierce anger."*

God has been warning the inhabitants of earth for centuries. Can people say He is cruel when after all His warnings and pleadings they don't listen, and He must, because He is holy and righteous, send judgment?

I think not.

The sixth vial:

The opening of the sixth vial sees the drying up of the Euphrates River and the amassing of a great army. The beast and false prophet have sent demonic spirits to the leaders of the world *"to gather them to the battle of the great day of God Almighty,"* (Revelation 16:14). *"And he gathered them together into a place called in the Hebrew tongue Armageddon,"* (Revelation 16:16). This army plans to destroy Israel and battle God.

The seventh vial:

The seventh and final vial sees a *"great earthquake such as was not since men were upon the earth, so mighty an earthquake, and so great,"* (Revelation 16:18). There has never been an earthquake like this. *"And the great city was divided into three parts, and the cities of the nations fell: . . . And every island fled away, and the mountains were not found,"* (Revelation 16:20). It destroys every island and mountain. Next, picture the cities of the world collapsing. All those high risers and skyscrapers will be rubble. Homes will also crumble. Towns, communities, all will be gone. This earthquake will level the planet.

On top of that, sixty to seventy-five-pound hailstones will come raining out of the sky, crushing everything that isn't already flattened. *"And there fell upon man a great hail out of heaven, every stone about the weight of a talent,"* (Revelation 16:21).

What the earthquake doesn't destroy, the hailstones will. And that means crops, if there are any left, as well as trees, plants, animals, weakened remaining structures, and those people who cannot find shelter. And what will man's reaction be? *"And men blasphemed God because of the plague of the hail; for the plague thereof was exceeding great,"* (Revelation 16:21).

Though words cannot accurately describe the horror of these seven years, Zephaniah 1:14-18 comes close: *"The great day of the LORD* (the seven-year Tribulation) *is near, it is near, and hasteth greatly, even the voice of the day of the LORD: the mighty man shall cry there bitterly. That day is a day of wrath, a day of trouble and distress, a day of wasteness and desolation, a day of darkness and gloominess, a day of clouds and thick darkness. A day of the trumpet and alarm against the fenced cities, and against the high towers. And I* (God) *will bring distress upon men, that they shall walk like blind men, because they have sinned against the LORD: and their blood shall be poured out as dust, and their flesh as the dung. Neither their silver nor their gold shall be able to deliver them in the day of the LORD'S wrath; but the whole land shall be devoured by the fire of his jealousy: for he shall make even a speedy riddance of all them that dwell in the land."*

Revelation 17 and 18 talk about the fall of Mystery Babylon, the Mother of Harlots—the antichrist's One World Religious System. Remember, when declaring himself god, the antichrist destroyed the One World Religion of the apostate church and created his own One World Religion, featuring himself as its head. Also destroyed is Babylon the Great—the antichrist's One World Government and economic system. The wrath of God is now complete.

Revelation 19 sees the return of Jesus on a white horse with His bride following. No longer the Lamb, He comes as King of kings and Lord of lords. And He is fearsome to behold.

The antichrist and false prophet, along with the armies of the world, are waiting for Jesus. It's laughable to think they, as created beings, actually believe they can overcome the Creator Himself! It shows how deceived they are, and how badly Satan has deceived himself. He still believes he can win.

Romans 1:21-32 describes these types of rebels. *"When they knew God, they glorified him not as God, neither were thankful; but became vain in their imaginations, and their foolish heart was darkened. Professing themselves to be wise, they became fools, And changed the glory of the uncorruptible God into an image made like to corruptible man, and to birds, and four footed beasts, and creeping things. Wherefore God also gave them up to uncleanness through the lusts of their own hearts, to dishonour their own bodies between themselves: Who changed the truth of God into a lie, and worshipped and served the creature more than the Creator, who is blessed for ever. Amen. For this cause God gave them up unto vile affections: for even their women did change the natural use into that which is against nature: And likewise also the men, leaving the natural use of the woman, burned in their lust one toward another: men with men working that which is unseemly, and receiving in themselves that recompence of their error which was meet. And even as they did not like to retain God in their knowledge, God gave them over to a reprobate mind, to do those things which are not convenient; Being filled with all unrighteousness, fornications, wickedness, covetousness, maliciousness; full of envy, murder, debate, deceit, malignity; whisperers, Backbiters, haters of God, despiteful, proud, boasters, inventors of evil things, disobedient to parents, Without understanding, covenant breakers, without natural affections, implacable, unmerciful: Who knowing the judgment of God, that they which commit such things are worthy of death, not only do the same, but have pleasure in them that do them."*

These people not only despise God but want to continue their evil lifestyle. And they encourage others to live evil lives as well.

But Jesus is about to put an end to it all. He opens His mouth and releases a sword (the word of His mouth), vanquishing the rebels in an instant. Following that, the beast and false prophet are cast into the lake of fire, while Satan is chained and thrown into the bottomless pit.

There is an interesting point worth mentioning. Since I have already covered the issue of the Nephilim in my book, *The Coming Deception*, I won't spend much time on it now. But briefly, fallen angels cohabitated with human women to create hybrids called Nephilim and Rephaim. They did this to corrupt human DNA and make man "other" in an attempt to prevent Jesus from coming as man to redeem us. Many in the Satanic Illuminati claim to be their descendants. This corruption is still going on today.

Daniel 2:42-43 describes the ten toes of Nebuchadnezzar's statue. *"And as the toes of the feet were part of iron, and part of clay, so the kingdom shall be partly strong, and partly broken. And whereas thou sawest iron mixed with miry clay, they shall mingle themselves with the seed of men: but they shall not* ***cleave*** *one to another, even as iron is not mixed with clay."*

Nebuchadnezzar is a type of antichrist, and the ten toes represent the world's final kingdom, the revived Roman Empire, which will be the antichrist's kingdom. It will not be as strong as the original Roman Empire. But as often is the case in Scripture, it conveys a double meaning.

In this revived empire someone or something will mingle themselves with the seed of men and not cleave one to another. That word "mingle" is *arab* and means, "commingle, mix to braid, to traffic as if by barter, become surety, a pledge, a guarantee, a kind of exchange, occupy." Seed means a physical seed. Cleave (*debeq/dabaq*) means, "to cling or join to." It's the same word used in Genesis 2:24. *"Therefore shall a man leave his father and his mother, and shall* ***cleave*** *unto his wife: and they shall be one flesh."*

This seems to imply that these men are hybrids, those whose seed has been corrupted by fallen angels and this time not because of "cleaving" sexually to their wives but by DNA manipulation. Currently, transhumanism (the making of human 2.0) employs the use of DNA manipulation. Labs worldwide are crossing human DNA with both animal and plant DNA in perverted experiments detestable to God.

Was this commingling in Daniel regarding the ten toes the result of a Satanic bargain by which these rulers gave up their status as true "men" for the pledge, the guarantee of global dominance, and the power to rule the world?

Whoever "they" are, the mix isn't good. It is weak because this kingdom will be *"partly strong and partly broken."* A quick look at the meaning of these words gives a fuller picture. Strong (*taqqip*) means "overpower." Broken (*tebar*) means "break in pieces, judgmental punitive activity." While partly (*qesat*) means "the end, the last of a thing; cut off."

This word study suggests that because both entities are only "partly" it means their end. They are the last of a thing and will be cut off. It also implies that the partly strong will overpower the other which will break in pieces as a punitive judgment against this kingdom. Neither one will last but be destroyed by Jesus before He sets up His kingdom.

Scripture also tells us that these Nephilim hybrids are an abomination to God and will be damned forever. Since a trial before Jesus, the Judge, will be afforded to every human who ever lived, does the fact that both the antichrist and false prophet are thrown into the lake of fire without one indicate they were *not* fully human? I think so.

Conclusion:

We have seen that the entire seven-year Tribulation is contained in Jesus' scroll; first the seven seals, which in turn contains the seven-trumpet judgments, which in turn contains the seven vial judgments. And all are unleashed by Jesus. He is in total control. Daniel 2: 21 clearly states that it is God Who sets up kings and removes them. He is the One who controls world events. And Isaiah 14:24 and 46:9-10 assure us that whatever God has planned will come to pass. It is set in stone.

And yes, for a season, Satan and his crowd will have their way. But God always gets the last laugh.

"Why do the heathen rage, and the people imagine a vain thing? The kings of the earth set themselves, and the rulers take counsel together, against the LORD, and against his anointed, saying, Let us break their bands asunder, and cast away their cords from us. He that sitteth in the heavens shall laugh: the LORD shall have them in derision," Psalms 2:1-4.

Proverbs 29:1 makes it clear. Those repeatedly corrected and warned by God, but who harden their hearts will be destroyed. There will be no remedy. Only God's wrath, (Romans 2:5).

2 Thessalonians 1:6-10 says, *"Seeing it is a righteous thing with God to recompense tribulation to them that trouble you* (the saints, believers in Jesus); *And to you who are troubled rest with us, when the Lord Jesus shall be revealed from heaven with his mighty angels, In flaming fire taking vengeance on them that know not God, and that obey not the gospel of our Lord Jesus Christ. Who shall be punished with everlasting destruction from the presence of the Lord, and from the glory of his power; When he shall come to be glorified in his saints, and to be admired in all them that believe (because our testimony among you was believed) in that day."*

Because the world, in large part, has lost its fear of the Lord and the understanding of His greatness, this is where they are headed. As in the days of Noah and Lot, people are going about their business, eating, partying, marrying; not paying attention to the signs of the times, unaware of the horrors ahead.

Revelation concludes by telling us that after the chaining of Satan there will be another seventy-five days of mopping up operations when the sheep and goats are separated, the earth restructured, and the resurrection of Old Testament and Tribulation saints. Then Jesus begins His one-thousand-year reign in Jerusalem during which time He, as the Jewish Messiah, keeps His promise to Israel by setting up a Davidic Kingdom of Peace.

All this time, the globalists have strived to create a one world government, but it will be Jesus who creates that global one world government and rules it. He is the stone from heaven that will pulverize all empires at the end of the age. Daniel 2:34-35 says, *"Thou sawest till that a stone* (Jesus) *was cut out without hands, which smote the image* (of the antichrist kingdom) *upon his feet that were of iron and clay, and brake them to pieces. Then was the iron, the clay, the brass, the silver, and the gold* (all the kingdoms of the world) *broken to pieces together, and became like the chaff of the summer threshing floors; and the wind carried them away, that no place was found for them: and the stone that smote the image became a great mountain, and filled the whole earth."* All too late the elites will understand Jesus' caution when He said, *"For what shall it profit a man, if he shall gain the whole world, and lose his own soul?"* (Mark 8:36).

Praise our great God! For believers, these are exciting times! Jesus will rule the world as King and Judge for 1000 years. Following that, He will create a new heaven and earth, which will be our glorious home for all eternity.

Something to think about:

God loves you more than you can imagine. Oh, how rich, how deep, how wide is His love! It passes all understanding (Ephesians 3:19). And He wants you to spend all eternity with Him.

To those who say, "I don't believe in God or the Bible," I say this: As a former cultural Christian who didn't believe in

Scripture or Jesus as Savior, I understand. But that didn't discourage God. Even when I was far from Him, He was there, protecting me in my folly, and orchestrating things in a way that could only be described as miraculous. Then when my heart softened, I finally prayed, "God **IF** you are real and **IF** Jesus is real, then I want to know you." And oh, how wonderfully He answered. God is no respecter of persons. What He does for one, He will do for others. And God is not offended by your questions. It means you are seeking, and that pleases Him. If you ask with a sincere heart, He will answer in a way meaningful to you.

Or, if you are one who has walked on the wild side and think you are too far gone and that God could never love someone like you, then rest assured, if you are sincere, He will not turn you away. He knows your name. He even knows the number of hairs on your head (Matthew 10:30, Luke 12:7). He has a book in heaven about you, which includes details of your life, His wonderful hopes, plans, and dreams for you. He's pulling for you and wants you to succeed. And He loves you no matter what you've done. In fact, no one could love you more!

But as we've already seen, works won't cut it. They never have. So, it's not a matter of cleaning up your act before you can come to Him. Remember, all our good deeds/works are like filthy rags compared to His holiness and righteousness. Only innocent blood can remove sin and make us righteous. So, praise God for Jesus! He paid the ultimate price. The problem is that while Jesus' sin payment is for everyone, it can only be appropriated by those who believe it and receive it, which means one must personally accept Jesus and what He did.

So, why waste more time? Come to Jesus now. Come to the One Who loves you most and knows you best. He is calling your name. If you want to answer, then pray this prayer and mean it:

Father God, I come before you in the name of Jesus. I acknowledge that I am a sinner and can't save myself. Forgive me for my sins and for trying to live a life without Jesus. I accept Him now as my Savior and want to make Him Lord over my life and to serve him all my days. Amen.

If you have prayed this prayer, angels are rejoicing in heaven! The next step is to get a Bible, read it, and connect with a solid Bible-believing church.

Love and Blessings,

Sylvia Bambola

Students For Supporting Classmate Who Brought In a Trump Flag; "Trump Brings Out Racism in Trashy People" - (Video) (thegatewaypundit.com)

29. The Dailywire, Megan Basham, August 30, 2021, 'Christian Evangelicals Are America's Taliban': Actors, Journalists Equate American Christians To The Taliban | The Daily Wire
30. WND, Bob Unruh, July 8, 2021, Gay chorus threatens: 'We're coming for your children' (wnd.com)
31. The Epoch Times, Brad Jones, November 20, 2021, Leaked Audio Reveals How California Teachers Recruit Kids Into LGBTQ Clubs (theepochtimes.com)
32. Harbingers Daily, David Fiorazo, November 22, 2021, Next Stage of Rebellion: Normalizing Pedophilia | Harbingers Daily
33. Gateway Pundit, Jim Hoft, October 28, 2021, Florida School Board Member Chaperones Little Children on Gay Bar Field Trip (thegatewaypundit.com)
34. Gateway Pundit, Julian Conradson, October 13, 2021, SICKENING: Loudoun County Schools Covered Up Rape of a 14-Year-Old Girl and Prosecuted Her Father To Protect Male Transgender Student Who Was Permitted to Use Ladies Bathrooms (thegatewaypundit.com)
35. Gateway Pundit, Jacob Engels, October 27, 2021, VIDEO: Journalist Reads Filthy Porn Book from School's Library at FL School Board Meeting - Board Members Call Police to Have Him Forcefully Removed for Reading Obscene Content Aloud (thegatewaypundit.com)
36. Gateway Pundit, Cristina Laila, September 15, 2021, Ohio Mayor Puts School Board on Notice: 'Resign or Face Criminal Charges For Distributing Child Pornography' (VIDEO) (thegatewaypundit.com)

37. Harbingers Daily, September 28, 2021, Parents Outraged After Sex Ed Program Asks Students to Role Play Gay, Trans Sex Scenarios | Harbingers Daily
38. Gateway Pundit, Jordan Conradson, December 8, 2021, EXCLUSIVE: North Carolina Parents Identify Over 100 Book Titles Containing Obscene Content, File CRIMINAL Charges Against Wake County School Board (PHOTOS) (thegatewaypundit.com)
39. WND, Bob Unruh, July 8, 2021, Gay chorus threatens: 'We're coming for your children' (wnd.com)
40. IAmAWatchman.com, from *Harbingers Daily*, Joseph Kerr, They're Coming for your Children – Welcome to I Am a Watchman!
41. *Washington, Examiner*, Asher Notheis, November 8, 2021, Nearly a third of millennials identify as LGBT, study finds | Washington Examiner
42. WND, Andrew Powell, August 8, 2021, What the devil? U.S. turns to dark side as Americans make Satan mainstream (wnd.com)
43. Thomas Horn & Cris Putnam, *Petrus Romanus* (Crane, MO: Defender, 2012), 449.
44. Cris Putnam & Thomas Horn, *Exo-Vaticana* (Crane, MO: Defender, 2013), 533.
45. Ibid., 535.
46. Thomas Horn, *Apollyon Rising 2012* (Crane, MO: Defender, 2009), 328.
47. Thomas Horn & Cris Putnam, *Petrus Romanus* (Crane, MO: Defender, 2012), 91.
48. Ibid., 90
49. Ibid., 244
50. Ibid., 466
51. Gateway Pundit, Joe Hoft, November 17, 2021, HUGE EXCLUSIVE: Archbishop Carlo Maria Viganò Calls on People of Faith to Unite in a Worldwide Anti-Globalist

Alliance to Free Humanity from the Totalitarian Regime (VIDEO) (thegatewaypundit.com)

52. Cris Putnam & Thomas Horn, *Exo-Vaticana* (Crane, MO: Defender, 2013), 211-212; Thomas Horn & Cris Putnam, *Petrus Romanus* (Crane, MO: Defender, 2012), 471.
53. Azcentral, Elizabeth Montgomery, Arizona Republic, May 6, 2021, Meet 'The Giant.' a 10-story movable statue that could come to Phoenix (azcentral.com)
54. September 4, 2020, Bill Gates Vaccine Ingredient Says it All : An Enzyme Called LUCIFERASE is What Makes Bill Gates Implantable Vaccine Work - VACCINE ID - Stillness in the Storm

Bibliography

Church, J.R., *Daniel Reveals the Bloodline of the Antichrist*, Prophecy Publications, P.O. Box 7000, Oklahoma City, OK 73153, 2010

Harris, R. Laird; Archer, Gleason L.; Waltke, Bruce K., *Theological Wordbook of the Old Testament*, Moody Publishers, 820 N. LaSalle Boulevard, Chicago, 60610, 1990

Josephus, The New Complete Works of, William Whiston, translator; Paul L. Maier, commentary, Kregel Publications, a division of Kregel, Inc., P.O. Box 2607, Grand Rapids, MI 49501, 1999

Lahaye, Tim; Hindson, Ed, *Exploring Bible Prophecy from Genesis to Revelation*, Harvest House Publishers, Eugene, Oregon 97402, 2006

Lamsa, George M., *Idioms In The Bible Explained and A Key To The Original Gospels*, Harper One, An Imprint of HarperCollins Publishers, 195 Broadway, New York, NY 10007, 1985

Salus, Bill, *Psalm 83 The Missing Prophecy Revealed*, Prophecy Depot Ministries, P.O. Box 5612, LaQuinta, CA 92248, 2013

Strong's Exhaustive Concordance of the Bible, MacDonald Publishing Company, McLean, Virginia 22102

The Perry Stone Hebraic Prophetic Study Bible, King James Version, Commentary Written by Perry Stone, Published in association with Fedd Books, a division of The Fedd Agency,

Inc., a literary agency, P.O. Box 341973, Austin, TX, 78734, 2019

The Zondervan's Pictorial Encyclopedia of the Bible (In Five Volumes), General Editor, Merrill C. Tenney, Ph.D., Regency Reference Library, 1415 Lake Drive, S.E. Grand Rapids, Michigan 49506, from Zondervan Publishing House, 1975-1976

Webster's New World Dictionary of the American Language, The World Publishing Company, Cleveland and New York, 1957

www.ingramcontent.com/pod-product-compliance
Lightning Source LLC
LaVergne TN
LVHW010558100826
845148LV00014B/2760

* 9 7 8 0 9 6 5 7 3 8 9 8 9 *